THE
ELDERCARE
911

Question and Answer Book

"A comprehensive source that provides all the answers to questions you've needed regarding an elderly parent. This book offers essential, practical, and candid advice on every aspect of eldercare! An invaluable resource!"

—Ken Dychtwald, PhD, president and CEO of Age Wave

"*The Eldercare 911 Question and Answer Book* is a comprehensive caregiver guide dealing with the most common to the sublime issues of caregiving. Unique topics are impressive, including information for male caregivers, the special role of women, life as a working caregiver, and lessons in feelings. This book is truly a departure from the typical caregiver guide and one that addresses the difficult questions caregivers often refrain from asking."

—Mark Warner, author of *The Complete Guide to Alzheimer's-Proofing Your Home*

THE ELDERCARE 911

Question and Answer Book

SUSAN BEERMAN, MS, MSW
JUDITH RAPPAPORT-MUSSON, CSA

Prometheus Books

59 John Glenn Drive
Amherst, New York 14228-2197

Published 2005 by Prometheus Books.

Inquiries should be addressed to
Prometheus Books
59 John Glenn Drive
Amherst, New York 14228–2197
VOICE: 716–691–0133, ext. 207
FAX: 716–564–2711
WWW.PROMETHEUSBOOKS.COM

09 08 07 06 05   5 4 3 2 1

Library of Congress Cataloging-in-Publication Data

Beerman, Susan, 1950–
    The eldercare 911 question and answer book / Susan Beerman and Judith
Rappaport-Musson.
        p. cm.
    Includes index.
    ISBN 1–59102–293–2 (pbk.: alk. paper)
    1. Aging parents—Care—Miscellanea. 2. Caregivers—Family relationships—
Miscellanea. 3. Older people—Care—Miscellanea. I. Rappaport-Musson, Judith,
1942– II. Title.

HQ1063.6.B446 2005
306.874'084'6—dc22

                                                              2005005102

Printed in the United States of America on acid-free paper

To the loves of my life,
John, Kim, Tom, Sweet Nicky, and Harriet—you are my sunshine.

—Judith Rappaport-Musson

To my loving husband, Alen, and children, Hal and Audra,
who give me the support and encouragement to fulfill my dreams.
I love you.

—Susan Beerman

CONTENTS

CONTENTS

DISCLAIMER

The information provided in *The Eldercare 911 Question and Answer Book* is offered with the understanding that the authors are not engaged in rendering financial, legal, or medical advice. Readers who require such advice should not consider this book a replacement for professional counsel, but instead should see the services of licensed financial, legal, and medical professionals.

PREFACE

Thank you! I found your earlier book very useful, but why didn't you talk
more about my "know it all" relatives. I need help to survive their visits!
—Stephanie, New York

You left out my special hell: I'm a working caregiver! We need more help.
—Sharon, Georgia

In *Eldercare 911: The Caregiver's Complete Handbook for Making Decisions*, we asked caregivers for feedback and we got it! Thank you for telling us how valuable you found our information to be and what a positive difference we made in your lives. We also appreciate the responses that asked us why we left out issues that were important to you. When we answered that no single book can address all the issues faced by millions of caregivers, many of you asked for another book. This is it.

The *Eldercare 911 Question and Answer Book* is a compilation of your experiences, questions, letters, and comments that delivers much more than general advice and recommendations that tell you *what* to do. *What* is important, but it's just not enough. If you read a book on brain surgery that told you *what* to do, would you feel comfortable stepping up to an operating table to remove a tumor from your parent's brain?! Of course not. Caring for your parent may not be considered brain surgery, but it can certainly be life altering for all concerned. That's why we're providing step-by-step directions in each chapter that actually show you *how* to solve current problems and also help you learn to become an advocate for yourself and your parent. In addition, most chapters have interactive worksheets that you can reproduce and carry with you for continuing support and encouragement.

The first chapter, "The Positive and Negative Impact of Caregiving," allows you to view the private passions and determination of other caregivers. You'll share their inner thoughts—guilt, stress, expectations, love, hate, anger, and fear—and gain strength from their sense of purpose as they become advocates for their parents. Chapter 2, "Saying *No* to Toxic People," helps you create strategies to cope with people who seem to thrive on making your life miserable. We're sure you'll find your "special person" among Know-It-Alls, Guilt-Trippers, Surprise Visitors, Sibling Battlers, Parents in Denial, or one of the other groups in our Top Ten Toxic People categories.

Caregivers who work were extremely responsive in voicing their needs for practical coping tips and strategies. Look for answers in chapter 7, "Life as a Working Caregiver." On another note, both men and women expressed a need for a better understanding of how gender roles affect the interpersonal relationships of caregivers. You'll find our responses in two dedicated chapters: chapter 4, "For Women Only," and chapter 5, "For Men Only." In addition, we have devoted entire chapters to three of your most difficult and persistent challenges: "The Rules of Intervention," "Breaking Away from Burnout," and "Living with Alzheimer's Disease."

"Family Matters," chapter 6, was created specifically for the many caregivers who find it difficult to gain practical or emotional support from family members. We urge the many men and women who feel as though they haven't done enough for their parents to sit quietly and also read chapter 10, "Lessons in Feeling Good about Yourself."

Many readers also asked us to discuss filling the void when a parent passes away. We hope chapter 11, "Life after Caregiving," will inspire the strength and courage you need to plan your journey.

Our response to the caregivers who asked for warm and loving thoughts that bring a few moments of serenity and encouragement late at night is chapter 12, "Words of Hope and Comfort." We hope these affirmations soothe your spirit and help you face the coming days.

Since the time we wrote *Eldercare 911: The Caregiver's Complete Handbook for Making Decisions*, the need for information and assistance has increased significantly. Science has continued to expand our parents' life expectancy. Its focus on treatments has helped slow our parents' decline from a variety of diseases and conditions and thus has been enormously successful. In the 1990s, the fastest growing segment of the sixty-five and older age group was people eighty-five years old and older.[1] As of this writing, some demographers believe it may be people one hundred and older![2]

As in past decades, society lags far behind science, and the consequences continue to build. For caregivers, expanded life expectancy often means not only additional caregiving years but the probability of a far greater degree of difficulty in their caregiving duties. As infirm parents battle the middle and end stages of Alzheimer's, Parkinson's, and other diseases, they are likely to need more in-depth assistance for many years longer.

Walk into any office building, any mall, any church or synagogue, any conference center, or any sporting event, and ask everyone you meet over the age of forty-five, "Are you an elder-caregiver?" The number of positive responses will absolutely astound you! Some will tell you how blessed they feel to participate in the caregiving experience; others will roll their eyes skyward and complain about problems stemming from a scarcity of practical information or a lack of help from others—the majority of caregivers receive no help from family members. Many will talk about the issues relating to the need to conduct eldercare activities from the workplace; others will relate the difficulties of time management while providing help for extended families, or burnout.

Eldercare 911 was the first step in our commitment to bring information and peace of mind to caregivers. As the scope of caregiving expands, caregivers need new approaches and additional information. It is our hope that *The Eldercare 911 Question and Answer Book* will serve that need.

Our conclusion is this: as people live to be much older, and unless families' demands and workplace responsibilities diminish, caregivers will continue to have problems that need answers. In fact, if asked what their number one need is, most will have a one-word response: *answers!* The wonderful caregivers we talked to told us:

> Not magic, but practical, workable answers that help us surmount the obstacles we face from the system and our families.
>
> —Celia, Illinois

> I want to feel warm again.
>
> —Fran, New York

> I want answers that help me laugh and allow me to cry without feeling guilty.
>
> —Annie, California

As before, we stand in awe and admiration at the power and dedication we found in caregivers' experiences and personal stories. You demonstrated once again how truly wonderful and amazing the human spirit can be. You also showed us that whether we are caring for our parents, spouses, or children, there is a universality that connects us and binds us all together. Your unselfish sharing of your most personal thoughts and feelings will help support thousands of other caregivers. On behalf of them, we honor you and thank you.

PLEASE CONTINUE TO WRITE US

If we missed your questions, visit www.eldercare911handbook.com and post your comments or questions on our Caregivers Connection bulletin board. Our Web site is packed with interesting articles that will help you solve problems. To contact us, or to subscribe to our free *Eldercare 911* newsletters (e-mail only) e-mail jrappaport@eldercare911handbook.com or suebeerman @eldercare911handbook.com.

Thank you for taking this journey with us.

Warmest regards,
Judith B. Rappaport and Susan Beerman

ACKNOWLEDGMENT

Special thanks to Carlene Race Tockman, LCSW, child and family therapist extraordinaire, for lending her guidance for the section on children and teenagers in the chapter entitled "Family Matters."

THE POSITIVE AND NEGATIVE IMPACT OF CAREGIVING

Dear Eldercare 911,

Believe me, nothing can prepare you for this.... It's the hardest thing I've ever done. As angry as I am, I would not have missed it for the world.

—Arlene, Canada

Caring for my mother gave me a better sense of how much I could endure and still survive. Looking back, it was a time of unrealistic expectations and unimaginable emotional and physical stress. It's easy to say that now—it was a great deal more difficult to look at it that way when I was in the middle of it. I can still feel the love I had for her, but ten years later, if I let myself, I can also still feel the guilt and fear. In the end, after my mother died, I had a new respect for life and for myself.

—Elaine, Georgia

It's like watching the approach of a tidal wave on a remote beach where there is nowhere safe to run. I'm so afraid. I just hope I can hold up.

—Beverly, California

Dear Caregivers,

These are just a few of the powerful emotions that besiege so many caregivers every day. Some are able to restore or maintain a positive balance in their lives; others are not as lucky and continue to feel the weight of their anger, fear, or guilt. Most are unprepared for the emotional turbulence they experience, and very few feel prepared to deal with it. Almost all, however, who have been through this experience can look back and pinpoint many of the situations that helped create their inner turmoil. Are these feelings always a part of caregiving? Are most caregivers troubled by them in one way or another?

The answer partially lies in the responsibility inherent in the title "caregiver." The scope of a caregiver's duties is so broad that no one person has the skills necessary to do it all. Whether you are living with your parent or trying to help from afar, caring for your parent can involve hands-on help or managing one or many needs. You may help with meals, insurance claims, home repairs, bathing, dressing, toileting, daily reassurance telephone calls, making and going to doctors' appointments, communicating with your parent's physicians, paying bills, hiring and supervising homecare workers, choosing a nursing home, finding community resources, getting transportation, doing grocery shopping, getting financial assistance, finding companionship, providing emotional support, and other duties.

When we accept the job of caregiver, we believe that we can help our parent; we offer our skills *to try* to keep a parent safer or healthier. The trouble begins when we forget that no matter how hard we try, even if we do the very best we can, our efforts remain only one small piece of the puzzle. To accomplish our goals, we are fully dependent on medical science researchers and physicians, as well as assistance and understanding from family and friends, employers, and a host of other people. We are even subject to simple everyday factors like the weather, which may prevent us from taking Mom to her scheduled doctor appointment and put us in the position of having to ask for another day off to take her.

No matter how hard we try, regardless of how deeply we love our parent or how much we just want to succeed because we said we would help, we actually have limited control. After years of battling the stresses and frustrations of caregiving, we begin to feel our limitations. The impact of that reality can change our attitudes toward ourselves, and our partners, children, parents, jobs, and homes—literally everyone and everything that *impacts* our lives. We can be swept away by emotions so powerful that they override our coping skills. When the impact is positive—as in recognizing your own strength or experiencing a family member's love—we may feel power*ful*. When the impact produces negative feelings like fear or guilt, we may feel power*less*. For example:

- Some caregivers are afraid that something bad may happen to their parents because they don't know enough to do *more* than they're already doing.
- Others are angry; they feel that *no matter how hard they strive*, forces outside their control can, and often do, change their lives.
- Too many caregivers feel guilty, wondering if their parents might be

healthier if they had done more, worked harder, taken more days off, paid more attention, or just found the magic key.

In all these cases, nothing could be farther from the truth! All any one of us has to give, all that anyone can ask of you, is what you are able *to give and what you* want *to give.* This truth is unassailable, holding firm from both an emotional and a logical viewpoint: when we have given what we are able to give, there simply is no more we can do because we have nothing left to give.

It's time to begin advocating on your own behalf by understanding that premise and finding peace in your life. It's time to learn to recognize and utilize your strengths to help you live with your feelings. This chapter is dedicated to that purpose.

A. THE IMPACT OF EXPECTATIONS

Dear Eldercare 911,

I'm caring for my mom and am having a really hard time with "role reversal." I read a lot about it when I became a caregiver, hoping it would help me avoid the unsettling feelings I had heard about. I thought I was prepared, but I'm not. As Mom continues to become sicker and frailer, for the first time my responsibilities include calming her fears and helping her make appropriate decisions about eating, bathing, and when to go to the bathroom. More and more often I feel as though I'm the parent and she's the child. She's always been a role model for me and this reversal of roles is much harder than I thought it would be. Equally disturbing is that at the age of forty-eight, for the first time in my life, I feel like I can't count on my mother to guide or comfort me if I need her. Sometimes that feels like the saddest thing that has ever happened to me.

—Inez, Pennsylvania

Dear Inez,

Your own words tell the tale—almost nothing can prepare you for a feeling this unsettling and different from anything you've ever known. You have to experience it firsthand. Learning coping skills may help keep your memories of your mother intact and keep role reversal from impacting your current relationship with her.

Your sadness is understandable. Adult children often find it difficult to accept that their previously strong parents are declining in health or physical stature before their eyes. After all, for many of us, these newly dependent parents are the same people who not too long along ago seemed invincible when they calmed our fears or dried our tears. We turned to them for shelter, love, security, and help with almost any problem. We *counted* on them to be there. We grew to expect the security of knowing our parents would be there *if* we needed help. Now, our expectations are no longer valid and we have to change our lifelong expectations and behavior.

Caregiving sometimes forces us to admit that our parents will not be with us forever, which in turn spurs a period of quiet, internal grieving. You may also experience fear, denial, helplessness, anger, or other conflicting emotions. It is important to discuss your feelings before they adversely affect your relationships with your children, partner, parents, and friends. If you have siblings, talk with them. You may find that they are experiencing the same emotions and they may welcome the opportunity to talk about them. Alternatively, consider discussing your feelings with a good friend, your clergy, or a professional counselor. These guidelines may help.

- It's important *never* to consider yourself as the *parent* to your parent. You aren't, and no matter how much assistance you provide, you *never* will be. You are a loving child, or a dutiful child, helping someone who can no longer help herself.
- Rather than treat your parent as a child, assume that she would like to remain in control of as much of her life as possible. You can help avoid both of you feeling that you have become the parent by bringing your parent into the decision-making process as often as possible.
- It is dangerous to ask a parent with dementia to make decisions outside her capability. (For further information on safe methods to give parents with dementia a voice and choice, see chapter 8, "Living with Alzheimer's Disease.")

Losing independence can lead a parent to depression and loss of self-esteem. If you have had a loving relationship with your parent, it's important to reassure her that you still love her and value her as your parent. It is equally as important to reassure yourself that you are acting as a loving, responsible daughter—not her mother. You are doing the best your can for your mother and that it is all she or anyone else has a right to expect from you.

Dear Eldercare 911,

My father has been ill for three years and I've helped Mom out with cooking, taking him to the doctor, paying bills, keeping them both company, and even moving into their home during critical periods so I could be there for them. I thought it would give Mom a break if I were there to sit with him or help with anything they needed. I love them both and am happy to do it. It would be nice, just once, to hear either one of them ask about me. Or call them just once and have them say something pleasant when I ask "How are you today?" Instead, I get the same complaints day in and day out. I have my own business and I work hard. I haven't taken a vacation in over three years since Dad became critically ill. I finally went away for a week. Just one lousy week. And I made sure I didn't go more than a few hours away by car so I could get back quickly in an emergency. While I was away, I called to check up on them. I said, "How are you?" and they both unloaded all their problems and aches and pains on me. There was nothing new, nothing out of the ordinary. Couldn't they have held it until I got home? Could they have said, "We're fine. Don't worry. Have a good time"? Am I wrong to expect them to care about my feelings once in a while? To give me just a little break? I'm fed up with the both of them! I'm still helping and I will do whatever it takes, but that really hurt me and I'll never forget it.

—Right or Wrong, New Mexico

Dear Right or Wrong,

It's easy to understand your feelings and they may be right on target, or not, or both. This is far more complex than a simple question of right or wrong. We don't have a lot of information, but from your questions, we'd guess you are a caring person who is concerned about your family and friends and that you show your concern when talking to them. These are wonderful traits, and regardless of how angry you may be at the moment, it's important to be true to yourself and to maintain your ability to connect with those you care about.

Think back and be honest with yourself: has your relationship with your parents changed since your father became ill? Was there ever a time when they were interested in your life? Or have you always served as a quasitherapist to them, allowing them to empty their problems on you? If nothing has changed, then it's time to accept the concept that they will not change. To protect yourself from further hurt, *you must change the way that you relate to them.*

On the other hand, if they have always been caring and this disregard for your welfare is recent or new, you may have to adjust your expectations to *what they are capable of giving at this time.* We don't know what your father's illness is, but he and your mother may be so caught up in their own health problems and potential loss of independence, impending death, or each other that they may not realize that they aren't asking about your health or happiness anymore.

If you had a different, more satisfying relationship prior to your father's illness, wait for a "good day" and try to tell them how you feel: "I understand how hard this is for you both to be living like this now, and I'm here for you. But it hurts me that you never ask me how I feel, or if everything is all right with me."

Being a caregiver is hard enough without the extra resentment and anger of being an "invisible" caregiver. Please remember that to decrease your frustration and anger you need to take care of yourself. If your parents can afford it, suggest that they hire a professional homecare worker to help take some of your caregiving duties off your shoulders. The worker can cook, help with transportation, sit with Dad when Mom goes out, help with Dad's laundry, change linens, and take care of many other time- and energy-consuming necessities. If your parents can't afford it, offer to contribute toward the cost. Use the extra time you gain to stay connected to your friends and allow them to help you, just as you would gladly help them.

B. THE IMPACT OF LOVE

Dear Eldercare 911,

This is a love story about my wife and her mother and the insensitivity of our friends. My wife, Martha, is fortunate in that she has a remarkably close relationship with her mother—in many ways her mother is her closest friend. Mom lived in her own apartment, but she was falling so often and using her emergency response system so much that the company wouldn't answer her calls anymore. We invited her to come live with us out of love. This was our well-thought-out decision. We wanted to care for her. Our lives changed, but she was a wonderful woman who had a cooperative personality; rarely was she difficult. We decided that we would move her to a nursing home if she became incontinent regularly and we couldn't control where she urinated, and if Martha could not lift her or help her when I wasn't home. We took pride in that we were able to keep her home as long as we did, although it wasn't easy. I know what we did isn't right for everyone. My job and our personal life combined with my mother-in-law's personality made this situation viable. Now that she's in a nursing home, our friends think they're commending us, but they actually are being inconsiderate and thoughtless with their comments. They keep saying, "I don't know how you did it. I can't imagine living with my mother." Or, "You must be glad your ordeal is over." Or, "You are both saints; how did you STAND it?" Why is it so hard to understand that we wanted her to stay as long as possible and that we miss her?

—Perplexed, Ohio

Dear Perplexed,

How lucky you and Martha are to enjoy such a warm, loving relationship with her mother. You are right about your friends being thoughtless, but we're guessing that you are also right that they are actually trying to compliment you. People often comment on topics based more on their singular experience than on the broader experiences of many people. This leads us to think that your friends were picturing themselves in your shoes, and not one of them found it pleasant. Or they may have been reacting to experiences they had heard about from others. Either way, the relationship you and your wife have with her mother is far outside their realm of knowledge and understanding.

To rectify their lack of experience and end their hurtful comments, we suggest you act promptly but in a more mature and humane manner than those who are causing your wife this pain. A confrontation may only further hurt your wife. Every time someone makes a remark that you find inappropriate, look the person in the eye and quietly reply, "I'm glad you brought that up so I could clarify our position and put this misunderstanding to rest once and for all. Martha and I invited my mother-in-law to come live with us. We love her and we're glad we could be there for her. We're sorry she couldn't stay longer." Alternatively, if your wife isn't within earshot and you have children, you may want to add, "We feel we are the role models for our children and we want to teach them that rather than love ending, love should increase when a loved one needs it the most." We hope this will silence their remarks once they've realized that they actually hurt you. You and Martha can then more peacefully continue your loving relationship with your mother-in-law.

Dear Eldercare 911,

My father had several strokes and entered a rehab facility for therapy in the hopes of coming home to live with my stepmother again. She took public transportation for over an hour each way to see him every day. She stayed all day, at least eight or ten hours. She talked to him, held his hand, kissed him, and never left his side. When the doctors said he'd never walk again, she yelled at them and fought with them to keep him walking. They did what she asked, but eventually they had to stop because his insurance refused to pay for treatment that obviously wasn't helping him. Against the advice of the doctors, the nurses, my brothers, and me, she took him home instead of leaving him in the nursing home. He couldn't walk, he couldn't use his hands, he was incontinent, but by some miracle, he could talk. My stepmother said that was enough for her. Even our kids got in the act and said, "Ruth, don't do it. It's too much for you." The social workers at the hospital set up a complete home-care regimen including physical and occupational therapy visits, nursing visits, and equipment that she emptied her husband's and her savings to pay for. We begged her to stop, but she refused to be diverted. She continued on what we thought was a fool's errand every day, all day and all night. Two years later my father took his first step with a walker. Six months after that he died. Thirty days later my stepmother, Ruth, passed from natural causes during a peaceful night's sleep. It was obvious to all of us that she loved him so much she couldn't conceive of living without him any longer.

—Five Kids Who Finally Understand What Love Really Means, Oregon

Dear Five Kids,

Thank you for this wonderful tribute to your parents. Your stepmother did much more than bring your father home. First, she showed a determination firmly rooted in love, respect, and loyalty to her partner and to a relationship that maintained its strength. Second, if only for a little while, she gave your father what we all need to face each day—hope.

To our readers: We do not advocate removing your parent from a nursing home in an effort to duplicate the story you just read. If your parent needed a nursing home before you read "Five Kids," the chances are that he still needs that care. If you have a loving relationship with your parent, show it by using the lesson in this story to advocate fiercely on his behalf in the nursing home and to teach your children to do the same.

C. THE IMPACT OF STRESS

Dear Eldercare 911,

I'm a single mother with a son in his turbulent teens. I had been searching for a move up the career ladder and recently found it in another city. When I moved, I also moved my mother from her nursing home to one in my new city. The new nursing home didn't work out, so I brought her home to live with me. We made a pact that when she needed more care than I could give her, she'd go back to the nursing home. Eventually that happened. Now I feel guilty for not having her in my home longer than I did. Even though I did my best, I feel as if I was deficient and somehow failed her. I also feel guilty that I can visit her only two or three times each week because I'm starting a new career and her nursing home is about forty minutes from me. Sometimes when she sees me coming, she claps her hands like a child and gleefully says, "Oh, I've been praying that you would come." That makes me feel so bad, but I just can't get there more often. My stress level is crushing me.

—Rhonda, New Hampshire

Dear Rhonda,

Moving a parent to a nursing home is one of the most heart-wrenching tasks that caregivers face. Our guilt and stress often keep hurting us after the move, because every time we visit our parent we also revisit and reassess our decision. When we do that, we bring up our original emotional turmoil all over again. Eventually the stress becomes so heavy it can feel like a weight. For most of us, nursing homes may not always be our first choice, but sometimes they are the best choice for a parent's safety and care. Other times it's the only choice that makes sense. Your parent may need more care than you can provide at home. The stress of caring for your parent at home may have caused you to become ill; the expense of caring for your parent at home may be more than you can afford; you may not have the physical space for your parent and/or a homecare worker; you may travel for your job and be away from home regularly; or you may have any one of a number of other valid reasons for having considered a nursing home.

One of the most important steps you can take is to recognize your *achievements*. You are amazing. We are in awe of the strength you've shown as a single mother who is caring for a teenager and an ailing mother while starting a new job in a new city without your old friends or family for support. In the midst of all this, you found a nursing home for your mother. Later, you brought your mother into your home and cared for her until she needed *more* than you could provide. Now you drive about one and one half hours, two to three times each week, to visit her. Rhonda, your love and feelings of responsibility shine through, and we applaud your efforts. If you feel as though you want or need to do more, here are suggestions that may allow you to increase your presence while you continue visiting on the same schedule. (You don't say what illness your mother has, so all these recommendations may not be suitable.)

- Visit a card store and buy several colorful cards that you can mail so that your mother receives them on the days you don't visit. You can write, address, and stamp them all at the same time, then mail them at appropriate times.
- Put up a pretty bulletin board in your mother's room and ask the aides in the nursing home to tack the cards to the board so that your mother can see them.
- Your mother might enjoy a VCR and old movies with stars she enjoyed as a younger woman. Speak to the administrator first to make certain that the nursing home allows the machine and will operate it for your mother. If your mother has difficulty hearing, but has good vision, ask the nursing home to set up the captions for the hearing impaired. If your mother shares a room and her roommate has no interest in watching the movies, earphones might be appropriate.
- Check your local library for Books on Tape. They usually come in a variety of formats—mystery, drama, romance, religious—and may entertain your mother for hours. Large-print books may be another option.
- Create a scrapbook or a photo album with old family photos as well as newer ones, and leave it for your mother to browse through when she feels like it. You can update the album regularly. This is a good way to keep her up-to-date on her grandchildren's lives and a wonderful way for family members who live out of town to keep in touch.

If you can afford it, reimburse the aides in the nursing home for their help with setting up the movies and Books on Tape. Some facilities frown on staff accepting monetary gifts from patients or their families. However, you may be able to purchase an inexpensive token of your gratitude. Even something small lets them know that you appreciate their help. They are often overworked and underpaid and have a great deal to do without adding extra duties.

The next time your mother claps her hands with glee, don't read any more into it than that she is happy to see you. Just kiss her hello and answer, "I'm happy to see you, too, Mom!" Then make the most of your time together and have a lovely visit.

Dear Eldercare 911,

Just talking about taking my dad to the doctor raises my blood pressure, which is already high enough thanks to caring for him. What do I have to say or do to make his doctors understand that he is neither deaf nor demented?! First, they have the nerve to ask ME what my father's problems are! Then, when he tries to answer for himself, they don't look at him. Instead, they look to me for confirmation while he's speaking to them. Even worse, when he asks a question, they reply to me. I keep telling them, "I'm not the one who needs help, why don't you talk to my father? He's here with us in this room. It's his problem. He's not demented and stop yelling at him—he's not deaf, either." My dad often tells me how hard it is to grow old—he says he feels useless because he can't do the things he used to enjoy. These doctors make him feel even more useless by assuming he can't think, either. They're stressing both my father and me! I'm sure if they would stop to think how embarrassing it is for him or how much they're hurting him, they would stop. I'm determined to change this. I just don't know how.

—Stressed and Not Going to Take It Anymore, Florida

Dear Stressed,

Good for you! It is cruel and careless for anyone to act as though your father is inferior or a "nonperson." Unfortunately, we see the situation you're describing all too often. It's a double-edged sword for the physician. Family members become angry when he talks "around" a parent, but his patients may be at risk if he doesn't. Too many physicians have seen their patients return for follow-up visits in far worse condition than they were at the beginning of their illness. Much of that can be attributed to patients' inability to report a problem or to understand or follow directions because of a lack of capacity, psychological denial of the problem, or hearing loss. When a caregiver is present, the physician may feel more comfortable getting information and giving instructions to the caregiver, trusting the caregiver to have a more accurate memory of the instructions and to follow through with the recommendations. This technique has saved many lives. On the other side of the coin are the patients like your father, who, though capable, are made to feel embarrassed or useless. Take the doctor aside and explain that your father hears well and is competent to report problems, ask questions, and follow instructions. The doctor may test your analysis. If he does, try to understand that the testing is for your father's safety. Once the doctor confirms your father's ability to take care of himself, your problem should be solved. If, on a future visit, the doctor forgets and reverts to talking to you instead of your father, gently remind him of your conversation or find another doctor.

D. THE IMPACT OF ANGER

Dear Eldercare 911,

I will spare you all the details of this ugly family scene, but here's the short version. My mother is dying and my father is ill. I wouldn't be surprised if he left us soon after Mom. I have been staying in their home, caring for both of them for the last few months. Last week, while I was away for twenty-four hours dealing with another crisis, my brother showed up to "help." He wanted copies of their wills, and he demanded $1,000 from my father for a room he and his wife had reserved for him in a nursing home in Ohio—thousands of miles from Mom and Dad's home and friends, and from me. My poor father was dumbfounded. This was NEVER a family discussion, much less a decision! He told Dad he had no choice, that Mom was dying soon and that Dad could not stay here in his own home. Mother was in tears, my father was furious, hurt, and almost in tears. All my parents wanted was for him to leave. When my father asked him how long he was staying, he bluntly said "Until the end." My poor dad was praying for a miracle. He wasn't thinking about "An End." They both felt like Ted was rushing Mom to her death. After a screaming match, Ted stormed out, without apologizing, like a fifty-six-year-old spoiled brat. We have not heard from him in ten days. This was not his decision to make, and I'm sure his stupid and cruel action has expedited my mom's decline. I got so mad at him for the hurt he caused that I almost had a stroke myself. I have never been that angry in my adult life. How could any child do this to his dying parents?

—Furious, Florida

Dear Furious,

You have every right to be angry at your brother's insensitively to your parents' feelings and yours. You don't tell us anything about your family's interaction prior to this time, so we'll ask: Has your brother always had a poor relationship with your parents or with you? Is he jealous of your relationship with your mother and father? Does he have a history of demanding money from them? If so, then his actions may be a continuation of years gone by, and the only real surprise might be the actual depth of his lack of feeling or respect for any of you. Under these circumstances, you may want to consider your future relationship with him carefully. And if you haven't already done so, we urge you to consult with an attorney to help protect your parents' assets.

However, if this was out of character for Ted, then think about what other motive he may have had. Try to speak to him about your perception of what he did without letting your anger control your words. You might tell him how hurt and surprised you were that he seemed to care nothing about your parents' feelings or yours—only about getting a copy of their wills and moving Dad to Ohio whether he wanted to go or not. He may surprise you yet again and tell you that because you've been helping your parents for so long, he wanted to do his part and this was all he could think of. If Ted truly hoped to help, he'll be sorry that he upset you and happy to cooperate when you offer to help him. This is an example of a more loving approach he can use when he talks with your parents: "Dad, Nora and I love you very much and we're going to do everything we can to help you recover. We know you don't like to talk about these things with us, but we can help you more effectively if we are financially prepared for whatever happens in the future. Do you feel up to talking now?" If he was trying to be a good son and brother but you're still having a hard time getting over the mess he made trying to help, you may be able to think of something he can do to repay you—like keep you company for a while and help you with some of your responsibilities during this very difficult time.

Regardless of what you find or decide, please take steps to help reduce the damage your anger may have on your health.

- Write out the entire scene. Don't worry about punctuation or spelling or continuity. Just keep writing until you've written down your feelings and have nothing more to say. This is a wonderful way to vent and work out your feelings.
- Exercise regularly with workouts or long walks. Relaxing baths can help soothe your senses.
- Don't forget your own nutrition while you're caring for your parents. Be sure you get the essential vitamins and minerals you need for the strenuous mental and physical challenges you face each day.
- Take a few hours off on a regular basis. Hire a home health aide to relieve you at least twice each week for a minimum of four hours each time. This is critical to your ability to continue as an effective caregiver.

If your anger does not subside, seek help from a mental health counselor or a medical doctor. It would be even more of an injustice if your brother's actions make you ill.

Dear Eldercare 911,

I always thought love was the most powerful emotion, but now I know it's anger. I go to bed angry, I get up angry, I spend the day in the same state. I'm angry at my parents for putting me in this position (caregiver without funds), I'm angry at myself for offering to help, I'm angry at my brothers and sisters for saying they would help and then not helping, I'm angry at my wife and children because they're angry at me! When we said we'd help my parents, we didn't realize we'd be doing it alone. We scrimped and saved for years so my wife could stay home with our children; now she has to go back to work. I work two jobs and never have time for my family. They're tired of it and so am I. I love them and I don't want to desert them, but I've done what I could do. Now I want help or I want out.

—Ready to Blow, Nevada

Dear Ready to Blow,

You're right. There is a large, dangerous storm brewing, and you need help. Your anger is so strong that we're afraid you may have become a "burned-out" caregiver: too stressed to continue effectively, *regardless of how much time or money* you contribute. You can read more about burnout in chapter 9, but the bottom line is this: at this point it may even be dangerous for you to remain in a position where you are expected to handle the emotional, physical, and financial strains that go hand in hand with caregiving. Please step back and read the options we're recommending to help you take a break from your caregiving responsibilities. It's very important to reduce your obligations as fast as possible before someone inadvertently gets hurt.

There are several things that you can do to help keep your parents safe and relieve some or all of the financial burdens you're carrying alone. Without assistance from the rest of your family, it will be harder—but still possible—to also reduce your time involvement, which will allow you to spend more time with your family. If you follow these recommendations, the people you contact will offer additional help.

- If your parents suffer from Parkinson's disease or Alzheimer's disease or another illness, call the dedicated organization (American Heart Association, Parkinson's Association, etc.) in your community and speak to a family counselor. Tell her what you told us and ask for assistance that includes benefits and counseling. You can find toll-free numbers or Web sites to help you locate these organizations in chapter 13, "Resources."

- If your parents are not incapacitated by a disease but are too frail to remain alone, call the Area Agency on Aging and follow the same procedure: tell them your story and ask for assistance. It's important to also ask for counseling to help you cope with your anger. You'll find the toll-free number in chapter 13, "Resources." The national organization will help you locate the branch nearest you.
- Ask these organizations for assistance in determining what financial or other benefits you or your parents are entitled to. Also ask for help to apply for those benefits. *There should be no charge for this service.*
- Ask these organizations to recommend an elder law attorney who offers a free consultation to find out if your parents are eligible for Medicaid benefits and assistance for healthcare, medications, home health visits, or even food. Medicaid is a federal program that is funded by the state you live in. Because individual states may have different components, the laws and regulations in one state may differ from those in another state. For that reason, it is important to speak to an attorney who practices elder law in the state where you'll be receiving benefits. This way you'll be certain you are complying with that state's laws. Look in the "Resources" chapter for help in locating one near your parents.
- It may be time to consider alternative housing for your parents. If so, Medicaid benefits may help with all or part of the costs.
- If either of your parents was in the armed forces, call the Veterans Administration (VA) for an appointment to determine if they are entitled to VA benefits: healthcare, medications, hospitalization, housing assistance, or nursing home care. You can also inquire online if you wish to do so. The VA can be complicated and you'll need to stay on top of this to help assure success.
- Ask the disease-specific organization or the Area Agency on Aging for help in finding a daycare program to help look after your parents during the daytimes. Many have a sliding scale fee—this means the cost is whatever your parents can afford. Some programs also provide transportation.
- If your parents can benefit from companions or sitters, call your church, synagogue, or the Area Agency on Aging and ask if they have a visiting service. Remember, these visitors will not change diapers, bathe your

parents, or administer medications. They will talk to or read to your parents, and watch TV, listen to music, or go for walks with them.

Don't be discouraged if you don't succeed on your first call. Keep trying. Please be specific and frank about the urgency of your feelings and your need. And one more thing: you were right the first time—*love* is the most powerful emotion. You've clearly shown your love by helping your parents when you were able. Now show it again and keep helping them by recognizing that it's time for someone else to take over for their sake and yours. Good luck.

E. THE IMPACT OF FEAR

Dear Eldercare 911,

My mother has Alzheimer's and lives in an assisted living community. I help pay the bills, but I don't visit her. I visited her twice, and as hard as I've tried, I just can't do it. I get as far as the front door of the community and I stop breathing. My heart pounds and what I really want to do is run away as fast as I can. I walk back to my car instead of going in. When I get in my car and sit down, I'm drenched from perspiration. I've never known such fear. I can taste it. My family is incensed. They don't understand how I can be so "awful" and "uncaring." I'm not. I love my mother. What I'm afraid of is that I'll get the disease—not from visiting her, but from the genes I inherited. And as long as I don't see her, I can suppress my fear. I know that sounds stupid, but my aunt had it too. My brother and sister are getting tested, but I refused. What do you think?

—Feeling Foolish, Louisiana

Dear Feeling Foolish,

You need make no apologies for the terror that you feel. There is certainly nothing foolish about it. Alzheimer's is a horrible disease that wreaks havoc on the lives of those who have it and their families. Hoping you never become a victim is a normal reaction. When a first-line relative has the disease, feeling more vulnerable is a realistic reaction. But the debilitating panic that you describe may have its roots in many factors and influences in your life, and likely impacts other areas of your life as well. Please consider speaking to your physician about your reaction, and if he suggests a more in-depth look into the reasons behind your dread, try your best to go forward with his recommendation.

Testing is a very personal and serious decision that should be made slowly and thoughtfully and only after you discuss your situation with a board-certified neurologist specializing in Alzheimer's disease (AD) *and* with a mental health therapist who can guide you through the aftermath regardless of the results. What are your sisters and brothers expecting from their tests? What are their plans if their tests are positive? Do they feel they will achieve peace of mind if their tests are negative? The same questions apply to you. What actions will you or they take if scans show the disease at work in your brain? Have you or your sisters and brothers discussed this with your spouses or partners, and children?

You have been brave enough to begin your quest for help by sharing your story with other caregivers. Stay strong and continue seeking help to find the peace of mind you are looking for. Once you come to terms with your own dread of the disease, you may be better prepared to cope with whatever lies ahead.

Dear Eldercare 911,

After my father-in-law passed away, my mother-in-law stayed alone in their apartment and grieved. Most of their friends had moved or died off over the years; even her doctor required a long bus trip or cab ride. In the thirty years they lived in that apartment the neighborhood changed from residential to industrial. The area wasn't safe anymore. I finally convinced my husband and his three sisters and brothers to move Mom to a wonderful assisted living community nearer to where we all live. She objected every step of the way; her fear of losing her independence was obvious. She had other fears as well: she was afraid the other residents would be "too old" and she feared she would never again see the possessions she had to leave behind—all the things you hear about all the time—but we finally made it. It took her about two months to adjust, and it was hell around here. She just kept telling my husband and his siblings that she wanted to go home, and the five of them talked every night about whether to take her out and move her back (they held on to her apartment in case she didn't like the assisted living residence). Then she began to change. She gained weight, socialized with people, went with the residents on trips to the theater and shopping malls—all the things people do when they have a good life. I think it was the first time she felt safe in years. But my family couldn't get over her past pleadings and never noticed the change. Two weeks ago my brother-in-law finally blew his cork. He took Mom out and put her back in her apartment—alone—without any consultation with the rest of us and without any plans for her future. He didn't think one day further than their "great escape" as he now calls it. A therapist told me he was reacting to *his* fear. When I went to see my mother-in-law my, heart broke. She's back to the withdrawn person she was before she moved. My husband is beside himself. We want to help her but we don't know what to do. We're afraid she'll die from loneliness and neglect.

—Patsy, Mississippi

Dear Patsy,

Your story resonates with thousands of caregivers across the country who have tried to help their parents and gotten caught up in the emotions of the moment. We agree with you; you're mother-in-law was safer and happier in her assisted living community. Many people who are resistant to the move at first find enormous benefits in the lifestyle of assisted living for the same reasons you described.

Let's talk about how you can help her. You don't mention anything about powers of attorney or guardianship or relationships within your family, so all these recommendations may not be appropriate. Choose the suggestions that will work best for you.

- Ask your husband to call a family meeting where you can talk to all his brothers and sisters.
- Talk to the social worker at the assisted living community and find out all you can about your mother-in-law's life from the day she moved in until the day she moved out. Ask if there is room for her to move back.
- Talk to her physician about what changes he may have seen, and talk to the wellness center director at the assisted living community.
- Then talk to your family. Ask them to listen and let you tell your story without interruption and to please keep an open mind. Then promise you will do the same for them after you've finished.
- Tell them what you found out and what your fears are. Be clear that you *have no doubt* that your brother-in-law acted out of love, but you are convinced he would have acted differently if he had been up-to-date on her status.
- Ask the family to talk about the way they see her now as compared to the way she was in her final days at the community.
- If you can't get a consensus, suggest hiring a professional care manager for a geriatric assessment. This is an independent report that will help you determine the best course of action for your mother-in-law's health, safety, and quality of life. Ask for a written report and be certain to confirm the fee before the assessment begins.

- If your family holds firm that they are not moving her back, end the meeting, but talk to your husband privately about consulting an elder law attorney about your options.
- When you meet with the attorney, ask about powers of attorney, temporary or permanent guardianship of the person and/or property, and other options the attorney feels you have. If your mother-in-law has full capacity, you will need her consent for this. Under the circumstances, she might give it.

Please act quickly. This will require strength and determination, but it's worth it. Your mother-in-law is lucky to have you as an advocate.

F. THE IMPACT OF GUILT

Dear Eldercare 911,

When Dad was nearing the end, he was in such bad shape that I had taken him to hospice for evaluation and a few days of respite. He ended up staying there. He no sooner arrived, when he fell twice and the doctor in charge ordered him to not walk anymore. He advised that my father would be better off staying there, where his medications could be monitored and nurses were available twenty-four hours. I felt like a traitor. In retrospect, I know it was the right thing, because his pain was becoming so unmanageable and he was bedridden and too heavy for me to help alone. I had just finished caring for my mother who died of cancer, and now so quickly again, the whole sudden need to deal with bedsores, bedpans, bathing—just the things to try to keep him comfortable—became insurmountable. I justify my decision through common sense, but that doesn't diminish the guilt that I've betrayed my father by not letting him stay in his own bed. But three years later, the question still haunts me: Did I kill him because I couldn't fix him? Will I ever get over this loss and confusion?

—Annie, Florida

Dear Annie,

How emotionally devastating and physically exhausting it must have been to care for two very ill parents. The enormous load of caring for *one* parent can be powerful enough to break down your defenses, but the added stress of caring for two parents who died so quickly, one after the other, can be even more costly to your physical and emotional quality of life.

We don't know how long you will continue to feel guilt and anguish. Neither we nor anyone else can tell you not to feel it, nor can we take it away from you. But we can give you hope: the answer to your last question is *yes,* you can eventually live with your feelings. And *no*, you didn't kill him because you never had the power to save him.

Often caregivers who feel that they are doing everything they can to help their parents end up feeling guilty when their parents die. Even though they know they've tried their best, they feel they should have found something more. When we ask "What else could you have done?" the answer is usually "I don't know. But there had to be something." Rather than consciously admit that they could not keep a parent from illness or death, many caregivers retain feelings of guilt for circumstances and outcomes over which they had no control.

Do you remember when you *promised* yourself, your parents, or your family that you could do more for your parents than anyone else, including medical professionals or hospice? You probably never made that promise because prior to becoming a caregiver you may not have taken on the burden of believing you could do more than was humanly possible. Many of our guilty feelings stem from forgetting that all we agreed to was to *try* to help. We didn't guarantee results because before we became overwhelmed, we saw the problem differently. Before you became intimately involved with your parents' suffering, it probably was clear to you that you would help them as best you could but that you had little or no control over most of their problems. Many times we feel guilty not because we didn't do our best, but because feeling guilty is often easier and less painful than feeling helpless.[1]

Try to concentrate more on how much you helped your parents—on the loving care you provided within your skill level and control. Because your father was in end-stage cancer, bedridden, and too heavy for you to manage, and because his pain was so severe, your continuing to care for him would more than likely have increased his pain and discomfort. Rather than worry about your own need to personally care for him, you did the right thing and put your father's needs first. Hospice is known for its ability to control pain and provide comfort during the dying process.

Consider asking your physician or hospice for a referral to a licensed therapist or social worker for grief counseling. It's time for you to ease your pain by learning to appreciate yourself for the caring person you are. We hope it also helps heal your heart.

Dear Eldercare 911,

If I didn't feel like such a dumbo, this would be funny. My mother is driving me CRAZY. I swear she invented guilt. It's pathetic to think that a ninety-three-pound, eighty-five-year-old, mildly demented woman who comes up to my shoulders can get the best of me, a criminal defense lawyer, every time! Last night when I called her, she said she was on a starvation diet and wouldn't eat until I took her out of the assisted living community I had just put her into a month ago. I bought right into it and worried all night whether I had done the right thing or not. Today, I went over there unannounced and found her eating a doughnut, which turned out to be *dessert* to finish off the soup, salad, and sandwich that she ate for lunch! A week ago, she gave me hell on the phone for putting her in an "institution." She said she was running out of there at the first opportunity and finished off her tirade with her traditional "I hope your children do this to you, Julia. You'll be sorry for what you did to me. God will take care of you." I took off work the next day and went over to see her and found her *dancing* to the live piano played by an entertainer who came in for the afternoon. She also had a piece of paper in her room from the current events meeting she had attended that morning and a note not to forgot the shopping trip to the mall the next day. The social director tells me she's one of their most active residents—that she socializes with everyone and enjoys herself tremendously. She looks ten years younger. I have three questions: Is guilt inherited? Do I have to worry about treating my kids like that? And is there a way to turn her off? She's been doing this to me for years, and I could use some relief from this torture.

—Julia, Nebraska

Dear Julia,

Pine no more; your wish is about to be answered. The clue to achieving the silence you long for is in the last part of your question, "she's been doing this to me for years." Your mother's habits are well established, and it is unrealistic to think that you can effect any change in the way she manipulates you. We're guessing she's won too many battles for too many years—in other words, her tactics have paid off, and so she has no reason to change them. The fact that she has mild dementia brings up two other points: First, since short-term memory is usually the first to be damaged, her guilt skills appear to lie in *long-term* memory. This means she has probably been "guilting you" for a *very* long time. And second, her dementia may be increasing and she may actually believe all or part of what she tells you when you're speaking with her. Either way, she's not going to change. All the changing has to take place in your role in this continuing melodrama.

Try this strategy: the next time your mother tells you she's going on a hunger strike, say the following: "Mom, I don't think you should do that, but if you really want to, that's your decision. I'm doing all I can to give both of us a good life and it hurts me deeply when you're angry with me, so I'm going to hang up now. I'll call you tomorrow (or later)." Then do exactly what you said and hang up the phone. You can call back later to see how your mother is feeling, or check with the community to see if she is taking part in the day's activities. A note of caution: if your mother's dementia has progressed, she won't remember your conversation and will continue her guilt trips. In that case, assuming you are still satisfied with her care, you'll need to remind yourself continually that her pleadings are based on patterns etched in years gone by. Try to end the conversation and pick it up again a little later—when she's forgotten and you can both enjoy talking to each other.

G. RECOGNIZING YOUR STRENGTHS

Dear Eldercare 911,

I didn't volunteer to be a caregiver. I just didn't know what else to do and felt that events were beyond my control. But learning to advocate for my father helped me develop a new sense of my strengths and capabilities. In fact, the skills I developed to be a more effective caregiver ended up giving me a control over my life that I could never have achieved on my own in a million years.

—Maria, Georgia

Dear Maria,

We hear the pride in your voice. Many caregivers feel the way you do and are equally as proud. They should be. Caregivers face new and life-altering challenges every day. Conquering those problems often produces new coping methods or leaves us with more productive life-management strategies. Those new skills make us happier and more in control. We celebrate your new strengths with you.

Dear Eldercare 911,

People who have known me for years are amazed at the advocacy skills I have developed. Being a caregiver pushed me into being very assertive on behalf of my mom, which is a big change from my Libra nature ... literally almost to kicking butt! I just don't have patience for cruelty or BS these days. And why should I? We had wonderful caring professionals, but we also had several who needed my newfound ability to make things happen when I'm roaring mad. I'm smiling now—what a hilarious thought! No one who knew me before this, not even my husband or my best friends, could EVER picture me roaring!

—New Lioness, Vermont

Dear Lioness,

Long may you roar! The world would be a far better place with less cruelty and BS, and we're sure your mother was glad to have your considerable vocal power working on her behalf.

Dear Eldercare 911,

I went to my mother's appointments with her in spite of my intense fear of physicians and hospitals. She was aggravated if anyone questioned her authority or decisions, but she wouldn't have stood up to them. I did it for her. I made them treat me and her with dignity and treat us as human beings with brains. I'm proud of that. It's my business to advocate for others, but this was very different. After she passed, I realized it was one of my most important accomplishments.

—Still Afraid, North Carolina

Dear Still Afraid,

In our eyes, you're standing at least an inch taller. It's much harder when it's personal, but you accepted your fear and conquered its limitations on your and your mother's lives. Well done. Stay strong.

Dear Eldercare 911,

Watching helplessly as my father died a slow, painful death was the most horrible experience I have ever had. Also, in some ways, the most liberating—it taught me what's important in life. It took all my willpower, but I've changed my life: I completely realigned my priorities, making me and my family number one on the list. For the first time in years, I feel like a husband and father, like a real part of my family, instead of just the guy who provides for them.

—Carlos, Indiana

Dear Carlos,

What a wonderful legacy your father left you—the power to love your-self and your family—the strength to fully appreciate what matters in life. Congratulations on your new life. Enjoy it.

Dear Eldercare 911,

What a difference it makes when you approach your idiot relatives nonjudgmen-tally—I know that sounds like a joke or an oxymoron, but it's not. Caregiving taught me who and what counts in this life. I know now that my opinion of myself is the most important one. Accepting your family for who they are and letting their BS roll like water off a duck's back—now, that's Strength!

—Sandra, Alabama

Dear Sandra,

Accepting your opinion of yourself as the most important opinion is a powerful positive image—so powerful that it strengthened you enough to accept your relatives for who and what they are. Well done!

Dear Caregivers,

You have the right to feel as loved and appreciated as the parent you are caring for does. *Recognizing your strengths* can help you reach deep within and bring forth the tremendous fortitude that you need to help survive and surmount the ups and downs of your caregiving experiences. But to maintain your stamina, to gain control, your new strengths need nourishment. Where and how you nourish your strengths is an individual decision. You may find strength in reaching out to your family and friends or in doing something that makes you feel good and worthwhile like painting, writing, or volunteering for a charitable organization. Or you may reinforce your strength from the words and voices of other caregivers who feel what you feel and think so many similar thoughts. In addition to all that you do for yourself, we hope that the worksheet on the next page, "Nourishing Your Strengths," will help you decrease your stress and increase your quality of life.

Nourishing Your Strengths

Caregivers know how far a little love and caring goes toward decreasing stress and increasing quality of life. Isn't it puzzling that those who are so good at giving this gift to others are so neglectful of themselves? It's time to show appreciation for yourself. It's time for you to feel as loved and cared for as the person you care for feels. If you can squeeze two minutes into your day—120 seconds—you can begin to change your life.

Take two quiet minutes each morning as you begin your day and repeat these four affirmations *out loud*. Add others that are specific to your life. You'll be surprised at how differently your day unfolds.

1. I know that my best is all that anyone, including myself, can ask of me. Starting today, I will believe that when I've done my best, my best is good enough.

2. I will not waste my time or energy on people who contribute nothing to my life but stress and self-doubt. From this day forth, I will answer politely, or not answer at all, and then I will move on.

3. I deserve to feel nurtured, and it is within my power to have that feeling. As of this moment, I resolve to maintain a quality of life that includes time for nurturing myself.

4. I want to value the good in myself as much as I value the good in others. Starting today, I will begin each day by giving myself the recognition I deserve for my accomplishments.

If there are other changes you'd like to make to help nourish your power, add them to this list:

5. _____
   _____

6. _____
   _____

2

SAYING *NO* TO TOXIC PEOPLE

A. SAVING YOURSELF: WHY YOU NEED TO SAY *NO*

Dear Eldercare 911,

I feel like I'm living in a permanent psychodrama! I'm constantly lectured by my aunt who thinks I'm not a good enough daughter to my mother, regularly bullied for money by my brother because I have Mom's power of attorney, expected to deal with Pop's never-ending demands for attention, and continue to raise three teenagers, work, and be a good partner. Who the hell wrote this script?

—Sharon, California

Dear Eldercare 911,

I live in Colorado, my mother lives in Texas. She has mild-to-medium dementia and lives in a really nice assisted living community. She continuously complained how unhappy she was in "this place" and finally guilt-tripped me into making an unannounced visit to Texas to see for myself. On the phone, she pleads to go home, but when she hangs up, she gets right back to sing-alongs or other group activities. She looks healthier, she's more alert, and she's in ten times better shape than she was at home alone or would be with me (I work all day). Even so, I still feel guilty.

—John, Colorado

Dear Sharon and John,

Like many other caregivers, you are on the receiving end of abuse from demanders and guilt-trippers, two of our top ten *toxic people* categories. We call them *toxic* because they are harmful to our emotional and physical health. Sometimes deliberately, more often because they are too self-centered to ever stop and consider any feelings other than their own, their words or actions

47

tear down our self-esteem or damage our relationships. They invade our privacy and our thoughts and leave only negative results behind. *Toxic people* may be devious, thoughtless, selfish, or controlling—but their goals are ultimately the same: they care only for *their* wants and needs. *You* matter little or not at all.

It's probably safe to say that most caregivers struggle with issues from one or more toxic family members. Learning to say *no* is one of the primary keys to maintaining your own emotional and physical health.

The facts are irrefutable.

- Caregivers often experience depression at three times the rate of others in their own age groups and are more likely to become physically ill themselves.
- More than 75 percent of caregivers receive little or no help from family members.

Think about this concept and you'll be halfway to saying *no*: *toxic people want you to accept interference or manipulation from them, but they feel no responsibility to offer you any concrete assistance unless that assistance helps them further manipulate you.* If you allow them to repeat their actions, you become an enabler. You actually *help them abuse you* by giving them tacit permission to continue mistreating you. It isn't easy to say *no* and maintain your new position, but if you're willing to learn, you can put an end to their power over you.

It's important to say *no* from a position of power and strength. You have both. All you need are the guidelines. After reading the questions, answers, and recommendations in this chapter, create your personal action plan and begin regaining control.

If you need additional support while you design your strategy, remember this overriding and lifesaving rule: *providing care to your loved one does not legally or morally require you to sign away your rights to take care of yourself and protect your own individuality.* This chapter will help give you ideas on how to deal with the *top ten toxic people in your life* and may also give you a long overdue laugh.

B. THE TOP TEN TOXIC PEOPLE

1. Demanders

Dear Eldercare 911,

My mother's a nag. There I said it, and a bolt of lightning didn't strike me down. When the home health aide called and said that my mother wants her to wash, starch, and iron all of the curtains in the house, I told her to forget it. When she called back and said my mom fired her, it was my turn to demand that something has to change.

—Marcia, New York

Dear Marcia,

We can all relate to parents and family members who have outrageous expectations and just don't know when to quit. They expect you to drop everything and serve their wishes. Demanders seem to have a poor attitude when you cannot fulfill their needs, and you might describe them as childlike because they require immediate gratification.

We know that the average caregiver provides assistance for approximately eighteen hours a week; some provide as much as forty, fifty, or more hours. The day-to-day demands of caregiving compounded by work, family, and social obligations leave many women and men physically and emotionally exhausted, with precious little time to take care of themselves. Most caregivers will admit that controlling their time is critical, and demanders are one of the biggest time eaters. Read on.

Dear Eldercare 911,

Please tell me what to do. My father begs me to take him to get a haircut in the middle of a workday. He keeps calling until I give in. I can't keep this up.

—Jacob, New Jersey

Dear Jacob,

Before you begin, take a deep breath and then say "I can't help you today (at this minute), but I'll be happy to help you on Monday." If he replies, "Monday is too late," or "Last time I asked you to take me to the barber you took me right away," explain that this is the best you can do today: "Dad last time when I took you to the barber right away I was on vacation. I had the time. I don't have that luxury today." It may take a great deal of your patience and strength, but remember it is very important for you to adhere to your decision. Remember to

- take a few extra minutes and allow your dad to express how he feels about the delay.
- reaffirm that you can take him for a haircut on another day.
- remind him that he is important to you, but at times you have other responsibilities that you cannot neglect.

Demanders resent boundaries because they see their needs as paramount to anyone else's. It is your job to set the limits as clearly as possible.

Dear Eldercare 911,

We are a family of three sisters and two brothers. Our brothers do nothing, see nothing, and hear nothing. As far as I'm concerned, Mom has three children. Our eighty-seven-year-old mother is independent, alert, and relatively healthy, but she is a "demander." She always expects everyone to jump and smile the minute she wants or needs something. We feel exhausted and want to stop this pattern of behavior. We try taking turns, but she still places too much demand on our time. How can we put an end to this vicious cycle?

—Janette, Michigan

Dear Janette,

Historically, your mother has demanded your time and energy. As children you may not have felt the burden of her needs as much as you do now. You and your sisters can change your mother's expectations and set specific limits of what you are willing to do. It is most effective if you face it together.

- Arrange a meeting with your mother at a time that is convenient for all of you.
- Decide on one spokesperson. This is important because if all of you address the issue, your mom will feel as if you are ganging up on her.
- Be very clear that you want to help her out. Try saying: "Mom, we love you and want to help you but we all have many responsibilities such as our jobs and our own health issues. We are available for you, but only

on specific days, at certain times. Let's talk about what arrangements we can make that will work well for all of us."

- Give your mom a chance to respond to your statement. She may be very emotional and angry, and she may try to make you feel as if you are deserting her. Reassure her that you are not abandoning her, but you are placing some limits on the amount of time you can attend to her needs.

- Try decreasing the time you spend with her in small increments. For example, if you have been available seven days a week, reduce it to four or five days for a few weeks. Then reduce it to two or three days a week. See what works best for you and Mom.

Remember, demanders require very specific boundaries. Changing the course of your mom's behavior will not be easy. Be strong and consistent, and it is our hope that your mom will begin to understand that you can help her, but at mutually agreeable times.

Saying *No* to Demanders

Over time a demander may begin to adjust to small changes and afford you the opportunity to work on setting new limits and effecting additional changes that work for all of you.

- **I will not be bullied.** I will be firm so that the demander learns that he may not always get his way.

- **I will set specific limits.** I will reinforce what I am willing or not willing to do for my family member.

- **I will be kind.** I will let my family member know I love her and care about her, but that I am not available upon demand except for emergencies.

---

2. Time Abusers

Dear Eldercare 911,

I wish I could buy my dad a talking clock. I would program it to say "John is unavailable Monday–Friday until 5 PM, because he works all day, and he only has Saturdays off to rest." Maybe then and only then will he stop making one appointment after the other and expect me to drop everything and drive him. The minute I feel like I have a few hours to myself, he schedules another appointment. I have to make him understand that this cannot continue.

—John, California

Dear John,

Family members who fill their day using *your* time as *their* time, even if you ask them not to, seem to develop a pattern of behavior that not only intrudes on your workday but even on the time you spend together. A time abuser is not considerate of your time and will abuse your time whenever he has the opportunity. You may try to limit your telephone conversations and visits, but your family member seems to ignore your requests and continues to talk on and on. You may offer to take your mom out for lunch, but by the end of the meal she is inviting herself for dinner. You feel angry and frustrated by the intrusion and the toll it takes on your time. The clock is ticking, and it is time for you to say *no* to time abusers. These examples will help you.

Dear Eldercare 911,

It's 11 PM and there I am in the middle of the twenty-four-hour mini-mart buying groceries with my eighty-seven-year-old mother. I thought it was a quick trip for milk and bread, but she further took advantage of me by taking more than an hour shopping for "odds and ends." I didn't get to sleep for hours and I had a 7:30 AM meeting. I just can't continue to be a midnight "shopaholic." What can I do?

—Kathy, Pennsylvania

Dear Kathy,

You might want to begin by saying something positive and reassuring to your mother. For example: "I enjoy spending time with you, Mom, and I certainly don't mind taking you shopping once a week." This helps the elderly person understand that setting limits on specific days and times does not mean you don't care about her needs. You may continue: "We can go shopping on Wednesday, Mom. Please make a list of all the things you need. If you have any grocery coupons, put them in an envelope so that we can take them with us to the store. We can pick up everything for the week. If that is not convenient, I can help you with your list and call in an order. The grocery store will deliver it to you the same day." This approach gives your mom some reassurance and options for her shopping needs. As an added bonus, consider the following two suggestions.

- Buy Mom a coupon folder or envelope specifically designed to help sort out grocery coupons by category, such as sections for produce, cereals, and paper goods. This organizer will help keep things easily accessible.
- When it is convenient for you, offer to take your mom out to lunch to make the most of your time together.

Be prepared for your mom to test your resolve and try to change your mind. Stay the course and you will achieve your goal.

Dear Eldercare 911,

Dad is on new medication and the doctor alerted us that he may feel sleepy, but he needs to take it. He really has his days and nights confused. The home health aide says she tries to keep him up during the day, but he somehow always ends up in his lounge chair or bed, mouth open, sound asleep. For the past few weeks he calls us between 3 and 4 AM, just to chat. He discusses his dinner or how much he paid for his new television. He is wide awake and we are exhausted and angry. Help us put a stop to this nocturnal chatter.

—Marilyn and Jeffrey, Massachusetts

Dear Marilyn and Jeffrey,

How frustrating it must be for you to receive a telephone call in the middle of the night, only to have the person on the other end begin a conversation about what he ate for dinner! You may want to ask your father if it is all right for you to talk to his doctor about his new medication. If he agrees, these steps may help you with your problem.

- Contact the doctor and tell him about the changes in your dad's sleeping habits. Ask him if this medication can be taken later in the day or if there is an alternative dose or medication that will not make him as drowsy.
- Ask the doctor if he feels your dad requires an evaluation to determine his cognitive functioning. If he thinks an evaluation is an appropriate next step, ask the doctor for a referral to a board-certified neurologist.

If the doctor says that there is no option, then suggest to the home health aide that if your dad had something interesting to do, he might feel more inclined to fight off the sleepiness during the day. A visit to a senior center for lunch, a game of cards, or a walk in the park may provide him with enough stimulation to stay awake during the day and make him sleepy for the night.

Suggest to Dad that before he calls he should look out the window to see if it is dark. If it is dark, you are asleep and you are not willing or able to talk to him. Make sure the home health aide reinforces your wishes. You can prominently place a sign next to his bed or wherever he keeps the telephone: DO NOT CALL MARILYN AND JEFFREY IN THE MIDDLE OF THE NIGHT UNLESS IT IS AN EMERGENCY! Encourage him to keep a notepad by his bedside to write down anything he wants to talk to you about the next day.

Saying *No* to Time Abusers

A time abuser needs you to remind him again and again that you love him. He needs to know that you want to spend time together and hear what he has to say, but at an appropriate, convenient time for you both.

- **I will set time limits.** I will remind my parent and family members that my time is not their time, and I am willing only to chat at appropriate, mutually convenient hours.

- **I will be consistent.** I will select the time of day that is most convenient for me (with the exception of emergencies) to reinforce my wishes. I will try not to deviate from the designated times.

- **I will provide options.** I will arrange for grocery or pharmacy deliveries if we can't find a mutually convenient time to shop. This will help you understand that I am trying to accommodate your needs. When we do shop together, I will set appropriate and reasonable time limits.

---

3. Work Disrupters

Dear Eldercare 911,

My boss is understanding about my mother's telephone calls, but even she has her limits. Mom usually calls once or twice a day, but yesterday she called eight times. Eight times! I have to put a stop to this.

—Jane, Florida

Dear Jane,

Many of our parents learned the value of a hard day's work by adhering to a strong work ethic, dedication to the boss, and loyalty to the company. When they look back, they can recall a time when they had a thirty-minute lunch and a five- or ten-minute break during the day. No one then would have ever considered asking the boss for time off to talk to a family member. Why would they think that at a time when many of us have demanding, twelve-hour-a-day jobs, our responsibilities are any less? Sometimes all we need to do is remind them. However, if your parent continues to call eight times a day, it may be a sign of physical or cognitive decline, and medical attention might be necessary. Please read on and see our recommendations to Maggie and Sam. They should help you put in a good day's work.

> Dear Eldercare 911,
>
> I have a full-time job. My healthy eighty-year-old father is a retired foreman who lives ten blocks away from me. I know that he is lonely. I offered to enroll him in a senior center or buy a new television, anything to keep him busy and away from the telephone. The telephone is his form of entertainment, and between 9 AM and 6 PM I am the star of the show. I need to close this show down before I lose my job. Help!
>
> —Maggie, Michigan

Dear Maggie,

Your dad sounds like someone who really would benefit from a reminder about "the good old days" when the hours on the job were devoted to his work and the men who worked for him. It is important for him to understand that you, too, have a job that you don't want to lose and that unless it's an emergency, the calls can easily wait until after you get home. Try these few steps to help your dad find other ways to keep busy and away from the telephone during working hours.

- Meet with your dad. Begin your conversation by saying: "Dad, think about what would have happened if someone had called you several times a day when you were at your job. I can't take personal phone calls at work. So unless you have an emergency, let's talk after 7 PM, after I get home."
- Talk to him about other ways of keeping busy during the day.
- Talk to your dad about enrolling in a senior center. Talk to him about

how he spent his leisure time in the past. Was he very sociable? Was he a loner? Did he enjoy school and learning, or was he more of a fishing and football enthusiast? Once you focus on what type of entertainment pleases him, you may find a class or a group at a senior center, a church, or a synagogue that specializes in something he enjoys. Knowing that the activity focuses on something he really likes may provide him with a new perspective.

- Set aside time for a periodic luncheon with him. This will give him something special to look forward to during the week.
- Talk to him about your ideas and ask him to give them a try just for you.

Give Dad peace of mind by reminding him that you are available for emergencies. Once he gets involved in other activities during working hours, the telephone calls should decrease and you can once again focus on your job during working hours.

Dear Eldercare 911,

I am an accountant and I have a home office. I usually work 8 AM to 6 PM. My seventy-eight-year-old mother and seventy-five-year-old father have some medical problems, but they are alert and basically very independent. They live in the next town and I try to see them two or three times a month. They think since I am home that they can call five, six, ten times a day to chat or even visit when they feel the urge. How do I stop the intrusions when it is very obvious that they don't get the concept of a home office?

—Sam, Arizona

Dear Sam,

It is time to provide your parents with a clear picture of a home office and how working at home improves your quality of life.

- Talk to them about why it works so well for you. Let them know how convenient it is to work in the privacy of your own home.
- Emphasize the fact that it saves you the cost of renting an office, transportation expenses, and traveling time.
- Explain to your mom and dad that working at home affords you the added flexibility to get things done at your own pace.
- Clearly state: "I love you guys, but between eight and six, I am working. Make believe I am in an office in a large accounting firm. Do

you think I could accept personal telephone calls and visits all day?"

- Suggest a visit to their physician for a complete medical examination if you think that their memory is declining. If this is part of the problem, they may be feeling more anxious and concerned about themselves and be reaching out to you for a sense of security.
- Ask your mom and dad how they spend their day. Do they feel lonely or bored? If they answer no, then let them know how pleased you are. However, be clear that you are not available for chitchat, but you are always available for emergencies. If they answer yes, that they feel lonely and bored, and they have clearance from the doctor, you may want to plant a seed about joining a senior gym, a senior center, or a church or synagogue group.

It's important for you to remember that you are a very supportive and caring son, even if you set specific limits and simply provide some options and alternatives.

Saying *No* to Work Disrupters

Help yourself to remain productive during the workday by reinforcing your needs and firmly letting your family member know that you mean business, especially between nine and five.

- **I will provide reminders.** I will provide a refresher course in old-fashioned work ethics to keep my parent off the phone during business hours.

- **I will provide options.** I will discuss appropriate, stimulating daytime activities to fill my parent's time and interest.

- **I will be available for emergencies only.** I will be clear that I am available for all serious problems but that I can't spend hours talking on the telephone or indulge in surprise office visits. All nonemergency calls have to wait until after office hours.

---

4. Surprise Visitors

Dear Eldercare 911,

I still don't believe it. My husband and I were exhausted from working, settling three kids to sleep, and getting Mom in bed for the night. The house was a holy mess and we were half asleep in front of the TV, when my brother-in-law shows up at the door. He came one thousand miles, unannounced! He had time off and was bored, so he decided to "drop in" and see how Mom was despite his having called and my husband having asked him not to come since this wasn't a good time for us. When my husband showed his anger and called him selfish and inconsiderate, he was stunned to think he'd done something wrong!

—Barbara, New Hampshire

Dear Barbara,

Your husband nailed it! Surprise visitors are selfish and inconsiderate of anyone else's needs and feelings. Some caregivers take them in stride or even enjoy the break in routine, but most caregivers' days are full to the brim without surprises. Spending unscheduled time with visitors often means rescheduling other duties. That multiplies the inconvenience of having surprise visitors because they also disrupt future days. Our emotional health can be affected in a negative manner as well by the extra draining of our already overextended inner resources. To add to the already significant emotional stress, if neither you nor your home is dressed for company, you may feel embarrassed—but if you refuse to let a family member or friend into your home, you may feel guilty.

Of course, it's your visitor who should feel embarrassed and guilty for putting you in this uncomfortable position. But since surprise visitors consider only their own needs, they usually have no concept of the physical and emotional disruption or inconvenience they cause. That means the job of enlightening them is up to you. If you pretend that "it's no bother," your visitor will surely continue his behavior, always visiting at his and never at your convenience.

To heal relations and prevent another visit, take these steps.

- Talk to your brother-in-law now before this becomes a permanent rift.
- Be clear about the inconvenience and establish definite boundaries: "Charlie, we asked you not to come last week because we had too many obligations and we couldn't make time for company. We'd like to see you and so would Mom, so let's try to schedule another visit."
- Assume that Charlie, like many other family members who are not full-time caregivers, has little or no idea of how much time and effort you and your husband put into caring for Mom. Remedy that on his next visit—by putting him to work helping you.
- Plan ahead for jobs he can help with: feeding Mom, taking her out for

a drive or to the mall, reading to her, helping change the linens on her bed, or simply sitting with her and chatting.

Whether you are cooking dinner or washing dishes, make certain you do not let Charlie add to your workload. He is Mom's son, and as such, you can reasonably expect him to carry part of the load when he is visiting.

Dear Eldercare 911,

I help my parents out around their house, helping them write checks for bills or whatever they need. I talk to them every day to make sure they're okay. They've suddenly taken to dropping in to visit without notice at any time of the day or night. Bonnie and I have been married less than a year. We're both building our careers, which necessitates long hours at work, so our time together is special. I want to be alone with my wife without worrying whether the doorbell's going to ring and my parents will come in and expect to be entertained for a couple of hours. How do I tell my parents that they have to call first? I've dropped hints, but they don't seem to pick up on them. I love them and don't want to hurt them, but we deserve some privacy.

—Dave, Kansas

Dear Dave,

You're right. You and Bonnie deserve to feel secure in the privacy of your own home. If hints aren't working, you'll have to be more specific. Try these suggestions.

- Since you help out around your parents' home, we're assuming you've checked the house for problems that may make it uncomfortable for them to stay there. If you haven't, that's a good place to start.
- Consider the possibility that your parents are simply lonely or bored. Perhaps you can help them get involved in a senior center, a synagogue or church group, or a volunteer organization such as a literacy program, meals-on-wheels, adopted grandparents, and so on.
- In addition, talk to them about their visits. Be specific and firm, but also gentle and kind. If possible, begin your conversation with something positive. For example: "Mom and Dad, Bonnie and I really enjoy your visits, but since we are all on such different schedules, it's really hard for us to drop everything and visit with you when you just 'drop in.' It would really help if you could give us a call first."

- If your parents are receptive, your problem is over, except for reminding them from time to time if they forget.
- If they respond negatively, you may hear "I am insulted" or "I guess you just don't want me around." Don't react to that statement. You can't win on that playing field. Take a deep breath, count to ten, and say, "Of course we want you, but we need to have some notice so that we can be available to enjoy our time together."
- If your parents don't want to discuss the situation and they walk away, just let them go for now. You can try again in a few days.
- If they agree but continue to drop in whenever they feel the urge to visit, consider the possibility that they don't remember the discussion and contact their physician for assistance in determining whether they need medical intervention.

If you don't find immediate relief, keep trying. The great oak tree begins with one tiny acorn—in your case, any small compromise beats no compromise at all.

Dear Eldercare 911,

Mom lives with my sister Caroline. Caroline has a bad habit of bringing Mom here once or twice a week, dropping her off, and saying "She's no trouble. I'll be back in a couple of hours." The problem is not that I don't want to help care for Mom; it's that Caroline never calls first or asks if it's convenient. Whether it's eight in the morning or eight at night, she just dumps Mom and leaves. I don't know how to say "no" to them.

—Wendy, Florida

Dear Wendy,

You don't say what your share of the caregiving responsibilities are, which leaves us wondering. Is Caroline overwhelmed with caregiving duties? Does she need a break or is she just irresponsible? It's sounds like a frank evaluation of Mom's support system is in order.

- Choose a time when you and Caroline can sit quietly and talk. Try to eliminate distractions so you can focus on the problem without interruption.
- Acknowledge Caroline's responsibilities in a realistic and appreciative manner. "Caroline, you've done a really good job with Mom and I appreciate the hours you spend."

- Now clearly set out your boundaries. "It must be hard for you to just 'hope' I'm home and drop her off the way you've been doing. It's also very hard on me. I'll be happy to help, but we need to arrange it before you come. I want your word that there will be no more surprises."
- You might need to reinforce this to make it stick, but the most important step is being honest with Caroline about how you feel and what you are willing to do to help.

Consider splitting the cost of hiring a geriatric care manager to help create a care plan that will give Caroline respite and give you the boundaries you need. Because the care manager is familiar with the healthcare community, she may be able to help you access affordable support services that will increase Mom's, Caroline's, and your quality of life.

Saying *No* to Surprise Visitors

Because we don't know when they're coming, it's unrealistic to believe we can control all "surprise visitors." We can, however, control repeat offenders by setting clear, firm boundaries that ask for an agreement "not to drop in without calling first." Follow these guidelines and see how energizing and satisfying it feels to take control of your time!

- **I will not feel guilty or embarrassed.** I have no reason to feel uncomfortable. It's my visitor who should feel that way for creating the need for me to refuse this or future visits.

- **I will be positive.** I will begin my conversation with how much I enjoy seeing my friend or relative, how much the friendship means to me, or how much I love the person.

- **I will set firm, clear boundaries.** I will tell my visitor that I prefer he calls before visiting and I would like him to please do so in the future. If I want to maintain the relationship, I will soften my message by setting a date to get together.

---

5. Know-It-Alls

Dear Eldercare 911,

I know people make in-law jokes, but this is no joke. My brother-in-law has a very bad habit of criticizing everything my husband and I try to do for their parents. He never actually helps, but he always has something to say. We are trying so hard to do what is right, but he is driving us crazy.

—Cynthia, South Carolina

Dear Cynthia,

Most families have at least one member who continually creates stress and self-doubt by always telling us what we are doing wrong, yet that person is never available to help or take over any caregiving responsibilities. This can make us feel so angry that we want to scream and strike out at him. But most of the time we keep it bottled up inside, because, after all, "it's family," and no matter how we may feel, we don't want to ruin family relationships. Sometimes it just takes a little preparation and a good solid answer to stop these people in their tracks. Keep reading for helpful coping skills.

Dear Eldercare 911,

My older sister, Pam, thinks she knows everything. Last week I was at Mom's house, doing the cooking and the laundry. Pam marches in and starts criticizing the meal and even the way I fold the laundry. She said I should have cooked the meat on the grill instead of in the oven and I should have folded all the towels with the design facing up. Once she gave her instructions, she left. I have to say and do something, but what?

—Nancy, Washington

Dear Nancy,

Before you explode with anger and frustration, it is time to call her bluff. Confronting Pam may not be the easiest thing you have ever done, but it will likely provide you with a sense of control and satisfaction. The next time Pam has anything to say, confidently respond by saying: "That's a great idea. I'm going to turn this over to you right now." Or "Since you feel that way, I hope you will consider this offer to share the responsibilities with me." That usually quiets down know-it-alls for a while. You may not always get help, but you probably won't be bothered as much. You can use these same responses over and over again. Remember, you are doing the best you can for your mom. With a little luck, Pam will put up or shut up!

Dear Eldercare 911,

I always thought it took years and years of medical school and training to be a physician. My sister, Cathy, is a secretary-doctor, or so she thinks. Although Mom has a wonderful geriatric physician, my sister insists on giving free medical advice to Mom. After she reads one article in a magazine, she has the cure for the disease. How can I impress upon her that Mom is in good and capable hands? Unfortunately, I am afraid that she may create more problems than solutions. How can I stop her from interfering?

—Lois, New York

Dear Lois,

There is an old expression "a little knowledge is dangerous," and in the case of medical advice it can be deadly. It's time to give your sister a taste of her own medicine. These three steps will help you make your point.

- Arrange for a time you can meet together in private. Begin by saying: "Cathy, you know I love you, but I am very concerned about the advice you are giving to Mom. Last week she told me you suggested a homeopathic treatment for her arthritis and she went out and bought it. I am grateful that she mentioned it to me. Did you know her prescription medication has many of the same ingredients as the homeopathic treatment? That means that Mom may be getting much more medication than is healthful for her. Please consider that although your advice is well-meaning, it can be very dangerous for Mom." Allow Cathy time to respond.
- If she is very angry or negative, repeat your concerns and suggest that you arrange a meeting with her and the geriatrician.
- Speak to the geriatrician beforehand and alert him to the situation. Ask him to repeat his medical advice directly to your know-it-all.

It is our hope that Cathy will begin to understand that she can remain a caring daughter without providing harmful medical interventions.

Saying *No* to Know-It-Alls

"Know-it-alls" truly aggravate, annoy, and antagonize us. If we permit them to continue on a path of least resistance, we enable them to order us around. It's time to put a stop to their orders and unsolicited suggestions.

- **I will be firm.** I will stop my family member in her tracks by calling her bluff.

- **I will be direct.** I will meet with my family member in private. I will prepare a dialogue that will clearly relate my concerns.

- **I will be vigilant.** I will reinforce my feelings and concerns whenever necessary. I will not hesitate to repeat my responses regarding the specific issues over and over again.

---

6. Guilt-Trippers

Dear Eldercare 911,

When my mother calls me, she expects me to talk until she's ready to hang up. If I say, "Only a minute, Ma, I'm late for an appointment," she says, "If you were calling me I would stop time for you. I guess talking to me is too much to ask of a busy person like you." And she hangs up. I always call her back and there goes an hour. I'm to the point where I can't stand to hear her voice. I need help.

—Jeannette, Georgia

Dear Jeannette,

Many of us have family members who have mastered the art of manipulating us by making us feel guilty if we don't do whatever they ask. They may begin conversations with "Oh, I know you're too busy, but . . ." or end the phone call with "Never mind, it's Tom who has always been there for me." Eventually, we may begin to believe their recriminations and try to do more.

The hardest fact to face is that for guilt-trippers, doing "more" is not a solution. You can never do enough to satisfy a guilt-tripper because each time you give in, your guilt-tripper experiences the thrill of success. When we let guilt-trippers rule our lives, we reinforce the concept that their bad habits work! They will continue their same laments no matter how much time, energy, or money you devote to them. To add insult to injury, "practice makes perfect." Eventually, Mom's practice will make her an expert. She will discover the exact buttons to push to achieve her desired result. Use the next two answers to create your own plan.

Dear Eldercare 911,

Every time my father calls me, he begins the conversation with "Bobby, if you're too busy to talk to me, I'll understand. . . ." If I say "Thanks, Pop, I am a little busy right now, can I call you later?" he says, "What have I done? Why are you mad at me?" By the time he gets done with me, I'm convinced I'm a lousy son. It's really stupid considering my wife and I shop for him, take him to medical appointments, handle his bill paying, help with just about everything else. How do I stop letting him make me feel like I don't do enough for him?

—Bobby, Maine

Dear Bobby,

You've identified the right button—guilt! You've got to stop letting your father convince you that you are someone other than a responsible son who may also have other interests in his life. Intellectually, you sound like you have already stepped back and know that the reality is totally different from your father's manipulative insinuations. Instead of being "too busy" for him, you are already contributing a significant amount of time and energy to help your father. Now it's time to teach yourself to control the emotional damage that your dad inflicts. Remember to check first to make sure your father isn't in danger. The strategy is simple, but it takes practice. The next time you can't spend time on the phone and your father asks "What have I done?" interrupt him immediately and say, "Dad, I'm happy to hear from you, but you have to accept that I can't always stop what I'm doing and spend time with you. I'm always happy to call you back later." If he continues with more guilt dialogue, interrupt immediately and say, "I'm sorry you feel that way, Dad. Sally and I are doing the best we can. I'll call you back later."

Dear Eldercare 911,

If my mother tells me one more time how "grateful she is" and "how much she thanks me and loves me for caring for her," I'm going to explode! I have friends who would give anything for a simple thank you, but her constant groveling makes me feel like I can never say no to her. I don't want her to think I don't want her thanks. I'm really confused.

—Amy, Nebraska

Dear Amy,

There's a fine line between being sincerely thankful and using appreciation as a manipulative tool. To help identify where you stand, ask yourself two questions:

1. Does your mother have reason to think that your relationship with her is changing and you will soon pay less attention to her? If so, then try reassuring her of your continued support. Try saying, "Mom, don't worry. I'm glad I can help you out and I'll continue to help you for as long as you need me." Consider a support group for her, or activities such as those at a senior center or a daycare program to redirect her focus.

2. Ask yourself if this has been your mother's normal pattern for years or has her behavior changed? If her behavior has changed, she needs medical attention to determine the reason.

If Mom has always been sincerely, but overly grateful, then it may be time to look at your stress level and try to get help. A little respite and regular relief from even a few of your caregiving responsibilities may ease your stress. Please consider that you may be dangerously close to burnout (see chapter 9). One of your best options is a caregivers' support group. Look for one at a nearby hospital, the local Area Agency on Aging, your place of employment, or, if she has a specific diagnosis, try the organization dedicated to your mother's illness (see chapter 13, "Resources").

If none of these is applicable and you are certain your mother is guilt-tripping you, it's time to take back control. First, recognize that guilt trips are thinly disguised threats: in effect, your mother is saying, "If you don't do what I want, then you will cause me pain because I'll believe that you don't love me," or "If you don't do what I want, then I'll cause you pain because I'll withhold my love from you." Accepting those threats as a way of life means you've agreed to become a hostage to your mother's fantasies and manipulations! Next, accept the fact that *you* will have to do the changing, not your mother.

Your goal is to change the way you respond. When your mother is overly grateful, say "thank you" once. Do not repeat yourself. When she asks you for something you cannot, will not, or don't want to do, say "Mom, I can't do that this week, but I'll try to help you out next week," or "Mom, I'm sorry but I can't afford that," or "Mom, you'll have to ask someone else for that. I just can't do it." If she persists, tell her "I love you Mom, and I'm doing the best I can, but I can't do that." Do not argue. After you've said "No," turn your attention to something else. You may never break your mother's habit of trying to manipulate you, but she will eventually learn that the subject is closed after you say "No" and stick to it.

Saying *No* to Guilt-Trippers

When we say *No* to "guilt-trippers," then concede and give in, we show them that if they continue guilt-tripping, we will eventually change our minds and say yes. It may be hard at first, but saying *No* and meaning it is the only way to regain control.

- **I recognize that "more" is not a solution.** I'm doing the best I can, and I won't let guilt-trippers shake my confidence and respect for myself. Their version is not reality; it's part of their scam.

- **When I regain control, I will keep it.** I recognize that if I reward my guilt-tripper's cooperation by reversing my decision, that may simply give them another way to manipulate me.

---

7. Parents in Denial

Dear Eldercare 911,

It was bad enough when Mom was sick but mentally intact. Now, I'm pretty sure she's losing it, and her friend is taking advantage of her financially. She also has trouble walking and I don't think she should be alone, but she keeps telling me to "butt out." She says she's fine and doesn't need my help. How do I make her listen to reason?

—Cecile, South Dakota

Dear Cecile,

Regardless of risk, *parents in denial* insist they "don't need" your help and advice and maintain they can manage on their own even when the signs of danger and decline are evident to you. If you feel frustrated, angry, and worried, you're in good company. Most caregivers face this problem eventually.

Many of the reasons parents avoid our help are obvious: some might be embarrassed to have to ask their children for help; others don't want to burden their children or take up their time with financial problems or caregiving duties. They would be surprised to learn that they create *more* anxiety or that they may inadvertently exacerbate their problems by not involving you and letting you help.

Alternatively, your parents may fully understand the consequences and be willing to take that risk because of not-so-obvious reasons. Many parents have witnessed their friends' children provide "help." Too often that help resulted in their friends partially or totally losing their independence because their children completely took over. They truly believed they were helping, but they left their parents without any input into their own future and without any hope of recovering their dignity.

This is among the most difficult and important decisions caregivers face. Before you act, dig deep within yourself and ask, "Is my parent in danger or is she just not doing things the way I want her to?" If your parent is in danger (financial exploitation *is* dangerous), do not take *no* for an answer. Act immediately. Report the exploiter to the police, the district attorney, or your local elder abuse hotline (call the Area Agency on Aging for the number). If your parent is not in danger, rethink whether or not you need to intervene at this time. Reassess the situation periodically. For a broader look at the picture, read Anxious in Ohio and Stan from Michigan.

Dear Eldercare 911,

Every time I call my parents, my mom says that my dad is in the bathroom, at his friend's house, playing golf, taking a shower, or somewhere far from the phone. This has been going on for months. They live in New Mexico and I visit them only twice a year, so I haven't seen them recently. My brother says I should stop looking for trouble and be glad Dad's so active, but it sounds fishy to me. What if they need our help? Should I be worried?

—Anxious in Ohio

Dear Anxious,

It sounds fishy to us, too, but neither of us can diagnose the problem without an objective eyewitness report. Try one of these options to help you gather the information you need in order to relieve your anxiety.

- Don't wait for your next scheduled visit; go now. The sooner you find out why your dad has been unavailable to talk to you on the telephone for several months, the faster you can help your parents if they are in danger.
- Ask your parents' neighbor or friend to visit on your behalf. You may find they were asked not to call you, but were hoping you'd call them.
- Retain a geriatric care manager for an impartial assessment of your parents' status.

Once you have the information you need to evaluate the situation, you'll be able to make the appropriate decision.

Dear Eldercare 911,

I just returned from visiting my mom in Arizona. She's always been a little eccentric, but this time I found some of her garbage in the refrigerator (she didn't remember putting it there), and one night when we were going to out to dinner, she used purple lipstick to color in her eyebrows. When she set a place at the table for my father who's been dead for fifteen years, I tried to tell her he wasn't with us anymore. She nodded and said, "I know, but he said he'd be back tonight." I tried to take her to the doctor, but she refused to go with me. I had to come home because of my job, but I haven't slept since I got back. I know I've got to do something, but where do I start?

—Stan, Michigan

Dear Stan,

This is a perfect example of real danger and of when to refuse to take *no* for an answer. From your description, your mother cannot adequately care for herself or make safe and sound decisions on her own behalf. It is no longer safe for her to live alone. Start by getting an accurate diagnosis. Take Mom to a board-certified neurologist specializing in dementia disorders. There are fifty or more medical conditions and diseases that mimic dementia symptoms. Many are treatable; some are totally reversible. Mom will need an advocate. If you can't return to Arizona to identify and help meet her needs, hire a geriatric care manager to work on your behalf. If the diagnosis is Alzheimer's disease, we urge you to contact the Alzheimer's Association for assistance and support.

Saying *No* to Parents in Denial

If you decide to step in and help your parent, it's important to judge "how much" assistance is necessary. For an impartial second opinion, enlist the aid of a supportive family member, your parent's physician, clergy, or a professional healthcare advocate. You may still meet resistance, but you will have the inner strength that comes with knowing you are doing what is required to help keep your parent safe.

- **I will gather the information I need to determine if my parent is really in danger.** If I find it difficult to assess the situation correctly, I will enlist the aid of a professional healthcare advocate such as a physician, a nurse, or a geriatric care manager to help evaluate my parent's status.

- **I will act immediately if my parent is at risk.** If I am certain my parent is in danger, I will not accept *no* for an answer. I will step in and act immediately to assess the danger and provide protection.

- **I will respect my parent's capability and desire for independence.** I will take over only as much as necessary to provide the help my parent needs. I will try not to take over any responsibilities that my parent wants to keep and can still handle safely.

8. Disappointers

Dear Eldercare 911,

My sister has an expression, "I'm here for you," but when we need her, she disappears faster than Houdini. Our mother has Parkinson's disease and she needs a lot of care and support. I know my limitations and I can't take care of Mom alone.

—Barbara, Washington, DC

Dear Barbara,

How often do the unfulfilled promises of our family members and friends hurt us? Unfortunately, the answer is that it happens more than it should. Chronic disappointments leave us feeling empty and alone. We always hope that the next time they will fulfill the promise, but they only disappoint us again. Approaching the people in our lives who disappoint us with their words and inaction can make us feel angry and very uncomfortable because they often respond to us with a heartfelt apology and a future promise. We want to believe them, and so we trust them again. Then we feel even worse when they fail us again. To ease your hurt, read Terri's and David's stories.

Dear Eldercare 911,

My sister, Andee, and I live within two miles of Mom and Dad. I don't work outside the home and she does, so I am the one who helps out the most. I ask her to give me one day a week off; that's all I need. Week after week she promises to take Mom and Dad for the day, and every week she breaks her promise. All I am asking for is twenty-four hours. What can I do or say to get her to keep her promise?

—Terri, Georgia

Dear Terri,

Your sister is not the only one. There are so many people who "talk the talk" but just don't fulfill a promise to anyone. Sometimes it helps to start with something small. Here is what you can say to your sister: "Andee, I'd really like to count on you, but in the past, you have reneged on your promises. If you would like to help me, maybe we can start with something that will not take the entire day. Could you pick up Mom and Dad's new medications at the drugstore on Thursday?" Consider this a test. If she fulfills this one request, then you can try again and hopefully increase her participation. If she does not help you with this one task, don't expect her to do anything at all.

Since you need the help, consider these options.

- Think about hiring a home health aide to assist you. Ask Andee to share the cost of the care. Let her know that you need a break and Mom and Dad need the care. This may be a way for Andee to help without actually spending time.
- Contact your local hospital or social service agency for a referral to a reputable homecare agency.
- Meet with the home health aide. If Mom and Dad are able and willing to participate in the interview process, give them an opportunity to meet her and ask her questions. Observe your parents with the aide. Do

they seem comfortable? Are they uncomfortable? If they seem comfortable, encourage them to try having the home health aide a few days each week. If they are not comfortable, contact the agency and begin the process again.

- Ask a close friend or a family member if she can spare a few hours each week to give you a respite. Be very clear on the amount of time you need, the day of the week, and what she will have to do for your mother. If she agrees, you may want to offer a monetary compensation. If she refuses payment, then consider buying her an appropriate gift to express your thanks.

You now have a few options to help relieve some of your caregiver burden if your sister does not agree to help you out. Remember, she may agree to help you, but then at the last minute she may renege. Protect yourself from your "disappointer" by being prepared with alternate plans.

Dear Eldercare 911,

Dad has some money, but he is really stuck in the middle; he has too much money for government assistance but not enough to pay for some of life's little enjoyments. I have been paying for my dad's daycare program, but it is too expensive for me to continue. My brother has the money and he promised to pay for the program. He has not paid the bill, so Dad will lose this program. How do I get my brother to see how much this means to Dad?

—David, Illinois

Dear David,

Your generosity and concern for your dad's quality of life is wonderful. When your brother promised to pay for your dad's daycare program, did you discuss the actual costs with him and when he would have to begin paying as well as the benefits of the program for your dad? If you didn't, the first thing to do is to have a conversation with your brother. You may say to him: "Please join me at the daycare program and see for yourself the pleasure Dad gets from the program, the staff, and his peers. I know it is expensive, and I hope that when things improve with my finances, we can share the responsibility. What about it?" By saying you hope to share some of the cost in the future, you are relieving him of some of the burden. Also, you've been paying up to now. Give him time to respond. If he says yes, make an immediate appointment at the daycare program to give him a tour of his investment. If he says no, then you will know that he is most likely not going to help now or in the future. You may want to consider another daycare program in the community. There are some programs that provide a sliding scale fee. The program will then determine the cost according to your Dad's income. Contact the Area Agency on Aging for a listing of these programs.

Protect Yourself from Disappointers

There is nothing as disappointing as an unfulfilled promise, except for a promise that goes repeatedly unfulfilled. Try a two-step plan to guard against "disappointers."

- **I will provide a test.** I will select something small that my family member or friend can do for me. If she fulfills that promise, I can hopefully follow with other requests. If not, I will know exactly where I stand.

- **I will protect myself.** I will prepare for disappointments by finding alternatives to my dilemma.

---

9. Sibling Battlers

Dear Eldercare 911,

It lasted one day. Just one day of working together and my sister and I were at it again, right there in the hospital. As if Mom wasn't on oxygen with a million tubes and needles in her. What's wrong with us? We're always sniping at each other, trying to be the final decision maker or to have the last word. After all these years, I don't expect us to become instant friends, but can't we manage to cooperate or be nice to each other for more than a few hours in an emergency like Mom's having a major stroke?

—Sonia, Arizona

Dear Sonia,

For you and your sisters and many others just like you, the ideal family that comes together and stays together in times of illness or crisis may seem as elusive as a fairy tale. It's the same way for most real families. It may take one day or thirty days, but eventually the feelings and issues that separated you in the past pop right back up to stress you out again because *those feelings and issues haven't changed in any way.* What's different is that something newer, and for a short period of time more powerful, has claimed your attention and moved old business—the reasons for your past adversarial relationship with your sibling—to the back burner of your emotions. Your love, fear, shock, or concern for your parent has temporarily taken center stage. While Mom is ill, try sitting quietly with your sister and express your feelings to her as well as you expressed them to us. Then ask her to express her feelings to you. At worst, your sibling may storm out and leave you with the responsibility during Mom's illness. At best, this may help open a dialogue for a long-term relationship and continuing communication.

Dear Eldercare 911,

My mother and father both live in my house. My family and I take care of their meals, their laundry, and their doctors' appointments. In fact, we take care of everything that they need or want. Believe it or not, that's not my problem. We've worked out everything so that my wife and kids all help, and we're doing fine. My problem is my sister. She visits once a month from a neighboring state and spends the entire visit acting superior. She wants to set up new routines, she insists her methods are more efficient, her food is healthier, her knowledge is broader; in fact, her "everything" is better than ours. She's very disruptive to our routine and our harmony. She has no concept of what it means to live with or take care of the two of them. She doesn't even stay the night when she visits. She's a big pain in the you-know-what to us, but my parents love her and I don't want her to stop visiting. And ideas?

—Pete, Iowa

Dear Pete,

First, consider the possibility that your sister is feeling guilty and overreacting to your having everything under control because she is not involved in caring for your parents. The flurry of activity and ideas may be her way of trying to show that she cares. Try this test:

- Ask her if she can help you with a task or two, preferably ones that she can take home and finish. This might help her feel involved enough to quit trying to run the show.
- If that doesn't work, ask her to spend some time alone with you.

Explain to her that you would value her help, but she needs to contribute something concrete, not just offer suggestions and then disappear again.

- Ask her if she would like Mom and Dad to come visit her for a few days. Tell her you'll send complete written instructions so that she won't have to wonder about any of the details.
- If that isn't practical, ask her what she feels she would be most comfortable doing. Then, do your best to accommodate her choice.

With a little luck, your sister will get the message and back off.

Dear Eldercare 911,

When I said, "Howard, I'm not comfortable with Dad's diagnosis. We need a second opinion," my brother said, "It's not necessary. Dad has so many doctors that one of them would have noticed if the diagnosis was incorrect." When I said, "Dad would be better off in an assisted living facility," he didn't wait for my reasoning and said, "No. He's better off at home." I start getting stressed and anxious days before Howard visits and am exhausted when he leaves. I can't take it anymore. How do other families handle this?

—Selena, Oklahoma

Dear Selena,

You haven't said whether saying "no" is Howard's traditional reaction to anything you say or if he's responding to caregiving issues in the safe mode. Could "no" mean "taking no chances" because he doesn't have enough information to comfortably say "yes"? Either way, the next time you want to be an advocate for your father, try these three steps:

1. Do your homework. Try not to approach Howard without serious backup. Explain your problem to a healthcare advocate or to one of your dad's physicians. For a fresh look at your dad's illness, it may be preferable to speak to a physician other than the one who made the diagnosis. Ask for a written opinion. Log on to the Internet and print out similar situations (see chapter 13 for resources) or visit several assisted living communities and bring back brochures. In other words, present Howard with expert opinions that make a persuasive case.
2. Listen to Howard's views on the issue. If he's simply being obstinate, look directly in his eyes and say: "Howard, I know we have our dif-

ferences, but this isn't about us, it's about Dad. Is either of us willing to endanger him to win an argument?" Then don't say another word until he answers.

3. You can help yourself by helping Howard understand that this isn't *your* suggestion; it is the recommendation of Dad's professional healthcare advisors. That means it's not a win-lose situation for either of you; it's about helping your father.

Old habits are hard to break, so don't expect miracles at the outset. If you can't make progress after several tries, you may need to find a way to help your father without Howard's approval.

Saying *No* to Sibling Battlers

Sibling rivalry usually stems from long-term issues that can take years to alter. These suggestions can help with the immediate effects of rivalries and ease the added stress on caregivers. Your "battlers" may continue to fight you, but your position will change: you'll pick your battles and plan your responses. In other words, you'll be in control.

- **I will choose my battles.** I will try not to work from years of habit and automatically respond to every comment, because I know that not everything is important enough to argue about or even comment on.

- **I will do my homework.** I will consult my parent's healthcare providers and research alternative housing or other changes and possibilities. I will give my sibling a list of the potential health and safety risks if my parent's situation/status does not change.

- **I will not attack in anger.** Before I respond, I will step back and think about why I'm angry. I recognize that a calm, measured response gives me more control and may help me diffuse the situation or even ignore it.

---

10. Caregiver Self-Neglectors

Dear Eldercare 911,

As I was screeching at my teenage son for something or other, I caught a glimpse of myself in the mirror. I shouted, "Hi, Mama!" The voice, the face I saw was my eighty-seven-year-old mother, but it was really me. Because I am so overwhelmed and exhausted, I feel like I have literally poisoned myself with neglect at fifty. I take care of her day after day, and she looks better than I do. I need help now.

—Reflecting in Maine

Dear Reflecting,

We need to banish forever the fable that burnout and self-neglect are unavoidable parts of the caregiver process. Caregivers who believe it are more likely to neglect their own physical and emotional needs. Many develop head, back, and shoulder aches, and digestive problems. Emotions are frail, anxiety levels are high, and fatigue and depression may overwhelm your body and your mind. Many of you compromise your health and well-being and in some ways you become "toxic" to yourself. It is not time to simply "say *no*," it is time to shout it—shout it so that your inner self can hear you loud and clear. It is time for you to believe that you deserve at least the same caring treatment you provide to your loved ones. We are not suggesting that you can or will make drastic changes overnight, but we are suggesting that you have the power to begin the process of self-awareness, insight, and progress toward taking care of yourself as well as you take care of others. Read on.

Dear Eldercare 911,

My name is Meg, but it could be Overwhelmed, Exhausted, or Disgusted. I have had it with my family. They take and take and give nothing back. My parents require a lot of my time and my teenage children eat up the rest of it. Sew this, cook that, be here, go there. I am ready to explode. I know that I should say "no" at times, but I just can't form the word. "Yes" seems to come easier to me. What can I do to save myself?

—Meg, California

Dear Meg,

We're exhausted just reading your question! We can only imagine how you feel. Begin by saying *no*. Recognize that there are times when you cannot change your responsibilities but that should not stop you from searching for alternatives. Stand back and take a look at your life. If you're too overwhelmed to do this alone, get a friend or counselor to help you. The trick is to decide what is the most important thing for you to do to take back some of your time. You may have to give up one caregiver responsibility. Here are a few simple steps to help you on your way.

- If you cook for your family members six times a week, decrease it to four and order one or two cooked meals, or serve a simple salad and sandwich.
- "Prioritize, prioritize, prioritize," when you can't be in three places at one time. You are in control and you make the decision. Be very clear to all your family members that in a twenty-four-hour day you must take time for yourself, and sometimes they will simply have to wait.
- Set the limits. You will find how empowering it is and that you actually have some time each day for yourself. More important, you will see and feel how much saying *no* improves your life.
- Check with your local hospital or social service agency for referrals to counselors and caregiver support groups.
- See the resource section in this book (chapter 13) for organizations that specifically help and support caregivers and will provide nurturing ideas just for you.

These options may help you take the first important steps to saving yourself and give you the strength you need to say *no*.

Dear Eldercare 911,

I am an only child, and my mother lives with me. I am so tired of taking care of her needs. A friend said I was suffering from "burnout." If I am, I am "burning out" slowly. It doesn't seem to end for me. I need to know how I can put out the fire and regain my life. I don't eat or sleep well, and the doctor said that I am compromising my health. Please tell me what to do?

—May, South Carolina

Dear May,

Burnout doesn't quite describe the anger, frustration, fatigue, and anxiety of caring for a parent. But you've actually taken the first step toward reclaiming your life. You recognize that you need help and it is time to free yourself from the fire within. It starts with making a list of priorities. Jot down as many ideas as you can think of that will make your life better, easier, and more enjoyable. Prioritize the list and number 1 to 3 as the most important.

1. Go for a physical exam.
2. Make a haircut appointment.
3. See a movie.

All are important ways to help heal your body, mind, and spirit. Decide on the best way to organize your day, and tackle one task at a time. Ask a family member or a friend to help you, or hire a homecare worker for a few hours each week. (See the section entitled "Demanders" for dialogue on asking for help from a family member.) You don't have to burn out, flicker, and melt!

Saying *No* to Self-Neglect

You have the ability to identify and reach out for what you need for continued strength and confidence. It is time to say *no* to self-neglect and *yes* to taking care of yourself.

- **I will practice self-awareness.** I will take the time that I deserve to decide what I need and want. Once I decide what I need, I will practice ways that I can help myself.
- **I will prioritize.** I will take one step at a time to enhance my quality of life.
- **I will be kind to myself.** I will be as good to myself as I am to the ones I love.

C. SURVIVING SAYING *NO*

Dear Eldercare 911,

I learned to listen to my heart and body. When I feel as if I can't do something for my mother, I try to get help. When I feel too tired to visit for an afternoon, I stay one hour. I think everything that I am doing for myself makes such good sense, but I still feel so guilty.

—Monica, Utah

Dear Monica,

Since we are emotionally attached to our family and friends, we sometimes experience feelings as if we were on a roller coaster. Sometimes these attachments bring us great joy, at other times, sorrow and guilt.

No one can tell you how to feel, and no one can make guilty feelings completely disappear. You may always have some feelings of guilt no matter what you do or how hard you try. What we can do is help you deal with your feelings of guilt. For example, if you feel guilty when you can't visit your mother as often as she likes, you may want to find some appropriate options. As one option, you can provide her with a hired companion to fill in some of the time you can't spend with her to keep her busy, or plan a special day for both of you to enjoy.

Even after you do the best you can, you may experience pangs of guilt when you say *no* to a loved one. Why? Sometimes no matter what or how much you do for your loved one, you feel that you should do more. In some situations, other family members make you feel that you are selfish or that you are trying to avoid certain responsibilities. At other times it is your own sense of duty that makes you feel as if you let your family member down.

- Saying no doesn't mean that you are abandoning your loved one; it means you are setting realistic limits.
- Saying no doesn't mean that you don't care; it simply means that you are taking care of yourself while taking care of someone else.

Being a cared-for, healthy caregiver is not only in your best interest, but in the best interest of your entire family. However, achieving a balance is very difficult when you expect nothing less than perfection. *Surviving saying no* means it's time to accept that your best is good enough for everyone, including yourself.

The most effective way to survive saying *no* is to stand firm and give yourself credit for all you are accomplishing. Don't allow the people in your life who disrupt, demand, abuse, disappoint, and surprise you at the most inopportune time to let you forget how amazing and strong you really are. Here are five simple reminders to help you say *no* and remain confident and in control.

Surviving Saying *No*

- **S**et limits. I will know what I can and cannot do for my family member.

- **A**ccept that my best is good enough. I will try not to second-guess myself.

- **Y**es, I will take care of myself. I will not allow my family and friends to burden me.

- **N**o to the pressures of doing everything for everybody. I will be a cared-for caregiver.

- **O**we myself a pat on the back. I will be proud of everything I accomplish.

THE RULES OF INTERVENTION

The question of when it is an appropriate time to intervene in your parent's life is a difficult one to answer. When as an adult child you are faced with this dilemma, it is important to ask yourself the following questions:

1. Is my parent able to care for his physical needs?
2. Is he receiving proper nourishment?
3. Is he capable of handling his finances?
4. Is he safe in his environment, whether in his own home or in alternative housing?
5. Does my parent enjoy the companionship of his friends and peers?
6. Is he receiving proper medical care and medication?
7. Is he clean, neat, and well groomed?
8. Does he appear anxious or confused?

If you have any of these concerns, then some form of intervention may be appropriate. The intervention may be as simple as cooking a few meals each week for your parent; meeting with the staff of a nursing home to make sure your parent receives what he needs, when he needs it; or finding an appropriate daycare program to provide your parent with a better quality of life. Your intervention may be as complicated as meeting with healthcare and legal professionals to determine the most appropriate plan of care for your parent, including selling his house and moving him to safer, more suitable surroundings.

It is not necessarily time to intervene if your parent is safe, high functioning, and is enjoying his quality of life, even if his way of doing things differs from yours. Take the time to observe your parent, periodically reassess his situation, and talk to him about any concerns you may have. If you feel you require help to assess your parent's needs, hire a geriatric care manager to help you and provide you with appropriate options to meet your parent's individual needs and financial situation.

Dear Eldercare 911,

This is a letter I wrote to my dad because he made me so frustrated and angry. He has heart disease, mini-strokes, arthritis, and mild dementia, but he is consistently noncompliant regarding all of these health issues. After a two-week hospitalization he was weak and he had difficulty walking. I hired home health aides to help him with his grooming, bathing, laundry, and cooking. When I wrote this letter, I didn't think it would make a difference, but I just wanted to let him know how I felt.

*   *   *

Dear Dad:

I wanted you to get this letter while I was on vacation, so you would get a chance to think about what I'm saying. I find it very hard to talk to you about this, mainly because I don't want to start a fight.

If you want to get better, you have to make an effort!

People are trying to help you, you see it as an intrusion, you call them "pests" and say it's torture. You want to sit back and not cooperate. You said you can't wait until Saturday because they [the aides] don't come. You said, "I only have to take this torture for one more week." Then what?

You must work and fight to get better!

It's easy to sit back. I often think you don't want to get better, and it hurts me. I'm sure you won't do anything to change your behavior, I just want you to know how I feel.

I love you.

—Lisa, Nevada

The voice of one caregiver reflects the feelings and frustrations that many of you endure every day as you try to help someone you love. Lisa's letter is a plea for her dad to live a better, healthier life. According to Lisa, she has spent too many long days and sleepless nights worrying about her dad and trying to do what she felt was best for him. When she finally decided to write this letter, it was because she just wanted him to know how she felt. Lisa's attempts have not ended—she continues to try and help her dad. With professional guidance, the support of her peers, and time, she has learned the difference between a battle and a war. She's learned to choose the most important battles and consciously ignore others. Her attempt at intervention is courageous. She continues to do what she can to help her dad remain safe and secure.

The important thing to keep in mind is that once you make the decision to intervene in your parent's life, you most likely will experience roadblocks from your parent, your siblings, and even from your own sense of insecurity. Intervention at any level is a difficult, arduous journey, but there are many ways that you can help yourself to do the best you can for your parent. This chapter will help you on your way.

A. NO GOOD DEED GOES UNPUNISHED

Dear Eldercare 9 1 1,

I am the primary caregiver for a tough, inflexible mother who suffers from dementia. When intervention of any sort is needed, this is my job because we live in the same community. My sister, Laurie, lives about five hundred miles away. When there is a problem, my sister is not particularly supportive and she says, "deal with it." Or when I do handle a situation, she tries to second-guess me at every turn. My mother views me as "the bad one" and my sister as "the good one." I sometimes have to intervene and take control of the situation for my mother's safety, like taking her cigarettes away when we found her smoking in bed. When it was time to move her into an assisted living facility, I simply dealt with what was necessary.

Any time there is a problem at the assisted living facility or Mom needs something, I am the one who intervenes or buys her what she needs. On the other hand, my sister calls her twice a day and regales Mom with the wonders of her four brilliant grandchildren. I can't remember the last time my sister actually visited Mom. I am tired of feeling like the bad guy when I know that I am doing what I can. Can you help me figure out a way to handle my mother, my sister, and my own feelings?

—Sam, Illinois

Dear Sam,

You describe your mom as inflexible and tough, but she is also suffering from dementia. Dementia may sometimes exacerbate an already existing strong personality. This may make the present situation even more difficult for you. We applaud your successful intervention by providing your mom with a safe, secure environment.

You may sometimes feel like the bad guy because Mom makes it difficult for you to feel good. It is not surprising that your sister feels that she can be cavalier and critical about what you do and how you do it, because she is not the one visiting Mom. We can't change your sister or your mom, but we can try to change the way you react to their negative comments and hostile behavior. Try these three steps to help you feel as good as you really are.

- Respond to your sister's next critical comment by calling her bluff. "Laurie, I am doing the best I can. Would you like to take over the caregiver responsibilities? If you agree, we can find Mom an assisted living community in your neighborhood. If not, and she is going to stay here, it is time you stopped being a critic and started being supportive." Don't say another word and let her respond. A dose of reality tends to frighten off second-guessing critics.

- Ask a staff member at the assisted living facility at what time of day your mom is the most alert and responsive to visitors. Many people who suffer from dementia are more alert and less agitated early in the day. Try to visit during those hours. If Mom becomes angry or aggressive, cut your visit short. One caregiver who regularly visits his mother at an assisted living facility told us that his mom often becomes angry and hostile. He shared his visiting method. "I take care of business. I visit with the staff members involved in Mom's care first, then I visit with her. If she starts to yell or become abusive, I calmly say, 'Mom it's been good to see you, but I have to go.' I leave with the information I need and the peace of mind knowing that she is well cared for by the staff. But most importantly I don't let her attack me for doing what is best for her."

- Make a list of all the things you feel you have to do to keep your mother safe and well cared for. Check off the things you have accomplished. You will probably be surprised to find that you have accomplished a great deal and intervened appropriately to provide your mom with the best possible care. Congratulate yourself for being a good son and a conscientious caregiver.

When your mom criticizes and your sister second-guesses you again about your interventions, think about your list of accomplishments and take a few minutes to feel good about yourself.

Dear Eldercare 911,

My father is alert, but he suffers from a serious cardiac condition. We don't have a strong, positive family history, and we never really communicated very well. I guess you can say we have a "transactional relationship." If I am not actually doing something for him, we don't have anything to say. Chitchat or an evening of television is not a part of our lifestyle. Dad is a critical man and he always was that way. Now it seems no matter what I do or say he is criticizing me for it. I feel very hurt because I know if I didn't intervene and help him he could not live at home as independently as he does today. I cook his meals, wash his clothes, and clean his house. How do you tell your father that he constantly hurts your feelings when you know that without your help he could never manage?

—Sylvia, Pennsylvania

Dear Sylvia,

We are sorry that you are experiencing so much hurt and pain. Cooking, cleaning, and doing housework are very time-consuming interventions. It is time to decrease some of your caregiver responsibilities in order for you to have time to heal and deal with your feelings. You say that Dad can't manage without you. Consider the following options:

- Hire someone to help you with one or two of the chores. A home health aide can do his laundry, cook the meals, and handle the light house-keeping. If finances are not an issue, then you can hire an aide from a private, licensed homecare agency.
- Interview the aide in advance, have her spend time with your dad in your presence, and be very clear on all the fees for her services. If finances are a problem, then you can contact your local Area Agency on Aging for possible referrals to sliding scale programs in your dad's community. Many community agencies base fees on a sliding scale that depends on an individual's income. The important thing is for you to step back and have someone else share in the hands-on, day-to-day responsibilities.

Once you address the concrete obstacles, take some time to deal with how you feel about Dad and your caregiver duties. You expressed that for years you and your dad have had a strained relationship. As a child the pain of criticism seems unbearable, and as an adult the pain is no less hurtful. The difference is that as an adult you have the resources to learn how to protect and save yourself. Since it may be difficult for you to express directly to him how you feel, you may want to write your dad a letter. This letter may con-tain specifics about incidences that upset and hurt you as well as how you feel today. The wonderful aspect of writing your feelings down is that you have time to change, add, or delete any or all of it. You can send the letter, read it to him, or destroy it. Remember, you don't have to be the one doing things for Dad; you can intervene effectively by providing the help he needs, and someone else can handle the day-to-day care. You are in control. Use this letter-writing tool in your own time, and in your own way.

B. YOU NEED A PLAN

Dear Eldercare 911,

My seventy-six-year-old mother is truly a piece of work. She has arthritis in her knees and hip, and it is very difficult for her to get around. I drive her wherever she has to go, and I help her with all of her banking. Over the years she has become very friendly and comfortable with the bank manager. He is in his late forties and I am in my early forties. She constantly tries to fix me up with the bank manager (embarrassing me completely). When it was time to reinvest one of her investments, she insisted that I had to cancel all my plans to make sure we had time to go to the bank in order not to lose a dollar and twenty-five cents in interest. However, when I try to discuss her future financial needs and the importance of meeting with an elder law attorney, she shuts down and she will not even discuss it. How do I get her to see that she will lose a lot more than one dollar and twenty-five cents if we don't plan for her future?

—Thoroughly Frustrated, New Jersey

Dear Frustrated,

Mom may not want to discuss the future, but you are actually in a perfect position to plant some seeds. Since you do her banking and you know her actual finances, you are way ahead of many caregivers, because you have access to the bank. Every time you take Mom to the bank you may want to open a dialogue regarding the importance of meeting with an elder law attorney. Try saying: "Mom, do you remember when we were here last month and you asked Jeffrey, the bank manager, if he wants to date me? Well, I won't forget that day, but something else happened that day that really started me thinking about things. We were planning to reinvest some of your money, and you were so worried about being a day late and losing a dollar or two. If we don't start planning for your future, you can lose a lot more money if you need homecare. How about a consultation with an elder law attorney or a financial planner just to see what they have to say?" Wait for Mom to respond. If she adamantly rejects the idea, let it go for now. You will have many more opportunities while you are doing her banking. If she agrees, make the appointment as soon as possible while you have piqued her interest.

Another way to bring this subject to the forefront is through the bank manager. You mentioned that Mom is fond of him. Let him do some of the work for you. Take a few minutes and meet with him without your mom present. Talk to him about her reluctance to consult with an elder law attorney or a financial planner. Ask him to engage her in a conversation regarding this topic and provide her with any literature that the bank has to offer about financial planning. You may find that your mom responds positively when her friend at the bank broaches this very important subject. Mom may see wedding bells, but you see a great opportunity to accomplish an important intervention!

Dear Eldercare 9 1 1,

Please help me come up with a way to entice my eighty-eight-year-old dad out of his house. Dad has diabetes and some cardiac problems. He suffers from moderate dementia and until recently he drove his car. I finally got him to give up his car. I told him that I needed a car because my lease was up and I was short of cash. It worked! He gave me his car. Dad has a home health aide twenty-four hours a day, seven days a week. She provides him with his meals, keeps the house clean, and even plays simple card games. She says he is doing fine, but I am getting another story from him. He tells my husband and me that he wants friends, lady friends. I tell him he can meet people at the senior center, but he finds excuses for not going. I don't get it. Can you help me?

—Margaret, Maine

Dear Margaret,

Dad is saying one thing and doing something else—no wonder you're confused. It appears that he is not sure what he wants, either. Because he suffers from dementia and might experience some confusion and difficulty expressing himself, you might want to look at things from a different perspective. Dad lives in his own home and he receives good care. He is safe and comfortable in familiar surroundings. You won the first battle. He says he wants "lady friends." Ask yourself if you are comfortable talking to him about what he means? If you are not comfortable discussing this topic with him, ask your husband to intervene. Perhaps Dad wants someone to talk to, have dinner with, or he is looking for a sexual relationship. The topic may be uncomfortable for you, but before you can help Dad, you have to be clear about what he wants. Because of your dad's diagnosis of dementia, if your husband learns that he is actually thinking about a sexual relationship, he may want to explore this topic further in the presence of your dad's physician. If you find that he simply wants companionship among his peers, you can look into a socialization program.

- Adult daycare programs provide socialization, interaction with a professional staff, and a nutritious meal in a supervised setting. The fees vary, and in some instances, there is a sliding scale fee based on your dad's income.
- Senior centers provide a variety of socialization and education programs. It's important to ask for a specialized dementia program. If the center does not have a specific program for people with cognitive impairment, ask the staff if Dad can attend specific senior center functions accompanied by his home health aide.
- Churches and synagogues often provide wonderful programs for seniors. Once again it is important to discuss your dad's appropriateness for the programs with the professional staff. Be sure that his home health aide can attend.

Margaret, before you rush to enroll Dad in any program, you may also want to speak to his physician. Dad's desire for new friends may also be a sign that he is feeling lonely and frightened. Since your dad has dementia, you may want to make an appointment for Dad with a board-certified geriatric psychiatrist. Once the doctor medically clears him to attend a program and then he decides not to, do not take this as a defeat. You have clearly tried to take care of his needs and tried to fulfill his wishes.

C. OBJECTIONS ARE A FACT OF LIFE

Dear Eldercare 911,

"Stop treating me like an infant. Everyone is right except me. Why can't you all leave me alone?" These are my mom's words when we remind her how important it is to lock her doors at night or to give us a set of keys to her apartment. Last week she left the door to her apartment unlocked and partially opened. A next-door neighbor was so concerned about her safety that she called me immediately. I am very glad that I gave her my phone number. She said Mom's door lock looks rusty, and it may be difficult for Mom to use her keys. The truth is that Mom always took care of everyone else. She was the consummate caregiver, and now we really want to help her out as much as we can. We are concerned because although she is very high functioning and independent, her memory is not as good as it was a year ago. She is hurt by our minor interventions, and it makes me very sad that she feels this way. How do you deal with someone who has enjoyed eighty-three years of independence and is really quite capable, but sometimes forgetful? How do you stop from feeling so sad for someone you love so much?

—Caring, Connecticut

Dear Caring,

There is something unsettling about a place we call "in between." This is a place between independence and dependence. It sometimes creates a sense of limbo that is often frightening and perplexing for the caregiver and the family member. It is a period of time that may last weeks, months, or even years. The amount of dependence may be as simple as a reminder about installing a new door lock and providing a family member with a set of keys, or as complex as moving someone to an assisted living facility or in with you if that is your choice. As hard as it is for you to understand that "in between" place, it is even more painful for your mom, who enjoyed a lifetime of independence. Most likely she is questioning herself and her ability to remain independent. Every time you remind her to do something, you also remind her that she is in a "place" that she doesn't like, she doesn't want, and that she wishes would simply go away. Because this problem will not disappear, you and Mom will be facing many obstacles together. The fact that you asked such a sensitive question is a credit to you and your desire to do what is best for her. Here is a sample dialogue that may help ease the way. Say it and then give her a hug. You are providing your mom with the most important thing of all, validation for an independent life for as long as possible.

The next time you are alone together you can say: "Mom, I think you are terrific. You have always been there for the family. Remember when Dad died, you tried to keep all of us from falling apart, and when my son was in college, you were one of his greatest cheerleaders. We know how much you enjoy doing things for yourself, and no one wants to take that freedom away from you. But sometimes we worry about you, and a simple thing like installing an appropriate lock and giving us a set of house keys will help keep you safe. It's one small thing we can do to help insure your ability to live on your own for a long time. We love you very much."

Your distress and strong feelings are understandable given the changes in your mom's level of functioning. These feelings make you hypersensitive and may cause you to question every intervention that is not only appropriate, but also essential for your mom's well-being. Here are three things to say to yourself when you begin to feel unsure or sad about the situation.

- I am doing the best I can to help my mom remain safe and secure in her home.
- I am providing her with appropriate support and care.
- I am helping her to live her life with dignity.

Once you begin to believe in yourself and what you are doing for your mom, both of you will reap the benefits. In time you will develop a more open and relaxed relationship that will allow her to communicate more candidly with you, and you to listen more effectively to her.

Dear Eldercare 911,

Our eighty-eight-year-old dad suffers from Parkinson's disease. A few months ago the doctors told us to start thinking about planning for his future needs. Dad is frail and he walks by himself, but he needs assistance with dressing, bathing, cooking, and cleaning. I am one of four siblings, and three of us are actually involved in helping him. Dad is not our problem. He is mild mannered and actually quite anxious to please us. When we talked about an assisted living facility, he didn't object. As a matter of fact, he said, "If I can't live with my kids, this is the next best thing." I guess one might think he was trying to guilt us into inviting him to live with us, but I think he was really OK with our decision. The problem is our oldest sister. She hates us! Because of our awful relationship, she attempts to sabotage everything we try to do. I think she sometimes has a problem accepting Dad's debilitating condition, and at other times I think she is just nasty. Dad seems to participate in family matters less and less, but our sister calls him behind our backs and tells him that we are trying to take away his money and freedom. Because she is being so destructive and hurtful, we decided if she is not on the "same page" about these important decisions, we will simply keep her out of everything. Due to recent dramatic changes in Dad's condition, we are moving him to a nursing home.

Should we contact our sister? Can you help us figure out a way to handle this very touchy situation? We don't want Dad caught in the middle and hurt by the bad relationship between my sister and me.

—Monica, Washington

Dear Monica,

Because of your dad's sudden deterioration, he is somewhat protected from this tension by his inability to understand and participate in the decision-making process. On the other hand, anger makes people do very unpredictable things. Although you tried to stop your sister's negative involvement by keeping her out of the loop, she found a way to reach Dad via the telephone. You handled this very difficult situation the best way you could; however, you may want to consider a few of the following options to respond to your sister. Most likely, if her anger and problems with the family persist, she will not be receptive to any of your overtures. This doesn't mean you failed your father; it means only that you may not be able to reach your sister in a way that brings all of you together.

- Meet with your other siblings. Decide if you want to approach your older sister or not. If you decide to approach her and involve her in this intervention, then it is time to have a family meeting. Whatever you decide, you may want to consult with an elder law attorney. You will want to know your legal rights if you move him into a nursing home.
- Decrease some of the stress by engaging a geriatric professional to facilitate the family meeting. The professional might be a family therapist or the social worker from the assisted living facility. The reason for the facilitator to be present is to keep you focused on the task of helping your dad and not on other extraneous or emotional issues that may cloud your thinking. Alert the facilitator to the family history and the recent friction.
- Contact your older sister by telephone or send her a note. The note will indicate that all of you want to get together to discuss Dad's future care needs. Plan the meeting in a neutral environment. Keep the note short and cordial. For example: Dear Older Sister: John, Mary, and I are meeting on Saturday, June 2, at the meeting room at XYZ Assisted Living Facility to discuss Dad's condition and possible transfer to a nursing home where he can receive the skilled nursing care he needs.

This meeting is only for the family, but a social worker from the facility will attend as a facilitator. We hope to see you there. Regards, Monica." Wait for her response. Don't do anything else. She may not contact you at all or she may simply attend the meeting.

- Meet with your siblings as planned. If your sister does not attend, then you know exactly how she feels and you may plan accordingly. If she does attend, allow the facilitator to do her job. Spend the time deciding the best possible plan for your dad. If you cannot come to an amicable agreement, you may want to meet with the elder law attorney for direction and other options.

If your sister attends the meeting, she is probably hoping for some type of reconciliation with all of you. This is often a difficult road, but in the best interest of your dad, it is worth the trouble.

D. SUCCESS COMES IN SMALL WINS

Dear Eldercare 911,

People tell me that I am unrealistic and that I expect too much from myself and the people who take care of my ninety-four-year-old dad. He lives in a small, suburban nursing home surrounded by gardens and trees. Dad has dementia, difficulty walking, and poor eyesight. I expect the staff to get him up, dressed, and involved in some activity. They say some days he is too tired to participate. I say they are not doing their job. Who's right? Am I being unrealistic? I think I'm just being a caring daughter.

—Linda, Florida

Dear Linda,

A woman caring for her eighty-eight-year-old disabled father told us that when she became a caregiver, her life changed in a way she never expected. She said, "I see what life is, what it can be, and what it should be. It allows me to be more real about life, like watching my dad light up because he catches a beach ball." When we asked her if it made her sad to see her father play a game we associate with children, she said no, that she felt a certain connection to her dad because she could see his world with her eyes.

Linda, you asked who is right. You can't put a right or wrong answer on caring and loving someone. Depending how disabled your dad is, you may be expecting too much from him on a daily basis. It would be very helpful for you to learn as much as you can about your dad's condition in order to understand some of his behaviors. Also keep in mind that sometimes the nursing staff needs a friendly reminder. The following suggestions may help you communicate better with the staff, and you may begin to see that small accomplishments are really big wins.

- Make an appointment to meet with the social worker or recreational therapist. A recreational therapist organizes and implements all the social programs at the facility. Prepare a list of your questions and concerns to discuss with the staff, such as: Does Dad enjoy being with his peers? Does he ever participate in activities or does he always need coaxing and direction? When he is alone, does he sleep or listen to music? Her answers will give you a better picture of his socialization skills and behavior. If he has always been a loner, he will be less likely to participate in group activities. If he appears to enjoy certain activities, ask if she can coax him a little more.
- Hire a companion who is trained in working with the blind or poorly sighted and who has basic training in dementia for a few hours a week to personally encourage him to join in the activities. Because he is blind and suffers from dementia, she can take him to the activities and describe what is going on in the room. This may add to his enjoyment.
- Create your own activity by talking to Dad about what he did and what he heard. Because of the dementia, he may not remember the actual event, but that doesn't mean that he did not have a good time while he was there. You can act as his memory and provide him with cues and information about the day. For example, if he attended a musical concert, say, "Dad, you heard a wonderful concert today at the park. The music was beautiful and the singer was sensational." If he says he did not go to a concert, you can change the subject and talk about something else, or gently remind him about the experience. If he acknowledges that he remembers the music, then feel free to continue talking about the event. If he seems to be getting anxious or frustrated, simply distract him by talking about something else.

Because of your dad's physical and cognitive condition, he may sometimes be too tired to participate in any social activity. His lack of participation does not necessarily indicate a neglectful staff. Continue to keep your eyes open and communicate with the staff on a regular basis. Showing your interest may inspire more effort on the part of the staff. You're doing what you can do to enhance your dad's quality of life, and he may be doing all that he can.

Dear Eldercare 911,

Call the doctor, check on the new prescription, buy the groceries, take my son shopping. I sometimes feel like poor Cinderella for my parents and family. Just call me "Cinderelder." I'm so tired, I just want to stop the mayhem and madness. I used to think I was organized and efficient, now I just feel overwhelmed. My mom died over two years ago and my eighty-nine-year-old dad is childlike and very needy. It is exhausting being his daughter. Did I mention that Dad lives with us? I gave up my job as a secretary to take care of both of my parents. When Mom died, it seemed natural for Dad to move in. Let me tell you about my dad. My friends think he is "cute," because he is full of life and jokes, and stories, but he is also filled with demands. He is physically and cognitively capable of doing many things for himself, although he has diabetes and heart problems. What can I tell you, Mom spoiled him and now he thinks it is my job to take over where she left off. Foolishly, I fell right into this plan, and now I'm stuck. Please help me win this losing battle.

—Battle Fatigue, Michigan

Dear Battle Fatigue,

In our lives we all struggle to complete tasks and finish our work. Most of us leave a pile of papers on our desk at the end of a workday and a load of laundry in the dryer because we don't want to fold it. It doesn't mean we are not accomplished or successful women and men; it just means we are simply human and we can only do so much at one time and in one day. Feeling "battle fatigue" or like a "Cinderelder" means that you are trying too hard and doing too much. It is time to take control and recognize your many successes.

Your particular battle is one that so many caregivers face day after day. It is a misconception that you have to win every battle. The reality is that every small battle you win is an achievement. One caregiver said, "I look at each thing I have to do and when I successfully accomplish just one thing, I say out loud, 'mission accomplished.'" Trying to do everything at the same time is impossible, but trying to do one thing at a time takes a little organization and the ability to delegate certain tasks.

- Talk to Dad about his strengths. Explain to him how important it is to his physical and mental health to do what he can for himself before he asks for your help.

- Approach him about how you are feeling and what he can do to help you out. For instance, you can say: "Dad, I am exhausted and I need your help. Can you pick up the milk at the grocery and then drop off the dry cleaning?" Wait for him to reply. If he is not receptive to helping you at the moment, try to get him to make a commitment for another day.

- Have a second conversation if he completely refuses. "Dad, we will have to find another solution to our problems if you don't want to help out. We can hire a companion who can help you with some of your daily activities and give me some time to take care of my own responsibilities." If Dad has the finances to pay for the aide, talk to him about the cost.

Stay firm! Remember to win this battle you have to remain strong and persistent. To remain emotionally and physically healthy, you must give yourself credit for all your accomplishments, big and small.

The Rules of Intervention

Intervening in your parent's life is very difficult for most adult children, but sometimes it is the only way to keep your parent safe and secure.

I will try to meet with my family. I will try to discuss my concerns with my siblings. I will try to impress upon them the importance of working together as a team to help our parent.

I will reach out to my friends and colleagues. The support of my peers is extremely helpful and comforting when I am involved in caregiver responsibilities.

I will contact geriatric professionals. Professional advice and guidance can help ease my way through the intervention process.

I will choose my battles wisely. There are some things I can change, other things I can't change. I will think, prioritize, and then act in my parent's best interest.

I will be prepared for roadblocks. If I understand that roadblocks are inevitable, I will not be discouraged easily. I will do the best I can to overcome each obstacle. I will focus on my parent's safety and well-being.

I will reward myself for doing a great job. I will give myself the praise I deserve for trying to provide my parent with the best quality of life.

Assess Your Parent's Risk Factors

These statements will help alert you to several potential risks. Complete each phrase with one or more of these statements. Circle the numbers that apply.

Remember, this is only a guide. If your senses tell you something is not as it should be, get help immediately. Enlist the services of a health-care professional to diagnose and treat the problem as quickly as possible.

1. My mother or father . . . (circle one or more)

1. has always been a pack rat, so the house has always had stacks of newspapers, mail, and other things standing around. (In other words, nothing has changed.)

2. used to be well groomed, but now wears stained clothes and/or doesn't bathe as frequently as he/she used to.

3. used to go out frequently, but currently refuses to go out except in rare circumstances.

4. shows none of the changes in numbers 1, 2, or 3.

5. has exhibited these and other warning signs in the past several months that signal changes that should be investigated by a medical professional.

If you circled numbers 2, 3, or 5, it is time for a professional geriatric assessment.

2. My mother or father . . .

1. takes several medications daily.

2. often forgets or becomes confused and doesn't take his/her medications properly.

3. takes multiple medications *and* drinks significant amounts of alcohol.

4. seems to take his/her medications properly.

5. is at risk because it is unlikely he/she can self-administer medications.

If you circled 2, 3, or 5, your parent may be at risk from a complication owing to the improper use of medication and alcohol.

3. My mother or father . . .

1. has been hospitalized more than once during the past few months.
2. has fallen and broken a hip or an arm in the last several months.
3. has stumbled or fallen more than once in the last several months, without breaking any bones.
4. shows no signs of having fallen in the past several months.
5. has poor balance or vision and is at risk for falls and the serious problems that may result from them.

If you circled 1, 2, 3, or 5, consider a medical evaluation by a board-certified geriatric specialist.

4. My mother or father . . .

1. has a vision problem severe enough to stop him/her from participating in activities even when wearing glasses.
2. has hearing problems severe enough to keep him/her from taking part in conversations or understanding even when wearing a hearing aid.
3. has difficulty getting around his/her own home even with a walker, a cane, or a wheelchair.
4. has little or no problem as long as he/she uses the appropriate assistive device.
5. is increasingly isolated because of physical limitations.

If you circled 1, 2, 3, or 5, your parent may require a home health aide or an assisted living facility.

5. My mother or father . . .

1. is unable to shop for or cook his/her own food.
2. seems to have lost weight in the past few months.
3. seems to have lost interest in food.
4. eats reasonable amounts of nutritious food every day.
5. is at risk for problems that arise from poor nutrition.

If you circled 1, 2, 3, or 5, your parent may require a medical evaluation to determine the reasons for the changes in his eating habits. Consider a home health aide or an assisted living facility to meet his needs.

6. My mother or father . . .

1. is increasingly confused and forgetful.

2. could easily be taken advantage of by unscrupulous vendors or con artists.

3. would probably let a stranger into his/her home.

4. has good cognitive ability.

5. is at risk for accidents and abuse because of confusion and memory loss.

If you circled 1, 2, 3, or 5, your parent requires a complete geriatric assessment and supervised care.

7. My mother or father . . .

1. could safely evacuate a building unassisted in the event of a fire.

2. could use a telephone and dial 911 in the event of an emergency.

3. is safe in the tub and/or shower unassisted.

4. feels comfortable and safe alone at home.

5. is at risk when he/she is home alone.

If you circled number 5, consider a home health aide or an assisted living facility for your parent.

FOR WOMEN ONLY

Dear Eldercare 911,

Many years ago I had a heated argument with a friend. She was a working mother and at the time I was a stay-at-home mom. I remember the conversation so clearly. She asked me if I was going to go to work. I answered that my children were my priority. She yelled back that her children were her priority and did I think I was a better mother because I stayed at home. Literally, our husbands had to break up the screaming match, and we didn't speak to one another for five years. Today, my children are teenagers, I have a full-time job, chronically ill and demanding parents, and intrusive in-laws. I never have a minute for myself let alone my husband.

When I look back on that fight, I realize that as women we sometimes place so much pressure on ourselves to be everything to everybody. Unfortunately, we also want and expect the rest of the world to validate what we do and how we do it. For some reason I finally realized that this is an impossible model to follow. I am simply exhausted. My family seems to pull me in a hundred different directions. I sometimes feel like there is no more to give. I know my sense of responsibility won't go away any time soon, and I know that I can't reinvent myself overnight, but I would like to give it a try.

—Ellen, Minnesota

Dear Ellen,

Many women find their caregiving responsibilities so physically and emotionally draining that they have no energy for children or other family members. As a result, their families may become distant or angry, even jealous of the time they spend caregiving. It is time to find a way to reclaim a part of life for yourself, rethink how you approach your problems and responsibilities, and reward yourself every day for doing the best job you can. Read on for additional information and tips.

A. DIFFERENT STROKES

Dear Eldercare 911,

For the past five years I have cared for my dad, and little by little I am losing him. He is a shell of a human being, barely seventy pounds. I am keeping him home, in my home to die. Everyone asks me why. I tell them it is the 3 Cs: Comfort, Care, Compassion. No facility will provide the kind of care he gets from me. I had let them take my mom to the hospital to die, and I will never forgive myself. I have help during the day when I am at work, but I am "it" at night and on the weekends. I don't sleep very well because I listen for his breathing. I guess that work is my salvation. I can divorce myself from the situation when I'm there. My friends try to get me to do things with them, but I never go out, and they don't understand.

They say that my life is like being in a coma. I would like people to understand that some of us want and need to do this. Can you help me explain to my friends and family that being a caregiver is important to me?

—3 Cs, Georgia

Dear 3 Cs,

The decision to be a caregiver is a very personal one. You have posed an interesting dilemma. Why do some people judge you when you do so much for your loved ones? Do the other people really feel compassion and concern for you? Or are they afraid this might happen to them? It is difficult to say. What is most important is how you feel and how you handle your caregiver role. You say that "work is your salvation" and you spend many nights "listening for breathing." In a sense you are providing your own intensive care unit, and this environment may eventually zap you of your physical and emotional strength.

You asked us to help you explain your commitment to Dad and the 3 Cs. We can't pretend to thoroughly understand why one caregiver feels a need to do it all and others don't want or need to take on this role. We feel the best way to help you is to provide you with a dialogue to use when you are confronted by well-meaning family and friends.

- To a family member: "I appreciate your interest and concern. I hope you understand that I am not planning to ask for your help, I am just asking that you respect my decision to do what I want and need to do."

- To a friend: "You are a good friend and I know you are worried about me. I have made a choice, and the way you can be my friend now is to support my efforts. Just be there for me. There will come a day when I will need you to give me a hug or hold my hand, but now I just need to know that you understand and you'll keep calling me even when I can't say a word."
- Don't hesitate to state your messages again and again. It may take your family and friends time to understand the choices you made.
- If you can, try to treat yourself to a day off once in a while. Even a few hours of relaxation will help refresh and rejuvenate you.

You have made a decision that will impact your life for quite a while. We ask only that you try to take care of yourself with the same strength and conviction that you care for your dad.

Dear Eldercare 911,

For several years I have been doing it all. When it was clear that my mom could not live on her own, we built an addition to our house to accommodate her needs. For several years she managed on her own. About two years ago she had a heart attack, and six months later she had a stroke. Because I have a full-time job, I needed help in the house, though I decided that I would take care of her at night. Since I wanted to be able to go out on the weekends, I hired part-time help on Saturdays. After a few months I fell into my weekday routine. Now I get up every morning at 6 AM and clean Mom up. I always have to change the linens on her bed. After I dress her, I prepare breakfast and feed her. Then the homecare worker arrives and I leave for work. Many days I receive phone calls from the aide because my mom has so many physical problems and complications. I leave work around five and go home to cook dinner. I'm exhausted, but I get up and do the same thing the next day. I want to do this for my mom, and I am not going to stop, but it seems to get harder and harder. My friends call me a superwoman. I am just wondering if I am being realistic? Can one person really do it all?

—Karen, Illinois

Dear Karen,

Can one person do it all? According to the magazines, movies, and television, women are born to do it all. Many of us try to do too much for too many people in our lives. The need to please seems to be inherent in many women, placing them at a high risk for exhaustion and a multitude of physical, emotional, and psychological problems. And some women are even considered superheroines, supercaregivers, and superdaughters. You have clearly stated that "you want to do what you can for your mother," yet you ask: Am I being realistic? If we follow the fictional role of a woman portrayed on a television drama, the answer would probably be yes, of course you can do it all. Just like the character in the show, you can do it in one hour with time to spare. However, if we look at what you do and accomplish in a twenty-four-hour day, the answer is a resounding *no*. You can't continue to live your life at such a frenetic pace without it harming you in some way. Allowing yourself to let go of some of your responsibilities may enable you to do what you want to do for your mom and not hurt yourself in the process. Try these three timesaving steps.

1. Think about hiring the home health aide a few more hours each day. If she arrives earlier, she can attend to your mom's early-morning needs. This will decrease a great deal of your morning workload.
2. Decrease your cooking time by preparing a few meals at a time and freezing them for another day. You can purchase freezer containers at your local grocery store. Label each one with the date the food was prepared and the contents of the package. This will help make mealtimes quick and efficient for anyone who takes care of your mom.
3. Talk to the home health aide about limiting her telephone calls during the workday. Explain to her that nonemergency problems can wait until you get home. (See chapter 7, "Life as a Working Caregiver," for more helpful ideas.)

Small steps are sometimes the most effective when you are caring for a loved one. In your special situation these suggestions may give you a few more hours a day to rest and relax.

Karen, you sound like an amazing woman, but let's try to look at this superwoman ideal in perspective. Take the time to read and think about the following advice.

Ten Steps to Being a New Superwoman

Sleep is important. I will maintain my strength and focus.

Understand my limitations. I will not berate myself.

Plan ahead. I will take time for myself.

Eat nourishing foods. I will eat well to help maintain a strong, healthy body.

Relax. I will relax whenever and wherever I can, even for a few minutes a day.

Work hard, but play just as hard. I will try to maintain some fun in my life.

Open myself to new ideas. I will try new ideas to help me through the day.

Maintain friendships. I will help keep myself well balanced.

Admit when I need help. I will get the help I need.

Nurture myself. I will nurture myself the way I nurture my loved ones.

We hope this helps you rethink about your caregiver role and how you can take care of yourself as well as you take care of your mom.

B. THE PERILS OF SELF-NEGLECT

Dear Eldercare 911,

I often wonder how self-destructive I can get. I thought I reached the height of it in high school when I rode on the back of my boyfriend's motorcycle at seventy-five miles per hour. One day we hit a rock in the road and we swerved into the bushes. It was a near miss. I guess in some ways that was a precursor to the rest of my life. I am divorced and I have two children in their early twenties. I'm a fifty-three-year-old bookkeeper for a large company, and my day begins at 8 AM and ends about 6 PM. I then rush over to my dad's house and fix him dinner. Dad had a stroke five years ago which left him partially paralyzed on his right side. He has a very nice lady who helps him a few hours a day, but he really wants me to do the cooking. My mom and mother-in-law are on the other side of town in a nursing home. Two for one! I feel guilty if I visit my mom and not stop in to see my mother-in-law. So I try to visit both of them two or three times each week. My time is never my own.

A few weeks ago I started to get pains in my stomach and back. I figured it was just indigestion from my frenetic lifestyle. I finally went to the doctor because the pain finally stopped me in my tracks. I have stomach ulcers and enough acid in my stomach to burn through a cement sidewalk. I'm on medication and a special diet, but my motor is still running at seventy-five miles per hour. Please help me, before I run this middle-aged motor out.

—Racing in California

Dear Racing,

It doesn't matter if you are a high school coed or a middle-aged mom, living your life at high speed is hazardous to your health and overall well-being. You are one of the lucky ones. It appears that your ulcers are treatable, and you may gain some relief from medication and diet. However, if you continue on this path, you may not be as lucky the next time. We want you to try to remember when you were on the motorcycle and felt invincible, until you hit the rock in the road and the bushes scratched your face. As a caregiver, three decades later and after a health scare, you are again proceeding at risk when you ignore the physical and emotional signs of declining health.

These three steps will help you begin to slow down your internal motor and help you back on the path to better health and emotional balance. While a better emotional balance will have a positive impact on your physical health, nothing substitutes for appropriate and timely medical intervention.

1. Decrease some of your after-work stress by increasing the hours of your dad's companion. Although he wants you to cook, you don't have to do it every day. Just by preparing two meals at a time you can save three visits each week. Have the companion stay a little later to keep him company and serve his dinner. If she stays only an hour or two later, the cost should not be significant. Explain to Dad that although you like to help him out, you are very overtired and it is affecting your health. If he complains, let him know that this is the best you can do for now. Be strong; it is time to reclaim a part of your life.

2. Reduce the number of times you visit the nursing home. Visiting your mom and mother-in-law once a week will help you reduce more of the after-work stress. If you are comfortable, talk to your ex-husband. Find out if he is already visiting his mom during the week. If he is making timely visits, feel free to decrease your visits. If he is not visiting often

enough, talk to him about hiring a companion to visit his mother once or twice a week. If you are on good terms, you may be able to share the cost of one companion who can visit both women on the same day. This will benefit all of you. If he is not approachable, then assess whether you can handle the expense on your own. Speak to the social worker at the nursing home for referrals to agencies specializing in companion care. Sometimes individuals who work in the nursing home are eager to earn extra money on their days off. Ask the social worker if she can suggest someone who is reliable and responsible.

3. Maintaining good health and emotional balance comes from an inner desire for things to be better. To help you achieve this goal, you also have to take the time to laugh and play. Decide what activity will make you happy and help you to relax, such as a game of tennis or a movie. Reward yourself by planning one activity each week and see how you feel. In time, you may add other activities to help you decrease the stress and increase the pleasure in your life.

In a race there is only one winner. Be a winner; let your motor hum by slowing down your race. Pace yourself and do what you have to do to keep yourself healthy and happy.

Dear Eldercare 911,

This is a list of things I found out about my dad from the doctor. It also includes the things I have to do for him to maintain his care at home. I have divided the list into two categories; specific health information and a "to do" list.

Health information:

Swelling is edema. Doctor suggests support hose
Dad's blood pressure is 160/90
Dad has unexplained weight loss from 180 to 153
I noticed a rash on Dad's left calf, contact the doctor
Doctor tested vision and reflexes
Tested muscle strength, minimal weakness
Doctor wants basic blood work done
Dad may have mild neuropathy, compression on spinal cord
Dad doesn't seem depressed
Doctor recommends a walker

To do:

Remind the aide to walk Dad in the hallway
Take Dad for a haircut next week
Take Dad to the podiatrist to have his toenails clipped

Last week I missed my own doctor's appointment, my fingernails are chipped and broken, and I haven't had a haircut in over two months. But I memorized Dad's blood pressure and I made an appointment for him to see the podiatrist before his nails break. Caregiving consumes all of my time and energy. I want a piece of my life back. Can you help me?

—Wendy, Massachusetts

Dear Wendy,

You are terrific! You created a personalized "caregiver shorthand" that includes almost everything you need to know in order to safely maintain your dad in his own home. Unfortunately, you left out the most important, precious person of all: you. Wendy, like many caregivers you have put yourself last for too long. Giving up everything to care for someone else is physically, emotionally, and psychologically draining, and it is not necessary. We are not expecting you to relinquish your role as the primary caregiver, but there are ways you can incorporate your role with the life that you want and deserve. Successful caregiving depends on a *cared-for caregiver.* Try some of these techniques to help you reclaim the important pieces of your life.

- Health alert. Too many caregivers suffer from a variety of medical problems because they don't listen to their own bodies. You said that you missed your own doctor's appointment, but you know Dad's blood pressure. It is time to know your vital medical statistics. It doesn't mean that you are paying less attention to Dad; it just means that you are giving yourself the same care and concern you give to him. Make an appointment for a physical examination and keep it. You are not just helping yourself; you are staying well for Dad.
- Delegate, delegate, delegate. On your list you indicate that you asked the aide to take Dad for a walk in the hallway. Since you are able to ask her to help with one task, you have the ability to ask her to help with something else. For example, your list indicates that Dad needs a haircut. Make the appointment yourself if you prefer a special hairdresser and want to arrange payment for the haircut, but ask the aide to

escort him to the appointment. At the end of this chapter you will find a worksheet to help you regain control of your time, aptly called "My Plan to Regain Control of My Time." (In chapter 6, "Family Matters," you will find another helpful worksheet called "Dividing Your Time.")

- Renew and refresh yourself. Everyone needs a little pampering now and then. You clearly recognize the need. According to your list, your dad needs his toenails clipped and his hair cut. So do you. Figure out how much time you need to get a manicure and your hair styled. If you can do it in one day, great; if not, take a few hours on two different days. Spend a little time preparing for your special day or days by looking through fashion magazines for new styles, colors, and haircuts. Make this minimakeover a part of your routine.

Caring for yourself is not selfish and it doesn't mean that you care for your dad any less. It simply means that you recognize that you are as worthy of a good life as your dad.

C. HUSBANDS AND PARTNERS

Dear Eldercare 911,

This is about my husband. By the time you read this, I may have clobbered my Bert on the head with a frying pan. He makes all the right noises, "Poor Rita, you work so hard" and "Don't worry, I understand," when I say I'm too tired to go out Saturday night. But if I need to talk about my father's illness, he becomes suddenly deaf. He says we've been talking about the same issues for years and I already know the answers. My dad's been living with us for five years. As he gets sicker, caring for him gets more complicated, and I don't always know what to do. When I try to talk to Bert about a problem, I expect a helpful suggestion or for him to brainstorm with me. But all I get is a few words, like "Sounds reasonable" or "Tell him no." Then he's finished. No continuing thoughts or comments about "how" to say "no" and what to do with the reaction my refusal will surely bring about. Then he goes back to his book or the TV. It's not fair. When his mom needed us, I spent hours thinking about ways to help her, but he's content with a thirty-second answer to my dad's problems. He thinks he's "been there" for me, and I end up feeling alone and miserable. Why doesn't he see that I need him to talk to?

—Tired of Talking to Myself in Ohio

Dear Talking to Yourself,

Reholster your frying pan! You've solved your own problem! You are absolutely right in believing you need someone to talk to about your caregiving responsibilities. You don't say how your relationship with Bert is outside of this issue, but you give us two clues that lead us to assume it's good: in your second sentence when you called him "my Bert" and that you seek and value his opinion on issues so that you can better manage your dad's care.

Bert sounds like he may be one of the many men who see problems and solutions in absolutes: you state the problem, they state the answer, and then they move on to the next topic. These men feel that they have "already answered the question," and they see no need to continue talking about it or even thinking about it. It's history for them. Many women, however, receive comfort and additional practical help from continuing the discussion and talking about "how" and "what if" and the value of one solution over another. Their experience is that very often this ongoing "brainstorming" leads to better and more palatable solutions.

But there is another, equally important truth. Regardless of gender issues, it may be time for Bert to start paying more attention to your needs. Caregiving is stressful and often very lonely. It sounds like you're giving Bert a free pass while you accept the entire caregiving burden. If you want him to participate, it's time to let him know his free pass has expired and you expect more from him.

The next time you ask for help and Bert gives you a quick two- or three-word answer, walk over to him and ask him to stop whatever he is doing. Stay in front of him until you have his undivided attention. Then calmly tell him how you feel. Here is a good beginning: "Bert, I really need you right now. Dad's care becomes more complicated every day and I'd feel less lonely and more comfortable talking things over with you. I'm confused over what I should do next, and even though your answer settles the question for you, it can't help me because you haven't told me 'why' you feel that way. Would you please take some time and discuss the pros and cons with me? I took the time to help you with your mom and now it's your turn—I need you to help me with my dad. Will you?"

If Bert can't fill your needs on this issue, try discussing your dad's care with a female friend or family member who is or has been a caregiver. Many women are natural connectors and exchangers of information.

If you feel you need further input, you have more options. Call the local

Area Agency on Aging or the community resource department of your local hospital and ask about a support group. Or contact a counselor at one or more of the resources in chapter 13. These resources are there to serve you and have answers that come from years of helping other caregivers solve similar problems.

Whether you end up talking with Bert or someone else, you'll find discussing your dad's problems with someone who will empathize and spend the time you need may help you work out solutions to situations that seemed insurmountable. You may also be surprised about how much better you will feel.

Dear Eldercare 911,

I'm a sixty-two-year-old divorced woman who expected to remain alone (without a husband) for the rest of my life. A year ago, I met a wonderful man. Keith and I began dating and fell in love. He's asked me to marry him and I have no doubts—I want to spend my life with him, but I'm afraid it won't work. My mother has Alzheimer's and she lives with me.

When she first became ill, we agreed that when I could no longer handle her alone at home, she would move to a nursing home. We've always been very close and I want to wait until the last possible minute to do that. Keith accepts my position and has offered to bring her to live with us in his home. I think that's asking a lot of him, but he says he can handle it. What are the chances that a sixty-four-year-old man who has never been a caregiver can do this? I love him dearly and don't want to lose him.

—Maryanne, Montana

Dear Maryanne,

It sounds like Keith doesn't want to lose you, either. Any man who loves you enough to make a wonderful offer like this deserves a chance to fulfill his promise. However, your anxiety about his lack of firsthand knowledge of the disease may be justified, so it might be wise to take certain steps to help his and your dream come true.

- First, we assume Keith has met your mother. If he hasn't, he is making a promise without a sound knowledge of the changes his vows will make in his life. That is unfair to all three of you. Introduce him to your mother as soon as possible.
- Next, talk to Keith about going with you to an Alzheimer's counselor for an impartial picture of what he can expect when you all live together. Is your mother incontinent? Does she wander? Will you need

to safety proof his home by locking up all chemical substances and sharp tools like dishwashing soap and knives? How would your life together be different than if you weren't caring for your mother? Addressing these issues will give Keith the information that he needs to make a more informed decision.

- We also recommend you speak with the counselor, alone or with Keith, to discuss at what level of need you will feel unable to care for your mother at home. (See "The Three Stages of Alzheimer's Disease" in chapter 8.) Discussing this with a healthcare professional may help prepare you for her eventual move and give you new insight into when that move may be necessary. It will also give Keith an idea of when you and he will be free to travel or experience other social activities. In addition, it will help clarify the financial responsibilities that lie ahead. Call your local Alzheimer's organization for a counselor or speak with your mother's physician.

As wonderful, loving, and caring as Keith sounds, every marriage has issues that develop over time. It is important to candidly discuss your mother's position in your and Keith's life together before your marriage. This will help you carry the least amount of anxiety into your new marriage and provide it with a solid foundation of trust and openness on which to build.

D. YOUR BODY, MIND, AND SPIRIT

Dear Eldercare 911,

How do I make my husband understand that after spending seventeen hours a day working and taking care of my mother, sex is the last thing I want? Do I still love him? Who knows? Maybe. Probably. I guess so. But it's been so long since I've had any time for myself, I can't imagine even spending a fun afternoon with him, let alone getting in the mood to make love. Right now, he's just another person who wants a piece of me. If I had a free hour, what would really turn me on is getting my first manicure in three years!

—Joanne, Arizona

Dear Joanne,

It sounds like your caregiving responsibilities and job have robbed you of a great deal more of life than intimacy with your husband! Like you, many women find their caregiving responsibilities so physically and emotionally demanding that they have no energy for companionship and no desire for physical intimacy at the end of the day. As a result, their husbands and partners may become distant or angry, even confused over why their wives can no longer find time for them. Some will become jealous of the time their wives spend caregiving. Whether you still love your husband or want an active sex life with him is important, but it takes second place to reclaiming your quality of life. In order to enjoy a meaningful relationship or friendship, you need enough time with yourself to willingly share some of it with another person. It's not easy, but it's worth the effort. Use these three steps as a beginning in your journey to change your life for the better.

1. First, write down three personal *pressure-free* things you would like to do if you had the time. *Pressure-free* is the key. Your goal is to enhance your life, not add more stress. For example, the manicure you mentioned is a good start and should help reduce stress. Why not add a pedicure? Or lunch with a girlfriend you haven't seen in a long time? If you feel that an afternoon or evening with your husband will be relaxing and joyful, make that one of the three activities. However, if you begin to feel anxious or irritable thinking about what to wear or communicating for three hours, then leave it off your list or you'll simply be trading one stressful situation for another.

2. Look at your list and choose one of the three things. Keeping your choice to only one will help you limit the time you'll need to make your goal a reality. Does one of the three make you smile and feel really good with anticipation? That's your choice!

3. Now, begin to revise your week to make time for your personal activity by removing something from your "to do" list. You have four options: delegate it to a family member, hire someone to handle it, reschedule it, or if it isn't very important, just forget about it.

This takes practice, but don't give up. Remember, *wants* are not the same as *needs*. Set the standard at separating duties that deal with healthcare and safety from other tasks or favors you perform. You reached this point by tending to everyone's *wants* except your own. When you remove something from your "to do" list, look for duties that won't compromise your mother's health or safety. Using that definition should open several windows of opportunity for you, but if you need help working out what to delete, use the worksheets at the end of this chapter: "My Contract with My Body, Mind, and

Spirit" and "My Plan to Regain Control of My Life." You can also use the worksheet at the end of chapter 6, "Dividing Your Time."

Once you begin caring for yourself, you may find that you have more time and inclination to communicate with your husband—on every level!

Dear Eldercare 911,

I love my mother and I'm aware that as long as I'm her caregiver I'll have more stress and less time than my noncaregiver friends, but somewhere in this daily grind someone has got to help me find a little time for me. I know this sounds unbelievable, but I haven't shopped for a new outfit in seven years. I'm always last on my to do list—that is, if I make the list at all! I've skipped eye-doctor appointments, physicals, and every other appointment. Now, I feel like I have no future. If I free up a few minutes, I'm too tired or depressed to do anything with them. I never knew how awful it was to lose hope, but what hope do I have for a life. Will I be a caregiver until I need a caregiver myself? I'm betting on you.

—Sheila, Tennessee

Dear Sheila,

Your question tells us that you're ready to bet on yourself. You've taken two of the most important steps in reclaiming time for yourself: admitting the realities of the situation and asking for help. Right now, before you finish reading this chapter, go to the telephone and make an appointment with an internal medicine physician and a gynecologist. Promise yourself that having taken this important step, *you will absolutely keep those appointments.* Be fair to yourself. Help yourself regain your optimism by being totally honest with both doctors about how you feel. A complete examination will help determine the best approach to help you feel better about yourself and help you regain enough momentum to begin to reclaim time for your personal needs.

Even though you may not be able to maintain the same amount of personal time that you had before you became a caregiver, it's critically important for your physical and mental health to find as much private and rejuvenating time for yourself as you can. That brings us to your second step: make another telephone call right now to have your hair professionally cut and colored if it needs it. Once again, it's important to *promise yourself that you will absolutely keep this appointment.* If you can afford it, why not consider a manicure and a pedicure? Often the little things in life give us enjoyment far beyond their cost.

Third, enlist the aid of a close friend, a therapist, or a support group if you can. Sometimes we find ourselves so deeply involved that it takes an uninvolved third party to help keep us moving forward on the right track.

Finally, use this outline to create a *contract with your body, mind, and spirit*.

My Contract with My Body, Mind, and Spirit

It is helpful to renew your contract every day by repeating your goals out loud.

☐ I will set realistic goals. I know I cannot undo in days what I have spent years creating.

☐ I agree to take small steps and let them accumulate into larger accomplishments.

☐ I will help myself by paying attention to my own natural body rhythms and schedule the most difficult tasks for my peak time of day.

☐ I acknowledge that there will be times when someone or something will not receive immediate attention. I will learn, by practice, when I can safely allow that to happen.

☐ I will learn to recognize when I give up my time because someone else has used guilt to manipulate me. When I see that happening, I will stop and correct the situation. If I waver, I will call a friend for support.

☐ I will understand that my past is behind me. I will learn from it, but I will spend my energies on my present and my future.

Signed _____ Date_____

My Plan to Regain Control of My Time

Week 1:

Pay close attention to your life this week. Take a fresh look at what you do, and rate each chore or duty as either "critical" or "can wait." Carry a small pad or piece of paper with you and write down everything you labeled "can wait."

Week 2:

Review your "can wait" list. Choose one duty that you can safely skip this week and use the time you would have spent on that chore for personal time. Consider permanently deleting this item or permanently delegating it to family, neighbors, friends, volunteers from community organizations, and hired help. If you're unsure which item to skip, reread number 3 in your "My Contract with My Body, Mind, and Spirit."

Week 3:

If you weren't able to permanently delegate or delete the item you postponed in week 2, then add it back to your list and choose a different "can wait" item to postpone this week. Again, use the time you saved on personal needs and consider permanently delegating or deleting this item.

Week 4:

Try to skip, delegate, or combine two "can wait" items to increase the time you have to yourself each week. Again, try to permanently delete or delegate the item to someone else.

Keep repeating Week 4 until you have increased your time by actually dropping or combining several responsibilities.

5

FOR MEN ONLY

Dear Eldercare 911,

I always thought I was pretty self-reliant. In fact, I can't remember the last time I asked anyone for help. But trying to care for my parents has finally brought me down. The problems remind me of a continuous loop tape; the same old message just keeps replaying again and again. When I am foolish enough to believe I have everything under control, they change the tape and I get a whole new set of problems that begins playing nonstop.

I'm a successful businessman so I expect unforeseen issues that need resolving, but I'm stumped here. To me, success is fixing the problem and moving on. It's pretty apparent to me that this is a different ballgame. Are there ever "ups" or will it be all "downs"? I'm not a quitter, so I'm in for the duration, but frankly, when I offered to help my parents five years ago, I never dreamed the job would be all consuming. How do I get them with the program?

—Fred, Delaware

Dear Fred,

You are not alone. Many male caregivers are surprised to find that the same strategies they've relied on for years to successfully meet their business goals fail to produce positive results when applied to eldercare. There are many comparisons, but the reason your results don't measure up to your projections is the same for all of them. Compare these two situations:

- Business strategies often move merchandise to and from the market, usually to sell and to make a profit. The staff that executes the plans usually asks to be hired. If they want to keep their jobs, *it's in their best interest to help the plan work.*
- Eldercare involves caring for people who are ill, frail, or have dementia, and who often don't want your help. They may be anxious and afraid that once you get involved, they will lose control and *you*

will make decisions without their consent that permanently change their lives.

If you're committed to remaining on this job, you'll need every bit of the self-reliance and ingenuity you seem to have displayed throughout your business career. You'll need to rethink your approach and look at each situation or problem with a different perspective. It's important to keep an open mind. You will almost certainly have to adjust your thinking to design a successful new strategy, but the bottom-line profit in this venture is peace of mind and a better quality of life for all of you. Read on.

A. GOALS, EXPECTATIONS, AND REALITIES

Dear Eldercare 911,

I'm in big trouble. A year ago, when my mother could no longer live alone, I convinced my wife to let her move in with us. The pros and cons looked good on paper: my wife and I are empty nesters and we had plenty of room; we could bring in homecare; Mom would cooperate because her alternative was a facility. I promised my wife that I would use my managerial experience to set up a seamless transition and a smooth ongoing program. I thought "How hard could it be to take care of one eighty-nine-year-old, four foot nine, ninety-pound woman?" We set Mom up in her own rooms in the house and felt good about our plan. After the move, we went back to our normal lives. As I look back, I can honestly say that the first day Mom lived here was the last day anything went according to that plan. Mom refuses to do anything that the doctor tells her to do. She has everything we have in her rooms: TV, phone, books, a computer, even a microwave and a small refrigerator. Yet she continually disrupts our life. She interrupts and then stays in our area every time we have guests and continually asks my wife to take her places (shopping, lunch, the doctor) instead of waiting until my wife has time. Yesterday my wife announced that either my mother goes or she does. What am I missing here? Where did I go wrong?

—Husband in Trouble, Iowa

Dear Husband in Trouble,

You've encountered a dilemma experienced by many male caregivers. You reviewed the problem, created a plan to resolve it, and expected everyone involved to act according to the script. Then, like so many others, you watched in disbelief as your carefully thought-out strategy began unraveling until it finally collapsed.

You and your family are involved in what some experts consider the most frustrating and traumatic situation you may ever encounter. The same goal-oriented, dispassionate problem solving that works well for inanimate uses such as budgets or revenue projections frequently produces the exact opposite result in eldercare. Once you acknowledge the existence of a human factor, you should have no trouble acknowledging that unless your mother and wife buy into your plan *before you finalize it*, it won't work. There are no finite answers. Sensitivity and flexibility are the keys to success.

If you want your mother to continue living in your house, and you want your wife to agree and participate, revisit your original concept. In reality, the plan you created was for Mom's physical move and ongoing care. This is only *half* of the plan you need to create a successful transition. To help create a better quality of life for all of you, add Part II: The Humanity Portion of Mom's New Life. These ideas will get you started.

- Consider what makes your life or your wife's life enjoyable? Friends? Family? Hobbies? Pleasure outings? All these are part of what your mother needs in her life as well. From many perspectives, socializing with you and/or your wife or joining you to watch TV or eat dinner might be considered normal family behavior.
- Clarify your and your wife's expectations for interaction with Mom. It is unrealistic to expect your mother to remain alone in the house without feeling lonely and wanting companionship. It is unrealistic and unfair to expect your wife to be Mom's only social companion unless your wife agrees to do so. If neither of you wants to involve your mother in your lives, then it's time to reconsider whether or not she should continue living with you.
- Consider Mom's previous lifestyle. Did she leave good friends behind? Or was she lonely, and did her expectations of the move include socializing with you and your wife? Did she leave a physician whom she trusted? Did she leave familiar stores and merchants where she shopped for many years? Has she gone from being a part of a neighborhood or a social group to being isolated in her room?
- If companionship is needed, hire a senior who works as a companion. Look for one who drives and enjoys the same activities as your mother does or used to enjoy. Interviewing and background checks on prospec-

tive candidates before hiring are a *must*. Choose two or three appropriate candidates and let your mother select the person she feels the most compatible with. The companion can accompany your mother to the movies, to the mall, on walks, to lunch, or just sit with her at home and talk, watch TV, read, and so on. (Note: Companions do not perform healthcare duties, so if your mother needs personal care, you may need to hire a home health aide.)

- Search out a senior center or a daycare program for Mom. Both provide socialization. Senior centers demand more independence; daycare programs provide varying levels of assistance. Some provide transportation. You can locate the centers near you by calling the Area Agency on Aging or a local hospital for recommendations. You can also check the phone book or the resources in chapter 13.

- You don't say how far away your mom's old home was. If she left a best friend behind in her old neighborhood and it isn't too far away, consider arranging transportation for regular visits.

- Ask Mom what she would like to do for interest and entertainment: walks, movies, rides in the car, shopping, lunch. If she's able to participate, her input may be the most valuable piece of the puzzle.

Moving exacerbates the uncertainties and insecurities that permeate the lives of our elders. Making a special effort to involve them in our lives or to help them maintain their own quality of life is one way to lessen the potential negative impact of the move.

Dear Eldercare 911,

After my mother died, I took my father to what I thought was a normal bereavement support group. He was the only man among eight women. The only part of the conversation he understood was when they tried to "hit on him." Two passed him their phone numbers! One woman actually invited him to dinner and another kept staring and smiling at him through the meeting. He wanted a support group and he ended up in a pickup bar for the bereaved! What were they thinking? They must have known that he had just lost his wife. Had they no shame? If I sound angry, I'm not. I'm furious! Now, Dad's refused to go back. So he's back in his house again, all alone. How is he ever going to get help?

—Rick, Maine

Dear Rick,

Believe it or not, what your father experienced is not unusual. In fact, it would have been more unusual for your father to have attended a meeting of all women and not have at least one of them make a pass at him! Even if more men had been in the group, your father might still have been "hit on." Elder men and women frequently approach the challenges of widowhood differently because of gender roles and practical issues. The reality of today's world is that women live longer than men. Once they are widowed, they are less likely to want to continue life alone, but they significantly outnumber their male counterparts. Although both sexes usually live a better quality of life with companionship, women are more likely to admit the need and actively look for a friend, a partner, or a husband. This can result in a competition to attract interesting available men. Another issue is that many women who were caregivers for their husbands for long periods of time—often five, ten, or more years—may have accepted widowhood long before their husbands died. This sometimes allows them to pursue a partner more quickly after a spouse's passing than those who remained in doubt or denial about the future. The net effect is that women often become the aggressors in pursuing a relationship. All in all, what your father experienced has almost become commonplace.

To help your father, seek private counseling from your local hospice organization or ask the hospital social work department for a referral. Be sure and tell the counselor about his first experience. Your church or synagogue may have a "men's only" group. There is no timetable for grieving—it may take weeks, months, or even years. However, if your father seems incapacitated by his grief, your best bet is to contact his physician for assistance. If he isn't eating properly, seems distracted or forgetful, doesn't join in family activities or socialize at all with friends, or is becoming more reclusive, his safety might be at risk. Alternatively, you can hire a geriatric care manager to help you find assistance or seek other guidance from the resources in chapter 13.

B. CONCRETE ANSWERS

Dear Eldercare 911,

I'm a retired military man. I've been responsible for tens of thousands of men and managed to keep them fed, housed, and clothed. That was easy compared with taking care of Dad. The problem is my wife, mother-in-law, and three sisters-in-laws need to talk about every decision for hours or days before we make a move. I sit down quietly with a pen and paper, create a task list for the next few days, and go to bed thinking everything is taken care of. They discuss each task so that several of them have input into every problem. Ask a simple question and that starts them off all over again. How can these busy women enjoy this endless rehashing of options that were clear as a mountain spring the first time around? They're strong women, and they laugh at some of the crazy solutions they bring up, so I don't think they keep talking because they are afraid to make a decision or to act on their solutions. Can you explain this to me? I love them all, and we're going to be doing this for years. How do I get some action around here? I'm waiting at attention.

—Colonel Bill, Kentucky

At ease, Colonel,

It sounds like the women in your life thrive on their connectivity and communication. Many women recognize that talking over problems with peers or friends can decrease stress and, in fact, often leads to better solutions than they might have found if they had faced these dilemmas alone. The camaraderie they create offers peace and release from tension, worry, or even guilt. This is especially true with sensitive and emotional situations. You mention that you will "be doing this for years." Long-term eldercare responsibilities, without the kind of coping mechanisms your family has created, often wreck the caregiver's health or marriage.

Look at it this way: For years society placed a higher value on men who were the "strong and silent" type than on women who were perceived as less strong because they talked about their fears and problems. Today, many Fortune 500 companies make many decisions based on the output of "think tanks" made up of men and women whose only responsibility is to talk about the company's goals and problems. These corporations understand that several brains attacking a single problem may offer more creative and cost-effective solutions. Having said all that, neither we nor your family, we're sure, want you to continue suffering. If their method of decreasing their own stress increases yours, that's unacceptable. Consider these steps as a beginning framework for a truce to prevent further escalation of your differences and to minimize the potential for open warfare.

1. Call a family meeting and explain your frustrations.
2. Suggest that in each situation there are certain things that need imme-

diate action and will not be impacted by other issues. Be prepared with one or two examples from past problems.

3. Suggest that you handle those "mandatories" while they finish working on the rest of the plan. Explain that disposing of those situations immediately will free more time for them and you to create strategies for the more difficult battles.

Dear Eldercare 911,

What the blazes is wrong with everyone?! I admit that I didn't volunteer or even happily accept the responsibility of caring for my father, but now that he depends on me, I'm determined to meet my obligations. My problem is that everyone else involved seems determined to create obstacles to stop me. The doctor says, "We'll see" or, and this one really floored me, "We don't know." If *he* doesn't know, who else should I ask? The daycare center expects to have an opening "soon." No amount of questioning or pushing for a more concrete answer can move them off that lame answer. What am I supposed to do with my father while I'm waiting for soon? I'm a CPA and tax attorney, not a healthcare professional. The physical therapist can't tell me "when" or "if" my father will regain the use of his left side (he had a stroke). I don't understand a world where professionals consider it normal if their clients take two steps backward for every one step forward. I only have one question: How the hell am I supposed to succeed when the rest of the support system continually fails me?

—Bart, Missouri

Dear Bart,

Here's the bottom line: when three and three no longer make six, it's time to look at the problem through fresh eyes. In order to help your parents, you need to have multiple options because there are no absolutes or guarantees in caregiving or in healthcare. Let's go back to your points. First, many of the best physicians are cautious when treating the elderly. As we age, our bodies absorb and react to medications differently. What works for you may be dangerous or even toxic for your father. Or science may not yet have created the medicine your father needs. Because the physician is dealing with a human body (as opposed to numbers), concrete answers and solutions aren't always realistic goals. On the other hand, you didn't mention the qualifications of your father's physician. We urge you to work with a physician who is board certified in geriatric medicine or in whatever discipline your father requires—

neurology, internal medical, cardiology, podiatry, and so on. If your current physician doesn't meet that standard, you might benefit from exercising your option for a *second opinion*. Whether you find the current physician is right on the mark or you find better care, you'll have taken a major step toward your goal of succeeding as a caregiver. The same approach applies to the physical therapist. Is he or she board certified? Expert in working with elderly? If not, find another source. Call the American Stroke Association in your area or call the national headquarters listed in the resource guide in chapter 13 and ask for certified therapists in your area. We hear your frustration loud and clear, but it doesn't drown out your intelligence. You know the answer for daycare: they have no way of knowing when a current participant will opt out of the program. For more help and support, ask your local chapter of the American Stroke Association, check with your local hospitals, and also call the Area Agency on Aging for additional daycare options.

You are absolutely right in believing that you cannot succeed without a support system. At best, caregiving is a series of wins and losses; at worst, it fits your description of one step forward and two steps backward. To reverse that losing position to a more positive one, create your own network for assistance and referrals. The resource guide in chapter 13 can help you locate some of the organizations you'll need. Above all, remember that most of the people you talk to will want to help you, but the system that *supports* them is overburdened to the point of bursting. Patience, a kind word, and a "please" and "thank you" will go a long way toward helping you generate the support you need to achieve your goals.

C. WIVES AND PARTNERS

Dear Eldercare 911,

I decided that it is hard enough taking care of my ninety-six-year-old father without my wife fighting with me every step of the way. She is really angry about the time I spend with my dad, no matter how much or how little time I spend with him. I know this is rough on all of us, but my wife, Mary is really a pain. One day I asked her to help me with one very specific problem and she said, "He's your father, you figure it out." I started to think about my situation and came up with my unique description of a caregiver's spouse. Here goes. The really lucky man has a wife who understands the situation. The lucky man has a wife who is at least willing to cooperate. The not-so-lucky man has a wife who is not a hindrance but who won't help, either. And the poor unlucky guy is the one who has a wife who makes his life completely miserable. Well, that's me. I don't know what to do so I just bite the bullet, but it's getting harder and harder. HELP!

—Sam, Louisiana

Dear Sam,

You are not alone feeling caught between family members. It is very common for a family conflict to result because a loved one feels neglected. Unfortunately, there are times in a caregiver's experience when one family member needs you more than another family member does. Feelings are hurt and emotions are fragile, but the reality is that you cannot be everything to everyone all of the time.

We are going to suggest a few things for you to try to help your situation. This may be tough because most men tend to do just what you are doing; they bite the bullet. Many men often find it easier to take control and physically do something about a situation rather than discuss it. Unfortunately, by not expressing your feelings, you appear to be hurting yourself and are not helping your wife understand why you do the things you do. One male caregiver wrote, "When my wife complains about something, I nod my head, mumble a word or two, and I'm done. What else am I supposed to do?" Some shut down emotionally in order to avoid any conflict or confrontation. We have some very simple techniques for you to try. Please don't cringe and close this book; try to consider some of our suggestions. It won't hurt and it may in fact help you. Your letter reflects someone who tries to be open and even sensitive. It's time to give you a voice to express yourself and how you really feel about your wife and the ongoing family tug-of-war.

It may seem hard to believe but it is possible that your wife may feel insecure about her place in your heart. A reassuring hug and a few thoughtful words while you are talking to her may help ease the situation.

- Begin by asking her to join you for a drive in the country or a picnic in the backyard. The important thing is for you to be alone and have the privacy to laugh and feel sad together. Keep in mind that you may never have her full support, but your efforts may help to initiate better communication and coping skills. Use some or all of the following dialogue to help you speak to your wife. "Mary, let's go for a drive in the country this weekend, just the two of us." If Mary disagrees, don't get discouraged, instead let it go for now and bring it up another day. If she agrees, you can say, "I was hoping we could have some time alone to talk about us and Dad. I know you and Dad did not always see eye to eye, so maybe we can talk about how you feel to help clear the air." Let Mary respond. If she says, "There's nothing to talk about," you can say, "There is a lot to talk about; we need to talk about you and me." If she says, "OK, I want to talk about you and me but not your dad. When do you want to go?" take full advantage of her willingness to talk about the situation, and during your time alone try to bring up the present situation with your dad and how she feels. Plan your drive in the country as soon as possible.

- Try not to discuss the sensitive and emotional issues during the drive. Driving is stressful enough, and you don't want to be distracted by a heated conversation. Find a quiet spot and pull over to have your chat. "Mary, I know the time I spend with Dad takes time away time from us, but it is very important to me. You know I love you and and our life together, but I need you to try and understand that taking care of Dad doesn't mean I love you any less." Give Mary time to digest what you are saying and give her an opportunity to respond and express her feelings. If she doesn't reply, you can add, "Mary, this is not forever, although it may seem that way now. I am not asking you to help me; I am only asking that you don't hinder me."

Mary will need time, a hug, or her hand held to get through this conversation. If she says that she is willing to not hinder your caregiving efforts, consider it a very successful intervention. In time, Mary may fall back to her old patterns of behavior, but now you have a new voice to help you express how she is making you feel. Use it to help you get through some of the difficult times. Remember, you are doing the best you can, and with a little reassurance from you, your family will recognize that your best is good enough for all of them.

Dear Eldercare 911,

My wife and I are so different I often wonder how we ever agree on anything. For years she has been the primary caregiver for her parents. Her dad died a few years ago and we are still very involved in her mother's life. I am happy to report that after a great many arguments she agreed to hire a home health aide to help her mom in her own home. Even though it has been difficult, on some level I think some of our bickering has brought us closer together. Caregiving gives us a common ground. The problem is we don't talk, we fight. I yell and she cries. I am a much stronger personality and she avoids confrontation. She is organized and I am not. She wants hugs, I'm not touchy-feely. I look at a problem and face it head-on and she wants to analyze it to death. I get impatient and in the end we just don't talk about it. Some things have changed for the better over the years. My wife always let her parents walk all over her, now she seems to have greater control and she is able to set limits. She doesn't always have a need to oversee everything in her mother's life. I know I am never going to be able to feel what she feels, but I really love her and I would like to try to understand her better. Any suggestions?

—Mark, Montana

Dear Mark,

Mark, you really have some good insights. And you are right, for several reasons. You will probably never feel the same way your wife does. First, we are talking about her mother with all of the emotional history and baggage. Second, oftentimes women and men take on the duties of caregiving in a very different way. Many men tend to look at a problem, find a solution, and then put it behind them. Many women look at a problem, find a solution, and continue to think about how they could do it better. It doesn't mean that one gender is doing something right and the other is wrong; it is just different ways of approaching and handling a problem. A common ground appears between men and women when they find themselves entrenched in a parent's life. When someone is entrenched in a parent's decline, it is all consuming. Most of the time it is not physically or emotionally healthy and it is generally not productive. In your present situation the important thing is that your wife has made some progress by hiring a home health aide and she is setting some significant boundaries.

Some male caregivers tell us the last thing they want to do is "communicate," but for better or worse, it is the one significant way men and women learn to understand each other. Try these few steps to help you open up and then close the emotional gap that is coming between you and your wife. We hope with time and a new understanding of her feelings and yours, your relationship will enrich both of you.

- Be direct. Tell your wife how you feel and that you really want to try to talk about how she feels and mean it! You can say, "I really want to talk to you. We seem closer because we have your mom's problems in common, but it also tears us apart because we fight about it. Let's call a truce."

- Set specific rules for your conversation, that is, no shouting and no walking out of the room in the middle of the discussion.
- Find the time to be alone and talk. Don't underestimate the importance of asking simple questions about how she feels about her mom and what makes her so on edge. You might be surprised to learn that she is afraid that her mom is going to die, or that she is fearful that as she ages she will be as dependent as her mother.
- Providing your wife with a venue to express her feelings may relieve some of her anxiety. Once she feels that you will not judge her for having these strong emotions, she may be more receptive to your overtures.
- Tell her how you feel about the situation. If you find it difficult to express your feelings, use whatever approach suits you. Brief and simple may work for you. For example: hold her hand and say, "Whatever is good for you works for me." This statement clearly expresses your support in whatever she does. You can also say, "Your mom is OK. I guess I never told you that I don't mind helping her, but I just want you to know for the future I don't want her to live with us. The thought of it makes me nuts and maybe that's why I yell." This revelation may be difficult for your wife to hear, but it may also help her understand why you get so angry. Give her time to respond and try to stay focused on the issues.
- Seal this conversation with a kiss or a hug. We know you are not "touchy-feely," but give it a try.

If you find this exercise helpful, then you can use the technique over and over again. If you can't seem to work through this problem on your own, it may be in your best interest to speak to a marriage counselor or a family therapist. You can contact your physician, a local hospital, or a social service agency in your community for a referral.

Dear Eldercare 911,

I have a problem that is very hard for me to talk about. My wife, Lois, is a good woman, but when it comes to her mom and dad, she's a witch. They love her, but she just doesn't like them. They're sick and need help with a few things, such as doctor's appointments and grocery shopping. The truth is, I really like them. When my parents turned their back on me, her parents reached into their hearts and pockets to help me through a financially difficult time. They supported me when I changed careers and gave me something my parents never did—confidence in myself. My wife has emotional problems and maybe they stem from her relationship with her parents, or not. I'm not a psychiatrist. I'm just a frustrated son-in-law who wants to help my in-laws. My wife says, "No way." Is there something I can say or do to turn this situation around?

—Unusual Son-in-Law, Alaska

Dear Unusual,

Family conflicts are often difficult to resolve because of deep, old wounds. You didn't give us your wife's actual diagnosis, but you said she had "emotional problems." Because of her problems, she may see and feel what you are doing as a betrayal of her. From what you said, you just want to give back to people who were kind and generous to you. Here are some of the ways you can begin.

- Talk to your wife. Be sure to set aside a specific time to talk privately. Begin by saying: "Lois, we've been together for twenty-two years and I know that you have very strong feelings about your parents. I acknowledge how you feel, and you know I'll try to understand. But I also have very strong feelings. When your parents helped me out, they were really helping both of us. Because of their financial support, we could afford the extra years of school we needed to follow our dreams. I'm not asking you to help them, only give me a chance to do something for them. Taking your dad to the doctor once every two weeks and grocery shopping with Mom once a week is something I can do. I will not involve you if you don't want to be involved. What do you say?"
- Give Lois time to respond. If she becomes agitated or argumentative, let it go for now and try again another day. If you try again and she still refuses, it may be helpful to look for therapeutic intervention from a trained mental health or marriage counselor. If she agrees, give her a kiss and a hug and thank her for being understanding.
- Don't overdo your involvement with your in-laws. You told Lois exactly what you would do for her parents; it is important to adhere to your promise. By doing so, you are proving to her that you not only respect your agreement but you acknowledge her helpful participation.

Your willingness to help your in-laws and your sensitivity to your wife's needs are truly wonderful. We commend your efforts and wish all of you good luck!

D. YOUR PERSONAL LIMITS

Dear Eldercare 911,

I've had it and I don't know where to turn. I take pills for my stomach, head, and back. I don't eat and I drink too much. People look at me and they just can't believe how I am taking this. I have a very good job, a marriage that endured thirty-two years of health problems, the teenage years, and the death of two of my best friends from my days in the army. All in all I guess I shouldn't complain, but my mother is driving me crazy. She was always mean and stubborn, but now she is very old, mean, and stubborn. I know she isn't safe living in our old house, but she refuses to let me help her. I am an only child, and when I'm around her, I feel like the little boy who lost his father at the age of five. She never hit me, but her words always made me cower. Grown men don't cower. What's wrong with me? Is there a way to help my mom?

—Henry, Nevada

Dear Henry,

For good or bad, each and every one of us is a product of nature and nurture. We are a combination of our familial genes, the houses we lived in, and the schools we attended. Everything that we do, everything that is done to us, makes us who we are today. You are no exception. It sounds like Mom was very controlling and overbearing, but you are a very strong man. The reason your strength is evident is that even though she sometimes made you "cower," you had the fortitude and ability to break away from her emotional grasp and make a home for yourself and your family. The fact that you are asking for help only reinforces the fact that you are much more than that five-year-old little boy. Small children simply don't have the resources to ask the right questions and fight the physical, emotional, and psychological abuse of adults. Too often children suffer the consequences. But as a strong adult, you have the power to protect the little boy and allow the grown man to do what he has to do for his mother.

Here are a few suggestions to help you begin the process.

- Hire a geriatric care manager to assess the situation, to support your efforts, and to provide you with a specific plan of care to meet your mother's needs. A geriatric care manager will charge a fee for the services she provides. Ask her for references and her fee schedule before you schedule an appointment. If you do not have the funds for private assistance, contact your local Area Agency on Aging for social services agencies or senior centers that provide similar services for a sliding scale fee based on your mom's income. As Joe from Nevada said, "Don't try to do this alone. It's OK to ask for help."
- Consider therapeutic intervention by a licensed social worker, a psychologist, or a psychiatrist. Some men think therapy is only for women, but the reality is that men benefit from counseling as well. Individual counseling may change how you look at Mom today and the problems you will face now and in the future. After years of suffering from emotional abuse you need to have a venue to vent your feelings with a qualified professional. Reach out to your family physician, local hospital, or social service agency for a referral. Interview the therapist, ask about his credentials and how often he deals with caregiver issues. Be sure you are comfortable with whoever you select.
- Contact a community hospital, your local Area Agency on Aging, or senior centers to find a caregiver support group. Ask for a group that is dedicated to men or already has some men in it. You may find that the friendships your form with these men will extend beyond the confines of the group. This type of support is invaluable because you begin to see more clearly that you are not alone.

Some men bring emotional baggage to the caregiving experience. Sometimes the baggage is light and easy to handle; other times it carries the weight of a steamer trunk. No matter how heavy the burden is, it sometimes needs the hands of a professional to lift it from your shoulders and help you through the experience. Don't shy away from getting the help you need. You have the strength to do what is necessary to help yourself and your mom.

Dear Eldercare 911,

I don't know how unusual my situation is, but I know it is very difficult. I am an only child, recently divorced, and the father of three children. My mom died and my eighty-four-year-old dad remarried over twenty years ago. My stepmother is eighty-five years old and she has two daughters. Dad and his wife always trusted me. As a matter, of fact I have power of attorney for both of them. My stepsisters are furious because they were not consulted about the power of attorney, and they want me out of the picture. They are very difficult and nasty, and the folks usually don't see them unless they (her daughters) need money. What has now developed for me is a multilevel problem. First, my parents expect me to do EVERYTHING for them. They want me to do the shopping, the banking, and plan the social activities. The second problem is the distrust that has developed between my stepsisters, my parents, and me. I find the whole situation intolerable and I need and want a way out. I just don't know what to do. I'm a financial planner and I'm used to things adding up, so to speak. This doesn't add up anymore and I need help. What can I do to take care of this problem or simply make it go away?

—Power of Attorney, Texas

Dear Power of Attorney,

Unfortunately, complicated family problems often don't change or go away because we want them to or because we try to wish them away. What can change is how we approach the problems and how we find solutions. In a world where reconstituted families are the norm, your situation is not as unique as you might think. You appear to have two significant issues: time and trust. Finding solutions to managing your time is a concrete problem. Facing the issue of trust is more emotional. This painful two-pronged problem combined with all of your other responsibilities is burdensome and exhausting. Let's try to approach this problem systematically. Try to look at it just the way you would add and subtract a column of numbers.

- Make two lists. On one list the things you do for your parents. On the second list jot down the things you would like to stop doing for your parents. For example:

  List A: 1. shop with Mom, 2. take Mom and Dad to the movies, 3. visit twice a week, 4. do the banking

  List B: 1. shop with Mom, 2. visit twice a week

- Decide if you can handle List A by yourself. If you feel that you need help, hire a geriatric care manager to help you accomplish your goals. If you want to attempt to pursue this on your own, contact a licensed homecare agency to help you find someone to take over the duties on List B. Many homecare agencies not only provide home health aides who are responsible for helping your parent bathe, dress, shop, and do laundry, but they employ women and men who are social companions or friendly visitors. This is someone who can escort Mom and Dad to the movies and then take them to the grocery store.

You will begin to feel less stressed once you alleviate some of your day-to-day caregiving responsibilities. However, tackling the trust issue is not going to be as clear-cut, and you will need help. As Jay from Michigan said, "I saw the handwriting on the wall and I knew I couldn't do it all on my own. I knew I needed professional help." Give yourself a chance to do what is best for all of you.

- Meet with a therapist, a social worker, or a psychologist who specializes in family issues. It is very important to find someone who is skilled in this area because it takes an experienced professional to facilitate a family meeting. Ask your medical doctor, the local hospital, or a social service agency for a referral. Most communities have agencies that deal specifically with family issues. If you hire a geriatric care manager, she can assist you with a referral and act as the intermediary between you and your stepsisters. Keep in mind that if you approach this subject without an intermediary, you can expect some resistance from your stepsisters, given the fact that they already don't trust you. Make an appointment to meet with the therapist. If you feel comfortable with him or her, then it is time to talk to the family. Ask the therapist to guide you, or you might want to try the following dialogue.
- To your parents: "Mom, Dad, we all know how difficult it has been over the past few years. Mom, your daughters don't trust me and I am not sure why, but the tension is getting worse and I think it is time for all of us to sit down and talk it out. I found a wonderful therapist who specializes in these kinds of problems. We only have to go once and try it. If you don't like it and you don't think it is helpful, we don't have to do it again. What do you say?" Let them respond. If they agree, it is time to approach your stepsisters. If not, ask them to think about it, and try another day.
- To your stepsisters: "I know that we have had our differences, but we all want to do what is best for our parent. I was hoping that we could all sit down with a family counselor and try to iron some of this out. My doctor referred me to a terrific woman who works with families. Mom and Dad have agreed and they are willing to give it a try. What

do you say?" Give them a chance to reply. Congratulations if they agree. If they adamantly object, you might want to take a different path and meet with the therapist yourself. A few private sessions may provide you with new coping techniques and greater insight to help you deal with your stepsisters and parents.

Your stepsisters may not change and Mom and Dad may still demand your time, but with the help of professionals and your own personal resolve, you will find the strength to find the best solutions to your problems.

Dear Eldercare 911,

My eighty-six-year-old mother is a wonderful, caring woman. She taught me how to be true to myself no matter what life throws my way. For the past forty years, she has accepted my life's partner, and she in fact is often my strongest advocate. Mom had a stroke about three years ago, leaving her partially paralyzed on her right side. She also suffers from dementia. She can walk with assistance, and she needs help with everything else. My partner, John, and I hired a home health aide to take care of her, but Mom is rapidly declining. The problem is that the home health aide lives with her and she isn't getting any sleep because Mom is becoming increasingly agitated and has confused her days and nights. Our intent was to keep her home forever. We're struggling with the idea of moving Mom to a nursing home. I find myself up at night in the middle of an internal tug-of-war. Mom made her wishes clear to me many years ago. She said, "Ken, I want to die in my own bed." I promised her I would do my best to abide by her wishes, but it seems to be getting harder and harder every day. John says he will support my decision and help me through the process. Please help.

—Ken, Texas

Dear Ken,

How wonderful that you and your mom enjoyed so many good and loving years together. She sounds remarkable and way ahead of her time. Your internal struggles regarding nursing home placement are a common caregiver problem. Fortunately, you have a supportive partner who will stand by you and help you through the process. We would like you to take a few minutes to think about what you promised your mom. You said to her "I will do the best I can."

The optimum word is "best." Sometimes even the *best* we can do leaves us feeling that there is more, but actually we have done it all. These five steps will help you make the "best" decision you can for all of you.

1. Visit three or four nursing homes. Ask to meet with the director of admissions for a tour of the facility. Look around at the residents. Can you picture Mom sitting in the dining room or recreational room? If the answer is yes, then continue.
2. Talk to the director about financial arrangements, room selection, nutrition, medical staff, medication management, and social activities. Bring your partner with you for another perspective.
3. Visit a second time at a different hour of the day. It is important that you see residents dressed and actively engaged in an activity, instead of still in bed.
4. Does the staff appear to be attentive to the residents? Do they address the residents by their names? Is the staff cordial and helpful to you? Keep detailed notes and the names of any contacts you make.
5. Continue the process by answering the following questions:

   - Does the nursing staff have the capability to handle your mother's physical and cognitive needs?
   - Do you think the surroundings and people will appeal to your mom? Is the facility clean? Are there any unpleasant odors?
   - Has the staff been open and communicative with you?
   - Do you fully understand the nursing home contract, financial obligations, and what Mom is entitled to as a resident?

Once you have answers to your questions, talk it over with John. The decision-making process is the most difficult when we don't have all the facts. Get the facts, and then make your final decision. Remember that you are keeping the promise you made—*you are doing the best you can.*

For Men Only: Reality Check

Successful caregiving is never a function of one great plan. It is a fluid process that depends on continuous management of the emotional and physical needs of both the care receiver and the caregiver, as well as practical consideration of the many pieces of the caregiving puzzle.

- **I will remember that my parent has a need for friends and peers to enrich his quality of life.** This is in addition to concrete, practical issues such as food and housing.

- **I will remain flexible.** If my plan isn't working, I will not automatically blame the participants. I understand that caregiving is a human experience and, as such, evolves as the needs and goals of the caregivers and care recipients change.

- **I recognize that eldercare plans are never final.** I will monitor, review, and revise my plan regularly to accommodate changing circumstances.

- **I will ask for directions!** Caregiving is new, uncharted territory. I will not let old habits or gender roles inhibit me from asking for help or prevent me from accessing the latest information. I will look for solutions that can help decrease my frustration and increase my quality of life.

For Men Only: You Are *Not* Alone

Many men are feeling the overwhelming difficulties of caring for an aging parent and find themselves struggling for answers. But there is hope and there is help. Take your time and read each statement. Check off one of the boxes: Sometimes, Always, or Never. Think carefully about your responses. You will be surprised to learn that when the going gets tough, everyone needs a helping hand.

	Sometimes	Always	Never
I have difficulty expressing my feelings.	( )	( )	( )
Even when I need help, I cannot reach out to my spouse, children, or friends.	( )	( )	( )
I expect my parents to do everything that I tell them to do.	( )	( )	( )
When things take longer than I expect, I become frustrated and agitated.	( )	( )	( )
I feel helpless at times because I'm really not sure how to be a caregiver.	( )	( )	( )
My spouse/significant other is not supportive.	( )	( )	( )
I feel like I am the only man in the world taking care of a parent.	( )	( )	( )
I lose my temper when my parent calls me several times a day in the office.	( )	( )	( )
I wish my spouse/significant other would handle the caregiving duties.	( )	( )	( )
When I ask for help, I feel like I am less of a son or a man.	( )	( )	( )

No matter how you answered these questions, remember that you are not alone. If you answered Always or Sometimes to several questions, it is time for you to find the help you need. See chapter 13, "Resources," for a variety of helpful information.

6

FAMILY MATTERS

A. DIVIDING YOUR TIME

Dear Eldercare 911,

Did you ever read a fairy tale where the wicked monster won? I loved my husband the first moment I saw him. When I gave birth to my daughter and son, I thought they were the most beautiful children I'd ever seen. For years, our small family was so full of love it was like a miracle. Taking care of my father-in-law has taken all that away. I used to do a few things for him, but as he got older and needed more, his care overtook my whole life. I never have time for Dave and the children anymore. They resent my not having time for them, and I resent that they resent me for trying to do as much as I can for all of them. I thought I was doing the best I can, but now I'm not so sure. I always thought that the only person I didn't have time for was *me*, but if we're all unhappy, something's wrong. I feel as though I'm doing all this for nothing. I'm tempted to just stop and let them all take care of themselves. After all these years, I'm not a good mother and I'm not a good partner. And he's not even my own father! I can't believe it's turned out this way.

—Unhappy Ending in Idaho

Dear Unhappy,

Don't close the book on your fairy tale yet. *Lack of time* is one of the most common complaints of caregivers. Some caregivers wish for "extra hours in the day," but that may not be the answer. In most cases, their duties would probably just expand to fill the additional time and nothing would change. Caregivers would continue to feel as though they were not paying enough attention to their children and partners, and would still pay little or no attention to their own needs. Most would be able to sign your letter as though they themselves had written it.

Your description describes the lives of thousands of caregivers. As our parents need more assistance, we take on more responsibilities. As our duties increase, they take more of our time. Because we have a finite twenty-four hours in each day, our time is limited. So when we spend more time caregiving, we have to take it from somewhere else: family, friends, ourselves—sleeping, relaxing, learning, working, and so on. When we withdraw time from a child or spouse and give that time to someone else, the family member can feel less valued—that is, "You're giving your time to him *instead* of me" —and that often leads to hurt feelings and resentment. There are two potential solutions: get help or get a new strategy to allocate your time.

Let's start with getting help:

- You don't mention whether your husband or children help with your father-in-law's care. If they don't, their lack of involvement has two important drawbacks. First, without firsthand knowledge of *what* you do, it is unlikely they can understand the complexity of the many needs your father-in-law has. A little involvement may go a long way toward helping them see how much time it takes to provide the assistance that he needs.

- As you continue caring for your father-in-law, consider which duties would be appropriate for your husband and children. Then ask them to help. Don't overload them—begin with one chore. Add others as they become more involved. And don't fall into the trap of thinking "It's easier to just go ahead and do it myself." We can assure you that caregiving is definitely easier when you have help.

- You don't say if you have professional help, but from the tone of your letter, we assume you don't. Consider hiring a homecare aide or a homemaker/companion for household chores. The aide can assist with dressing, bathing, shopping, cooking, and washing your father's clothes and linens. The homemaker/companion can do all of that except the dressing and bathing (homemakers/companions are not allowed to perform "hands-on" duties). If your father-in-law has funds, he should bear the cost, or at least part of the cost. Even two or three afternoons a week can make a significant difference in the amount of time you have to spend with your family.

- If you meet resistance from your husband, remind yourself, and him, that the person you need help with is *his* father. If your children object, remind yourself that we all learn by example and practice. You have set a good example by taking on this obligation and helping yourself.

"Getting smarter," the second piece of the time-management puzzle, refers to learning a simpler way of managing your time. The key to dividing your time is to separate what *must* be done for health or safety reasons from what people *expect* you to do. That includes managing your *own* expectations.

Separating *must do* tasks and leaving the remaining items for another time requires planning and practice. We've simplified the process to enable you to start today. Use the worksheet at the end of this chapter, "Dividing Your Time," to help you try to regain your family's quality of life.

Dear Eldercare 911,

My wife, Lydia, recently found out that her mother has been an alcoholic for several decades. We found this out when a hospital called and surprised Lydia with the message that her mother's documents named Lydia as having power of attorney! Her mother was ill, unstable, and refusing treatment. The hospital didn't feel that her mother was capable of making sound decisions on her own behalf. We live over one thousand miles from her mother and care for a daughter with special needs. Lydia was able to convince her mother to enter a psychiatric hospital for treatment, and we thought the situation would get better. Were we ever wrong! As best as we can reconstruct, this is what happened. While Lydia's mother was in the hospital, she signed a new document naming Lydia's aunt as having power of attorney. Then the aunt told the administrator that Lydia had no desire to help, that she only wanted to gain control of her mom's assets. The administrator of the psychiatric hospital accepted the aunt's word and the new power of attorney, and released her mother who promptly disappeared. Lydia's mother was found, three months later, living off alcohol and drugs, and suffering from malnutrition and dehydration. Lydia ended up with an emergency guardianship and caregiving responsibilities that she has no time for, plus an aunt who still tries to circumvent everything Lydia does and continues to tell vicious lies about her. Lydia never wanted this responsibility. She says she'd gladly give it up to her aunt if she could keep her mother safe, but she can't. Lydia's afraid something might happen to her mother if she doesn't try to "do her duty." She says she feels guilty enough as it is for never guessing her mom's secret and blames herself for "being so blind to what was happening." Or she wonders if she really saw it and was in denial along with the rest of the family? Our daughter, who has an acquired brain injury, needs our full attention. Lydia's mother is tearing our family to pieces. I just can't stand by and do nothing. I keep thinking there must be something I can do.

—Ron, Georgia

Dear Ron,

What a heavy load you and Lydia have taken on your shoulders. You mentioned you were over one thousand miles from your mother-in-law. If you saw her infrequently and you were not trained in addiction problems, it could have been easy to miss the signs, so your wife should not blame herself for that. Lydia may have heard this before, but we'll try to reinforce the thought: how much guilt would she have to feel to change her mother back to her previous self? There is no answer to that question because whether you feel guilty once a day, once a week, or every minute of every day, it doesn't matter. *No matter how much guilt you feel, or how heavy that burden feels, Lydia's guilt will have no impact on her mother's dependence on alcohol and drugs.* Only professional treatment and counseling could change that.

Alcoholism is a disease. The illness is progressive; without treatment the addicted person will continue to drink. Unfortunately, no one, not even someone who loves her as much as Lydia does, can help Lydia's mother. The only person who can stop Lydia's mother from drinking or abusing drugs *is Lydia's mother herself.*

Some professionals estimate that every alcoholic affects as many as four other people. If you start the count, you'll probably find that premise true for you and your family. Before your family suffers any further, we urge you to consider these steps:

- Contact Al-Anon (www.al-anon-alateen.org), the wonderful organization that assists families of alcoholics for counseling and support. Lydia is likely to find comfort by communicating with other family members who have felt the same pain that she has, and who may share strategies that will help her cope.
- Whether Lydia participates in the Al-Anon program or not, you should do so. The support and counseling offered by the program will help you maintain the physical and emotional health you both need to continue to care for your daughter.

These two seemingly small steps can be monumental in turning your lives around. Alcoholism's destructive affect on families—guilt, anger, and frustration—is well documented. Professional counseling and assistance is the most effective way to regain control of your life.

B. TALKING TO YOUNG CHILDREN

Dear Eldercare 911,

I am forty-one years old and I have three young children, ages nine, seven, and two years old. My seven-year-old son is very quiet and tends to shy away from grown-ups. On the other hand, my nine-year-old daughter is outgoing and vivacious. The little one is a typical energetic toddler. All the children have had a close relationship with my mother. My mom has Alzheimer's disease and on some days she's better than others. She often forgets things she promised the children and often calls them by my brother's and sister's names. Sometimes she gets agitated and she yells at them. My son gets teary, but my daughter usually just goes off and plays. Until a few weeks ago Mom lived at home and I used to bring the children over to her house to visit. Rather quickly Mom's condition went from bad to worse and I had to move her to a nearby nursing home. I try to visit two or three times each week. I am always on edge, and my children are feeling the brunt of my emotions. Our home was always calm and now my son calls it "the noisy house." In addition to everything that we are struggling with at this time, I am struggling with two other problems. Is it OK to bring the children to the nursing home to visit Grandma? And when Mom was living at home, I didn't really say much to the children about her condition. I think it's time. How do I explain Grandma's condition to my children?

—Karen, South Carolina

Dear Karen,

There is no perfect way to present this kind of information to young children, only a way that works well enough for you and your family. You said that the children are probably feeling your emotions, and you are right! Children are very tuned in to their parents' emotions, and your children are probably no different. If you try to hide your feelings, they still will know it; this is true even for your youngest child. Children as young as eighteen months old have their own identities, and even though they may not understand everything that is going on, they usually can sense that something is wrong.

Your mom's erratic behavior and memory loss may have frightened one or more of your children, and you need to explain her actions in the simplest terms. It is important for you to be aware of your own feelings about the situation. Your children will get cues from you on how to handle different aspects of what is happening to your family at this time. Try to be very conscious of how you approach the subject; your attitude, tone of voice, and body language will reveal a great deal to the children. If you decide to take them to the nursing home, remember it will most probably appear like a hospital to a young child.

Review the following suggestions and dialogue before you make a decision.

- Ask yourself, what frightens my children? Is it the dark or a fast-moving train? How do they deal with their fears? What makes them cry? What makes them hide? Remember any trauma to a child may stay with him. You want to spare your children as much as possible.

- Think about your motives. Why do you want to take your children into the facility? Do you think the visit will be good for Mom? Or do you want to be a good child to your parent? It's important for you to explore your feelings before you bring the children.

- Ask your children how they feel about visiting Grandma in the nursing home or hospital.

- If you decide to take them, prepare your children for the visits by reading books about hospitals and nursing homes. You will find appropriate books on this subject at your local library or bookstore. Purchase a toy doctor bag. Use the medical props to help give your children a sense of what to see and expect in a hospital or nursing home setting.

- Speak to the facility personnel about your upcoming visit and then clear your visit with the staff. Ask what times of the day are the best to bring small children. On the day of the visit, be sure that your mom does not have any infection or fever.

- Never bring a sick child into a facility or a child who has a compromised immune system.

- If possible, bring one child at a time to visit your mom. This will give you an opportunity to devote time to your child and observe his reactions during and after the visit.

- Ask Mom if she would like to see the children. She may not always remember who they are, but you may be able to trigger her memory. Bring pictures of the children and identify each one. You can tape a small piece of paper onto each picture to identify the children's names and ages. Because of the dementia, she may not make the connection, but you can give it a try. Let Mom hold the pictures and look at them for as long as she likes. If you decide to bring the children based on a favorable response from Mom, don't be surprised if the day you visit she is not receptive. Patients with Alzheimer's disease have good days and bad days, good hours and bad minutes. Mom's attitude can change very quickly from loving to angry.

- When you prepare the children for the visit, you might want to role-play with even the youngest child. Use a doll and say things like "Poor Grandma is not feeling very well, but she loves you so much." Reinforce the dialogue right before the visit.
- Approach your older children by saying: "Let me tell you how Grandma has changed. Sometimes Grandma forgets things, but she will always love you inside. She may not be able to say she loves you anymore, but the feeling is still there. I thought we may want to visit Grandma on Thursday. Would you like to come with me?" If your children say yes, suggest that they draw a picture for Grandma to hang up in her room. If any of your children do not want to go, reassure them that it is OK with you and that you and Grandma love them no matter what they decide.

Visits are taxing on any patient. Keep the visit short and have an exit plan. Try to bring someone to help you with the children. If your mom displays any aggressive or agitated behavior, remove the children from the room. Let them stay with your friend so that you can visit a little longer. If the visit becomes too difficult for you, make sure that your mom is safe and secure, give her a kiss good-bye, and visit on another day.

Dear Eldercare 911,

My eighty-eight-year-old dad is dying and my eight-year-old daughter and ten-year-old son know that something is wrong. I just don't know how to tell them what is going on. I also don't know whether I should allow them to go to the funeral? Can you help me?

—Miriam, Wisconsin

Dear Miriam,

Most important, your children need and deserve an honest, supportive answer. Because this is a difficult time for you and your family, it may help you to draw from your personal philosophy of life. If you are religious, you may want to use your belief system to help guide you in your discussion with your children. If you do not have strong feelings one way or another, there are many books in your library and local bookstores written specifically for curious, sensitive children that will help you present the complex subjects of death and dying.

When you feel that you are ready to talk to your children, you may want to begin the conversation with a simple, caring statement: "Grandpa was very, very old and he died. He will always be in your heart because you loved him very much and he loved you." Reassure your children that even though Grandpa is gone, there is always someone to take care of and love them. Each child will react differently depending on his grasp of the subject and his individual emotional development and personality. You will be able to determine your next steps by how your children react. If they appear content with your response, then they have probably heard enough. If they continue to question you, keep your answers focused on the specific questions. It is important for you to understand the question before you answer it and give them as much or as little information as they seem to want and need. When you are under stress, you may find yourself talking on and on unnecessarily. It is important to stay focused and on point.

Some people feel that it is not in the best interest of the children to attend a funeral service. Other people feel that children should attend given the support of family and friends. Once again your religious and philosophical beliefs and convictions may help you make the best decision for your family. Think about the following recommendations.

- Know your children. If they frighten easily or they are very sensitive, you may want to think twice about bringing them to the funeral service.
- Prepare an activity bag with a few items to keep the children busy, such as a coloring book and crayons or a small, silent electronic game. Ask a responsible adult to take the children outside to play quietly for a few minutes, if they become restless.
- Have an exit plan. If you decide to bring your children to the funeral, it is essential to have a calm and quiet way for them to leave if it becomes necessary. Bring a babysitter, a neighbor, or a friend to assist you. Allow the children to leave and go home with that adult if it is necessary.
- Be compassionate and nonjudgmental if they leave the funeral parlor or the service. When you return home, tell them that you understand that it was a hard day for them and you are not angry or upset with them. Give them as much opportunity as they need to ask questions and talk about how they feel.

Talking about death, dying, and funerals is difficult for even the most sophisticated adults. Answering your children's questions openly, simply, and honestly will help them to understand the sadness in your home and the reason for your tears.

C. TALKING TO TEENAGERS

Dear Eldercare 911,

My eighty-one-year-old mom is always in and out of hospitals. She has kidney disease and a severe cardiac condition. I am an only child, and I feel the full burden of her care. I am divorced, and I work a nine-hour day as an office manager. When Mom is in the hospital (which seems to be every other day), I visit her after work and get home about nine or ten o'clock at night. If she is home with her home health aide, I visit every other day for a few ours. My fifteen-year-old daughter, Beth, is usually watching television when I get home and she doesn't talk to me. She's a good kid, but I'm worried about her and how she is handling my absence. I know that I probably don't have to see Mom as much as I do, especially since we have a wonderful aide, but I can't help myself. Being an only child is sometimes very lonely. Even if I cut down some of my visits, I still must work long hours to support us and I still have to see Mom. Before Mom's illness took over my life, Beth and I talked and enjoyed each other's company. I miss her. What can I say to my daughter? She is alone too much of the time. How will I know if she is in trouble?

—Dina, Iowa

Dear Dina,

So often caregivers find themselves struggling to do what is best for every member of the family. Your conflict is clearly very painful. Intellectually, you recognize that maybe you don't have to do as much as you are doing for your mother, but your heart is telling you something else. We hope that in time you will take your own advice and give yourself a well-deserved break from some of your caregiver duties. In the meantime, it is important for you to be able to talk to your daughter about your situation. Try this dialogue to jumpstart your conversation: "Beth, I really miss our time together. I know our life has changed since Grandma's illness, but I want to try to spend more time with you. Can we try to set aside one evening every week or one day on the weekend to be together—a real girl's day or night out. I will clear

Wednesday night or Sunday? You decide and we can do whatever you want to do. How does that sound?" Beth may be very pleased with the idea or she may look at you and say "whatever." The "whatever" may indicate that she doesn't believe you or she is so angry that she can't respond favorably. If Beth is not receptive to your suggestion, let it go and try again the next week. If you are still not making a connection with her after a few attempts, it may be time to talk to a family therapist. You may want to meet alone with the therapist and when the time is appropriate ask Beth to join the sessions.

If she does respond favorably, be sure to keep your commitment for your special time together. In preparation for your date with Beth, try to arrange for a friend or a home health aide to spend time with Mom in the hospital. Give yourself more time to spend with Beth on a school night by asking your boss if you can come in a little earlier in the morning and leave a little earlier at the end of the day.

Because you raised some very valid concerns about Beth's behavior, it is important for you to be aware of some of the warning signs that indicate something may be wrong. If your daughter displays one or more of these signs, get help immediately. Meet with the guidance counselor, the school social worker, or the school psychologist, or make an appointment with a private, licensed therapist.

Look for these changes in lifestyle and attitude:

- Serious acting-out behavior such as drinking alcoholic beverages or using nonprescription drugs.
- Eating disorders such as weight loss from anorexia or bulimia, or weight gain.
- Self-mutilation, also known as "cutting."
- Changes in grades.
- Changes in friends.
- Changes in sleep patterns.

Once you and Beth begin to communicate about the situation, she may be more open and ready to make some changes. With your support and the guidance of professionals you and your daughter may eventually regain your close relationship.

Dear Eldercare 911,

My son is a very kindhearted teenager. He does very well in school and he is a good athlete. Believe it or not, I actually like his friends! My husband died, and for the past few months we have been living with my mother-in-law because I am facing financial problems. My mother-in-law is the only member of my family who offered to help us out. She is the caregiver for her mother and father, and we all live in an old apartment in the heart of a quiet suburb. The rooms are small and there is only one bathroom. Things get very harried in the morning when we all have to get ready for work and school. My mother-in-law is so stressed all of the time. For some reason she picks on my son and asks him to do everything for her like mop the floors and help change Grandpa's clothes. On top of that, she takes her anger out on him, and yells and calls him horrible names. I've asked her to stop because she is hurting his feelings. She says that she can't help herself, and then she always says, "You think I should yell at his grandparents. They are old and sick; he can take it." How awful is that answer? I am stuck here for now, but I can't continue to allow my mother-in-law to hurt my son. What can I say to get her to stop? How do I tell him that his grandma really loves him when she treats him so badly?

—Roberta, Massachusetts

Dear Roberta,

Children are adaptable and resilient, but it helps them to understand what is happening around them and why. You are in a difficult situation because of your financial problems, and for now, you and your son are in the middle of a very stressful household. Your mother-in-law's behavior is understandable given her caregiver burden, but it does not excuse her or give her the right to make everyone, especially your son, miserable. There are some things you can try to do to help her see that her behavior is detrimental to your son as well as to the rest of the family.

- Talk to your son in private. Try to find the time to spend a quiet evening with him at a favorite restaurant, or plan a day out and be tourists in your own city. When you are together, try to encourage him to talk about how he feels about living with Grandma. Talk to him about helping out with specific chores. Give him time and understanding to respond to you.
- Don't be discouraged if it takes more than one dinner or outing together. If he says that he hates living with Grandma, explain to him that because of your financial problems, you do not have a choice right now. Assure him that he will have everything he needs and someone will always take care of him. If he indicates that he doesn't understand

why Grandma yells at him, try to explain to him that when Grandma feels stressed, she acts out by yelling at him. Remember, he may say he understands and doesn't mind, though he may still be hurting. Remind him that Grandma's behavior is not appropriate and you recognize that he is not the one at fault.

- Talk to him about the household chores. Explain to him that sometimes we all have to do things we don't necessarily like to do. Provide him with a few options by giving him a list of a few specific chores. For example you might say: "Grandma needs help with the vacuuming once a week. She also needs you to take out the garbage every night after dinner, and Grandpa likes to have someone read the paper to him. Can you help Grandma?" If he says he hates to vacuum but he doesn't mind reading to Grandpa, ask him to vacuum once in a while as a favor to you. Tell him that the garbage duty is his responsibility. Let him know how proud you are of him for helping out in the house and how proud he should be of himself.

- Have a heart-to-heart conversation with your mother-in-law. Tell her that you understand that she feels stressed and that you appreciate that she has given you and your son a place to live. Tell her that you spoke to your son about helping out with specific household chores. Let her know exactly what he will do and on which specific days. Explain to her that he agreed to do some things on a regular basis, but he will help with the vacuuming once in a while. If you are able, you may want to volunteer to vacuum and take that burden away from your son.

- Talk to your mother-in-law about hiring a home health aide to help out with some of the other caregiver duties. Present this idea as something that will benefit her parents as well as the rest of the family. Plan ahead and provide her with the names of licensed homecare agencies as well as the fees for service. If finances are a problem, find out about sliding scale fees–based programs in your community. These programs are based on an individual's income. Contact the local Area Agency on Aging for specific information and referrals.

- Talk to your mother-in-law about how she treats your son. Let her know that she is causing him a great deal of pain and that no matter what else is going on in her life, she cannot verbally abuse him. If she agrees, ask her to have a talk with your son to reassure him that she loves and cares about him and that she will make every effort not to hurt his feelings.

The stress of caring for loved ones, compounded by several members of one family living in very small quarters, is extraordinarily difficult for anyone. It is important to keep in mind that no matter how hard you try to make this situation work, there may be rough days ahead. Your willingness to try to find a solution is commendable, and you should be very proud of yourself.

D. MANAGING EXTENDED FAMILIES

Dear Eldercare 911,

My stepmother never remarried after my dad died. She lives alone and is determined to remain in her own home until she dies. My five brothers and stepsisters and I all think she's unsafe to stay alone and that she needs someone with her. That's all we agree on. They think that because I'm divorced and have no children, I should move in with her and take care of her. I think they're out of their minds. We need someone to mediate.

—Not in a Million Years, Alabama

Dear Not,

We agree—your brothers and sisters are out of line for assuming your marital status determines whether or not you become a live-in caregiver for your mother. *You are the only one who has the right to make that choice for yourself, and you have done so.* Now you need to be firm and let your siblings know that door is closed. Instead of mediation, you need *options.*

- Consider hiring a professional geriatric care manager to assess and evaluate what your mother needs to remain safely independent in her own home. Ask the care manager to estimate the cost for an assessment that includes a written report and recommendations for a plan to help your mother remain at home. Ask the care manager for the minimum as well as the optimal plan.
- Explain to your brothers and stepsisters that the care manager will help you find a solution. Be clear that since the solution will benefit all of you, you expect them to share the cost of the assessment.
- You'll want to know about physical, emotional, mental, nutritional, and environmental risks, including the safety of the physical structure of the house (steps, wiring, sharp corners on cabinets, uneven surfaces) and risks for falls (your mother's gait, leg strength, uneven floor surfaces, whether she uses appropriate lighting).

- Be clear that you want to know which of the recommendations may be covered by your mother's insurance or other benefits, including local community services.

When the report is ready, call a family meeting and decide whether you and your family (including your mother) can afford the cost. If you cannot afford it and your mother is too unsafe to remain alone, try to explain the problem to her and convince her to move to safer quarters. If she refuses and is fully competent to make her own decisions, your only choice is to watch her closely and use as many of the care manager's recommendations as you can to help her stay as safe as possible.

Dear Eldercare 911,

My husband Walter's job necessitates his traveling for three to five days almost every week. It's been this way for the entire twenty-six years of our marriage without a problem. We have three children and a good life. In the last two or three years, Walter's father has become very forgetful and confused. He is very demanding. He also yells or barks orders at everyone. That's probably a throwback to his days as a drill sergeant in the army. His mom is a diabetic and has had a couple of heart attacks. She's too frail and too ill herself to handle my father-in-law anymore. On any given evening, he may wake up and decide he wants to go out to dinner at four in the morning. Last week he was fighting the war in his sleep and he accidentally hit her. Now she's afraid to sleep. She can't go on like this and, frankly, I can't either. When Walter is traveling, I get their calls for help. That's bad enough. Even worse is that when he's home, they know it and call more frequently. The result is that Walter spends so much time handling problems at his parents' house that we hardly ever see each other. He keeps thinking he can set things up so that everything will run more smoothly. Please don't tell me to "set boundaries." We've asked them not to call at night except in an emergency, we've tried not to be sucked in, but it just doesn't work. Walter's been trying for almost a year and nothing's changed except our marriage—it's deteriorating. We need a solution.

—Christy, Oklahoma

Dear Christy,

You're right. You need another solution, and you need one quickly before your father-in-law accidentally hurts himself or your mother-in-law and your marriage deteriorates further. You are also correct not wanting to bother with setting boundaries again because that approach won't work here. People with dementia *cannot remember* what you asked for or what they promised, so those kinds of boundaries aren't an option. There are, however, other types of boundaries that may help lower your stress.

- Talk with your husband and let him know how you feel about losing time with him when he's home and about your handling problems when he's traveling. Kindly and gently explain that you agree his parents need assistance, but you think it might be time to consider more effective ways of helping.
- Start with a physician's visit. Your father-in-law should be under the treatment of a board-certified geriatric physician or a neurologist specializing in dementia. Memory loss and confusion are present in many conditions and diseases, some of which are treatable or reversible. An accurate diagnosis will help you plan for long-term needs.
- If your father-in-law's current abrasive behavior is different than it was in the past, ask the physician for help controlling his outbursts. Also, ask the physician for help controlling non-emergency nighttime calls.
- Hire a homecare worker who is experienced with dementia patients to help in your in-laws' home. She should be able to resolve many problems without your involvement. This should also help decrease the burden on your mother-in-law.
- It is unsafe for your father-in-law to have access to a car. If your mother-in-law cannot keep the keys from him, *remove the car.* (We don't have specifics, but based on your description we also wonder whether it is safe for your mother-in-law to drive.)
- It is critically important to provide alternative transportation so that your in-laws can still shop, visit friends, and go to their physicians.
- Finally, consider whether your mother-in-law and father-in-law would be happier and safer in an assisted living community where they would be safe and their needs would be met by trained professionals.

Hiring a homecare worker or moving your in-laws to an assisted living residence could help lower your anxiety level by giving you the freedom to schedule your visits to his parents and leave enough time for you and your husband to enjoy each other's company again.

Dividing Your Time

It would be unusual for all your duties to have the same "due date" for completion. Although family members may "want" things immediately, you can decrease your stress by prioritizing and separating "wants" from true "needs." This allows you to refuse or reschedule without feeling guilty. This worksheet makes it easy.

1. List up to five pending responsibilities in the left-hand column.

2. Using the definitions below, circle the appropriate Time Code for each one.

    Priority Code #1: "Needs" that require immediate action for safety, financial/legal deadlines, or similar reasons.

    Priority Code #2: "Needs" that require immediate action but are not life threatening.

    Priority Code #3: "Wants" (not "needs") that are very important to me or to my family but do not appear to impact on our safety or health.

    Priority Code #4: Less important items.

Listing and coding your duties will give you a clear picture of exactly what you have to do now and what can wait until you have time. You'll have enough information to divide your time.

First take care of Priority Code #1 duties. These are the issues that require immediate action for health and safety reasons. When you have time, move on to Priority Code #2 where needs may require immediate action, but you can wait to handle them because waiting will not put your family in danger. When you have additional time, move on to Priority Code #3, and finally to #4.

RESPONSIBILITY	ASSIGN PRIORITY CODE
1._____	1 2 3 4
2._____	1 2 3 4
3._____	1 2 3 4
4._____	1 2 3 4
5._____	1 2 3 4
6._____	1 2 3 4
7._____	1 2 3 4
8._____	1 2 3 4
9._____	1 2 3 4
10._____	1 2 3 4
11._____	1 2 3 4
12._____	1 2 3 4
13._____	1 2 3 4
14._____	1 2 3 4
15._____	1 2 3 4

LIFE AS A WORKING CAREGIVER

Dear Eldercare 911,

My supervisor told me to find a way to take care of my personal issues on my own time. I don't have my own time. There are so many things I have to take care of for my dad during office hours. The insurance company keeps me on hold and the grocery store accepts orders only between nine and ten in the morning, just when I'm in meetings. The doctor's office opens Monday and Tuesday at 9, and then closes from 11:30 AM to 1:00 PM for lunch. It's closed completely on Wednesday and reopens Thursday and Friday at 11, but then it closes again at 4. If you call after 5 PM, you are connected to an answering service message that says, "If this in not an emergency, please call during regular office hours." It's a very bad joke. My boss is furious. He caught me using the company fax machine to send papers to my dad's insurance company. I need this job and I am running out of options.

—Larry, Pennsylvania

Dear Larry,

Millions of caregivers like you are trying to balance workplace and caregiving issues. The bad news is that although many experts continue to try, no one has found the answer. The good news is that even though we can't solve these problems completely, we can help reduce the time you and other caregivers spend on eldercare issues and try to alleviate some of the pressures you're feeling.

Many major US corporations report that there are billions of dollars lost each year in productivity owing to eldercare issues handled from the workplace. Telephone interruptions, days off, and lack of focus on the job are just some of the problems faced by employers and employees. Workers often feel torn between a sense of responsibility to a loved one and a sense of duty to their jobs. Inability to handle both caregiving and workplace responsibilities routinely forces caregivers to opt for early retirement, to miss promotion opportunities, or to close their small businesses. For caregivers to remain emotionally healthy and productively employed, it is important to decrease workplace anxiety and interruptions, organize caregivers needs, and create solutions to relieve the pressures and fear that come from clandestine caregiving duties in the workplace. Read on for helpful tips and information.

A. CONTROLLING WORKDAY INTERRUPTIONS

Dear Eldercare 911,

I guess you can say I'm selfish, I want my time. I want to do the things that I want and need to do, especially at work. My seventy-nine-year-old dad just doesn't understand. It is an understatement to say that the phone calls in the office are annoying, but his surprise visits in the office are killing me. Actually, they are much more than annoying; they leave me too drained to work. Business is stressful enough without Dad's constant interruptions. He doesn't really understand the concept of a real emergency. An emergency in his life is different than mine. He seems to feel that if he doesn't deal with a problem right away, then it will get worse. Unfortunately, I have to deal with his emergency attacks every day. I am lucky in one respect. I work with great people and when I'm on the phone screaming at my dad, they all nod their heads in sympathy. My boss knows when I'm on the phone with my father and she is really kind to me, but I just have this feeling that she wonders how much of her time I am wasting on these phone calls. Please help me. I really like my job and I really love my dad, but the two responsibilities are a deadly combination.

—Lillian, Wisconsin

Dear Lillian,

We can empathize with your predicament. Feeling torn between your family and a job creates an emotional tug of loyalties. Your boss sounds like a terrific person, but she pays you to be on time, alert, and conscientious. When business is involved and money is at stake, everyone reaches a limit. Your dad wants you to be his confidant and personal problem solver. It sounds like Dad is used to your responding immediately to his many emergencies. His expectations are really quite simple; he sees himself as number one on your "to do" list. Keeping both your boss and your dad happy while taking care of yourself will take a little planning and prioritizing. Try these four steps to help you find a balance that satisfies your boss, your dad, and most importantly, you.

1. Before you talk to Dad, carefully print a list of emergency situations on white paper using a nice black marker. This will keep things neat, clear, and easy to read. When you meet with him, ask him what he considers an emergency. Listen to his response without making any comments. Once he is finished, suggest to him that the only *real* emergencies during business hours are medical and safety issues. For example, an emergency situation may include an unexpected visit to the doctor or the hospital, or if there is a major problem in his home, such as a flood in the basement or a fire. Anything else most probably can wait until you're home from work. Place the "emergency list" near the telephone that he uses most often. Ask him to refer to the list and think about it before he calls you. You may never see a complete change in Dad, but you may see a reduction in the telephone calls.

2. Order and install a personal emergency response system, sometimes referred to as PERS. Your dad wears a button around his neck, and if he needs assistance, he presses one button and help is on the way. Talk to Dad about the benefits of being able to reach for help if he falls in the bathroom or if he does not feel well. If he is concerned that having this system will make him appear dependent, explain to him that by installing this safety program he is giving himself the support he needs to continue living independently. Let him know that this will give him and you peace of mind knowing that twenty-four hours a day, seven days a week, help is available.

3. Let your dad know that your boss frowns on unnecessary workday interruptions and personal telephone calls. Tell him that you are afraid that your job may be in jeopardy if things don't change soon.

4. Talk to Dad about setting aside a few minutes during your lunch hour to chat. Although Dad says he has an emergency, he may just be feeling lonely and speaking to you for a few minutes may make him feel better. Ask him to keep a list of things he wants to talk to you about after work hours. If you arrive home from work at six o'clock, ask him to call after seven, or whenever it is most convenient for you. Begin doing this on a daily basis and then slowly decrease the amount of time and days you are on the phone. In time you and Dad will hopefully find a comfortable compromise.

Juggling work and family is exhausting and time-consuming. By setting boundaries and providing Dad with an emergency response alternative, you are on the way to spending less time on the phone and more time at your job.

Dear Eldercare 911,

My brother, Ken, and I are in our fifties and we share many of the caregiver duties. I guess you can say we divide things up. He does the driving to and from doctor appointments and he takes Mom grocery shopping. He is very helpful especially to our eighty-seven-year-old dad who had a stroke a few years ago. Dad has problems walking and with his speech. On the other hand, our eighty-year-old mom suffers from arthritis but she is sharp and full of gab and nag. I am the designated listener. Now you'd think that was an easy job: think again. My parent's illness has impacted on my work day after day. Mom is a computer whiz and she instant messages me dozens of times each day, complaining about my brother or the next-door neighbor. If I don't answer her, I feel guilty, and then I spend so much time with nonsense. These electronic interruptions are as bad as a ringing telephone. I am interrupted during business meetings, in the middle of a negotiation, or during a meeting with my supervisor. There is no limit to her messages. I am a basket case and basically useless on the job. I know how to electronically shut down the e-mails, but I don't know how to emotionally shut down my feelings. HELP!

—Karl, New Mexico

Dear Karl,

You sound like a genuine nice guy who is probably the designated "listener" because you are usually patient and understanding. It's time to use those virtues in a new way and talk to your mom about her behavior. You describe her as someone who has the gift of gab. She may not actually be speaking to you, but the computer is her voice. For many seniors it is a lifeline to family and friends. Mom may not understand her impact on your life because she is so involved in her own needs. Try to use your excellent communitcation skills to discuss her behavior. There is a very fine line between explaining to a chatterbox that you want to "listen" to her and explaining to her that her e-mails are irritating interruptions.

- Try this dialogue. Use as much or as little as you need. "Mom, I would like to visit with you on Tuesday. I know Dad goes to bed around 8:30, so I would like to come over after he is in bed. Is that OK with you?"

Wait for a reply. She will probably ask what you want to talk about, and you can be as straightforward as you want. "We need to talk about the e-mails in my office. I will tell you more about it on Tuesday. Please have a pot of coffee and some of your good cookies." Asking for the coffee and cookies sets a friendly, familial tone for your meeting. Adversaries don't usually share cookies.

- Be prepared for your talk with Mom. On the day of your visit you can say, "Hi Mom, thanks for having me over." Let her serve you the cookies and coffee. It will help decrease some of the tension. "Ma, Ken and I have tried to give you and Dad our time and attention. Because of his schedule, Ken is able to help you out with the shopping and driving you and Dad to medical appointments. I can't do that because of so many time constraints on my job. That's the problem. I can't continue to respond to your e-mails in the office. We can set a time of the day to chat or e-mail after work, but I cannot take any more workday interruptions. If there is a medical emergency or safety problem, you can call me in the office." Let Mom reply. If she is angry and upset, you can acknowledge her feelings. "Mom, I know this is difficult for you, but my job is on the line. I am not pulling the plug on our communications; I'm only limiting them to certain times of the day. OK? Can we give it a try?"
- Allow Mom to respond once again. No matter what her reaction is, remain firm yet comforting. In other words, be yourself.

In time Mom may grow to understand that you don't love her any less because you have other responsibilities that take your time and attention.

B. SETTING LIMITS

Dear Eldercare 911,

When someone does something nice for you, you feel like a really miserable person if you don't appreciate it. I am an only child. My dad is a wonderful, happy, healthy, active seventy-seven-year-old man. Mom died three years ago and Dad retired from his very corporate job. I work in the corporate sector. I have my own office and secretary, and a huge responsibility. Here's the problem. We live and work in a large metropolitan city, and Dad lives twenty blocks from my office. Every day he stops by with a container of coffee and two muffins (he reminds me how much I like toasted corn muffins) and then he says, "Sally, you've got to eat." I say, "Dad I have work to finish today or else I will be in the office until ten o'clock tonight." He says, "But you have to eat." And it goes on and on. How do you tell someone who means well that he is driving you crazy? How do you stop the nice guy from being so nice?

—Sally, Illinois

Dear Sally,

Dad is retired and he probably misses the smell, the rush, and the exhilaration of a busy office. Many retirees struggle with free time after years of being in the throes of a frenetic work environment. Dad has a double loss: the loss of his job and the greater loss of your mother. He is trying to fill his emptiness with a cup of coffee, a corn muffin, and your companionship. Unfortunately, it is not the solution to his problem.

Let's begin with the premise that Dad most likely is not going to change his habits. How can you help Dad find a better, more productive way to spend his time, and in the process free yourself from the daily coffee breaks?

- Take a little time to think about who he is and what makes him happy. Answer these five questions, before you go any further.
    1. What are Dad's hobbies?
    2. How did he and Mom spend their leisure time?
    3. Do you consider Dad a sociable person or is he more of a loner?
    4. Does he stay in contact with old friends and colleagues?
    5. What makes him happy, besides spending time with you?
- Begin by making a list of his hobbies. Include things like reading or watching old movies. Think about your parents' social life. Did they go dancing or did they enjoy dinner in a fine restaurant? Questions 3 and 4 will give you a sense of his interest in socializing and maintaining friendships, or renewing old ones. What puts a smile on Dad's face? Does he enjoy a drive in the country or a golf game?

Once you compile your answers, you will have a very good picture of who Dad is today. Before you meet with him, try to put some of the information together.

- Begin your conversation by saying: "Dad, you are the best. I know you feel lonely sometimes and I know I have to eat, but the two things don't always go together. I want to spend time with you after work, but I can't spend time during the day. I have been thinking a lot about you, and I have a few ideas. Will you take a few minutes and hear me out?" This is one situation where it may serve both of you if you make every effort to present your case, then give Dad a chance to reply.

If your answers indicate that he is very sociable but that he has lost contact with friends, suggest a reunion at a conveniently located restaurant. If he loved a good golf game and his golf buddies have moved away or died, suggest that he take a lesson or two to refresh his game. He can then ask the golf pro if he knows of any other retirees who might enjoy a round of golf. If dancing is his thing, contact a local dance studio and inquire about a seniors night. Many senior centers cater to the social needs of very active men and women. He may find a specific group of men he can relate to and with whom he can discuss the ups and downs of retirement. Dad may also enjoy lunch and a card game with other healthy retirees or devoting time to a charitable organization. The job market is another option to explore. Many large corporations are hiring retirees as consultants. The belief is that the retiree is reliable, experienced, and available. Check into local companies that may have a senior-specific hiring program.

- Refer to the resource section of this book (chapter 13) for additional information.

Present your ideas to Dad. Give him plenty of time to think about your suggestions and allow him to ask questions. Initially he may reject your ideas, or he may welcome some of them. Whatever he decides to do or not do, it is your job to maintain the new boundaries you have set for your relationship. By providing him with options, you are not abandoning him; you are simply redirecting his wonderful energy.

Dear Eldercare 911,

We own a family business. My brother and I are actively involved in the day-to-day organization. Mom and Dad both worked in the business for over fifty years. Mom is frail and weak and she stays at home with a home health aide. Dad recently had a heart attack and a mild stroke. He is having difficulty walking, and he is not as sharp as he used to be.

The problem is that he wants to spend time in the office and be near the action. One of us picks him up at eight o'clock in the morning and we take him home sometime in the afternoon. Dad requires help in the bathroom and at meals. The women in the office are wonderful to him, and they all chip in and help out. The time he needs takes away time from their work responsibilities and definitely infringes on our workday. Dad was always generous to us and we know it means a lot to him to "work" in the office, but we have to set some limits. We don't know how to do it. Can you help us figure out a way to help Dad continue to feel a part of the business he began five decades ago and at the same time free up our time to do our jobs?

—Two Sons, New Jersey

Dear Two Sons,

Your Dad is lucky to have you for sons. Your sensitivity to his feelings and your appreciation for the things he did for you is commendable. The solution to your problem is to develop a balance that provides your dad with time in the office to feel useful and important and time for you to do your work. Although the women in the office are generous with their time, their job descriptions do not include tending to Dad's needs.

You can accomplish this balance by delegating other people to take care of Dad's needs: someone to serve as a driver and someone else to attend to his personal needs. This is a three-step action plan. You may appeal to your dad's sense of business and fair play if you approach this in a businesslike fashion.

1. Plan a meeting at a time that is convenient for you, your brother, and Dad. Decide in advance who will be the spokesperson. One of the purposes of this meeting is to make your dad comfortable and not make him feel as if you are ganging up on him. As you mentioned in your letter, Dad is not as cognitively astute as he used to be, so it is important to keep that in mind as you discuss this matter. However, don't underestimate him, either. He still appears capable of working in the office under specific limited conditions. Let Dad know how you feel about him and how you appreciate the confidence he has shown in both of you. For example: "Dad, we wanted to meet with you today to let you know how much we admire you and how much we learn from you. Unfortunately, we do have a little problem, but with your consent we have a solution." Your dad will probably want to know what the problem is, and it is your obligation to firmly and clearly explain the situation.

   "Dad, your experience in this business is invaluable, but since the stroke it is a little more difficult for you to get around. We love having you here, but we can't spare the time during the day to take care of your needs. The women in the office are great, but you know that's not their job. Let us tell you what we have in mind." Dad may feel uncomfortable with this subject, so it is important to give him a chance to think about what you said before he responds. If he is not willing to discuss the problem at this time, let it go for now and then try again at a later date. If he is ready to hear your suggestions, continue with steps 2 and 3.

2. Talk to Dad about the benefits of having a professional caregiver assist him with all his needs during the hours he is in the office. Suggest that you and Dad interview a home health aide who can help him in the bathroom and with his meals. Explain to Dad that this will give him the freedom to work in the office as much or as little as he wants without worrying about everyone else's needs or schedule.

3. Arrange for a car or taxi service to pick up Dad and the aide at a designated hour in the morning and then again at a specific time during or at the end of the workday. If he is reluctant to pay for the car or taxi service, then suggest that you split the fee. Explain to him that it is beneficial to you, too, because it saves you time and increases the hours you can work in the office. Keep in mind that some home health aides have driver's licenses and drive their clients on a regular basis. Be sure to check the specific regulations and guidelines in your city and state. A licensed homecare agency can provide you with the information you will need.

Dad may need time and your understanding to accept the help he requires to remain productive and active.

C. TALKING TO YOUR BOSS

Dear Eldercare 911,

I am in a most unusual situation. I have several coworkers who take care of their parents. One woman spends every weekend with her mom, and another man takes his dad to doctor appointments when he can. We have developed this bond that is very unusual, even for close colleagues. Our jobs are primarily based on "projects." Each project has a deadline and everyone has his responsibility to complete the task. At present, both of my parents are in the hospital, and Dad will probably need a nursing home after this hospitalization. The social worker said Mom could probably go home with live-in help. I have a job to do and a boss who doesn't like delays or excuses. My colleague, Bill, said he would cover for me and do my end of the project. This would give me the time I need to attend to my parents' situation. I feel so uncomfortable asking him to do this for me. I guess in part I don't know if or how I could make it up to him, plus I feel like such a sneak. I know that the right thing to do is to talk to my boss, but he is tough and I don't know how to approach him. Please help!

—Marvin, Florida

Dear Marvin,

Caregivers often have a clear understanding of each other's dilemmas and needs. Although your colleague empathizes with your situation, he may be placing his job and yours in jeopardy if your boss discovers the project "cover-up." In order to maintain everyone's job security, it is important for you to face your boss and talk to him about what you require. Keep in mind the following three points when you meet with your boss.

1. Prior to the meeting with your boss, determine how much time off you need and what you are willing to do to get that time. For example: Are you willing to work weekends to make up the time? Are you willing to use a few vacation days? This may give you enough time to handle your caregiver responsibilities.

2. Before meeting with your boss, talk to your generous colleague and see if the offer still stands. If the offer is still good, talk to your boss. State your problem clearly. Provide as much information as you need to make your point. Leave out any of the graphic medical details. It is not necessary and in fact in may turn your boss off. Explain to him that Bill is willing to pick up the slack for you on the latest project. Ask his permission to work out the details with Bill.

3. Wait for an answer. If he says no to everything you have discussed with him, it may simply mean that he does not have the ability to accommodate your needs. However, if he is able to help your special situation, it is likely that you and your boss will be able to come to some agreement.

Your honesty and willingness to find a fair solution to your problem should go a long way with your boss. Try not to personalize the situation if your boss cannot accommodate your needs. His decision-making ability may be limited by corporate constraints.

Dear Eldercare 911,

When I took this job with a large corporation, I was sure that working 9–5, five days a week was something that I could manage. I've been at it for several months, but now I find myself in a pretty serious predicament. My eighteen-year-old son was in a car accident and has a broken leg, and he will be at home for at least six weeks. My mother fell in the backyard and she is hospitalized for a hip and a wrist fracture. From the hospital she will be transferred to a rehabilitation facility for a few weeks. To add to the drama, my dog was injured while she was playing with my neighbor's cat. We rushed her to the veterinary hospital. When my mom was alert enough to hear about the dog's problem, she said, "Anne, you look exhausted. I'm almost afraid to open that bag of goodies you brought today. I wouldn't be surprised if you brought me dog kibble and sent the dog a bouquet of flowers!"

She's right. I am exhausted. I need a new work schedule, but I don't want to give up my salary to get it. Before I talk to my boss I have to be ready with some ideas. What are my best options?

—Anne, Pennsylvania

Dear Anne,

It is amazing how often we think that nothing else can happen and then it does. You certainly have your hands full, but you deserve kudos for recognizing that you cannot continue to juggle all your responsibilities without making some immediate changes. Keep in mind that although these circumstances are overwhelming, your involvement at this intense level is time limited. It is our hope that Mom will recover in a few months, your son's leg will mend, and the dog will be scampering around.

Given your work hours, it is very difficult to reach every doctor, your insurance companies, and other resources after 5 PM. You need time during the day to take care of your current caregiver duties. It is time to meet with your boss, but before the meeting, ask yourself these questions:

1. How many hours a day do I need to take care of my family's needs?
2. Can I work some full days and some half days?
3. Do I have vacation or sick days that I can apply to the time I need?
4. Does my company have any policy about taking a leave of absence for personal emergencies?

To help you get the answers, you need to do the following:

- Contact the human resource department of your company. Meet with a counselor before you meet with your immediate boss. Find out the answers to your questions as well as any other options you may have for alternative work hours such as a flextime schedule. Flextime allows you to arrange your hours according to your needs. For example, you may want to work 7:30–3:30, Monday–Friday. This will give you an hour and a half during traditional work hours to handle any important telephone calls or make other essential contacts to help your family.
- Decide which options are the best for you. When you meet with your boss, be prepared to present your needs and wants clearly. As a courtesy, let him know in advance what the meeting is about so he has an opportunity to prepare the information he requires. Remember this should not be an adversarial meeting; you are both on the same side.
- State your needs and then listen to what your boss has to say. He may be able to accommodate you, or he may have certain corporate limitations. Talk to him about a temporary flextime schedule if that works best for you, or discuss the possibility of taking a day or two off each week by using your vacation time.
- Try this dialogue: "Mr. Smith, I appreciate your time today. As you know, I am in the middle of several family medical problems and I need time to take care of my responsibilities. I love my job and I am anxious to do what I can to accommodate your needs. Can you help me figure out the best schedule for both of us? I have some information regarding my vacation and sick days. I also was wondering how a temporary flextime schedule works for you?" Give your boss an opportunity to respond. We hope that he will have the leeway and authority to find the best solution to your problem. If he can't accommodate all your needs, talk to him about a compromise. For example: if the company policy doesn't allow for flextime hours but you can use your vacation days, use as much or as little as you need to get you through this crisis. If he needs you in the office every Monday for meetings but he can give you Tuesday and Thursday off, try to work with him.

Approaching your boss may be intimidating and uncomfortable, but you have a legitimate problem and you have several options to accommodate the company's needs and your own. By preparing for the meeting, having potential solutions ready, and giving your boss advance notice, you are showing him your professionalism, concern for the company, and respect for his time.

D. SAVING TIME

Dear Eldercare 911,

My friend Jenny and I need help. We have known each other for over thirty years. We've been through so much together and now we are both care-givers. My consulting job keeps me very busy from 8 to 4 Monday–Friday, but I stop by every day after work to help my eighty-three-year-old mother with something or other. Jenny is a teacher and her eighty-eight-year-old Dad lives in the next town. She is there at least three or four times each week. When we compare notes we laugh, because we are doing the exact same things for our parents. We clean the stove, check out the food in the refrigerator, and throw away old medications. Amazingly, one day we found an hour to meet for coffee, and we both could not get over how exhausted we looked. We found out that we both existed on a few hours of sleep. Why? Do you know what I do at 1 AM? I iron shirts or wash floors, because it is the only time of the day that I have to do it. Sometimes I even cook for the next day. Jenny tells me that she gets up at 4 AM to cook dinner because she is too tired when she comes home from work at 7 PM. What's wrong with us? We need help.

—Two Friends, South Carolina

Dear Two Friends,

Nothing is wrong with you; you are just doing too much and working too hard. It is time to take back control of your lives by utilizing the organizational and management skills you both have used as a teacher and as a consultant. In your jobs you probably had projects to complete and deadlines to meet. Think about any one situation that took time, energy, and creativity. Draw from the success of that experience and recreate how you approached the project and how you finally completed it. For instance: If you had a long-term project that took six months, how did you organize your assistants or staff? What steps helped you the most to complete the job? What things did you do that were not helpful? You will probably learn that you used some very simple timesaving steps to complete the task.

Complete these sentences as a guideline and write the answers on a piece of paper.

1. The first thing I did when I worked on the six-month project was

_____.

2. After I made a list of what I had to do, I delegated certain tasks to

_____.

3. My project was complete and ready on time because

_____.

Once you complete your "project questionnaire," review your answers to help you get a clearer understanding of how you saved time and energy. Apply the same method to approach your caregiver duties.

- Prioritize the things you have to do for your parents and yourself on a weekly basis, and then decide what you can handle every other week. For instance, instead of ironing at night, think about delegating an hour or two on a weekend. If it is financially possible, hire someone to help you with the house cleaning. Investigate agencies in your community that provide a cleaning team to handle the housework once or twice a month. You may find a referral to a reliable company through many homecare agencies. Remember, sleep should take priority over clean floors and dust. This approach may not only save you a few hours every day, but it may in fact be beneficial to your overall health and well-being.

- Think about who can help you with some of the duties. Consider hiring a home health aide to handle some of your parents' activities of daily living. Activities of daily living include cooking, laundry, dressing, bathing, and light housekeeping. Contact your local Area Agency on Aging, the local hospital, or your parents' physicians for a list of licensed, bonded homecare agencies in your community. Interview two or three aides without your parents. After you make an appropriate selection, involve your parents in the process by having a meeting with the aide and your parents at a mutually convenient time.

- Think about how and why you satisfactorily completed your project at work. Did you prioritize your workload? Did you get the help you needed to complete the task on time? Did you stay focused on the important things and let the less important items go? Use the success of your personal method to help you prioritize, reach out for help, and take charge of your caregiver responsibilities.

You have the power to take control of whatever you have to do. You said that you found an hour to have a cup of coffee with Jenny on one of your busiest days. If you use the methods that have been successful for you in the past, then one hour a day may develop into several hours of sleep, relaxation, and peace of mind.

Dear Eldercare 911,

I have a good job and a great boss. She is very supportive of her staff and when any one of us has family problems, she is encouraging and very kind. I was telling a friend of mine how nice my boss is when I have to deal with my father's medical problems, insurance questions, and a bunch of other stuff. My friend asked me if I realized how many hours a day I spend on caregiver duties. I laughed and said, "Hours, I probably spend two or three hours each week." She challenged me and said one day this week I should keep a log of the number of telephone calls I make and how long I am on the telephone. She said I should be sure to calculate only the calls related to my caregiver responsibilities. I accepted the challenge. I couldn't believe what I found out. At the end of the day I had made nine telephone calls and spent a total of two hours, out of the seven I work, on caregiver-related problems. Two hours! Would you believe that was a light day? This can't continue; my boss is going to figure out that I am getting paid to be a caregiver not her secretary. How can I save some time during the week to take care of the things I have to do for Dad? I really don't want to be an unemployed caregiver.

—Mindy, New Hampshire

Dear Mindy,

Millions of working caregivers share your problem when they use company time to handle many of their caregiver duties, such as telephone contacts with doctors, pharmacists, insurance companies, and social service programs. Many feel the way you do, torn between a fierce loyalty to an employer and a sense of duty to a parent. We want to thank you for your honest and open accounting of the time you actually spend on caregiver duties during your workday. It takes a great deal of courage to own up to the fact that you are doing two jobs at the same time and for the same salary. You're right to think that any day now your boss will figure out what you are doing and end your ability to make caregiver-related telephone calls during work hours. To save time and your job, you may want to try our four-step approach: organize, prioritize, assign, and communicate.

1. Organize all the telephone numbers you need in advance. One client always complained that he could never find the doctors' phone num-

bers when he needed them. He showed us his makeshift telephone directory. He kept dozens of business cards in a small envelope without any logical order. We suggested that he use one of the following methods: plastic card holders that can be inserted into a three-ring binder, a small handheld personal computer that can also hold additional important data, a small pocket-size address book, or the worksheet, "Essential Telephone Numbers," found at the end of this chapter.

2. Prioritize the most important telephone calls you have to make during working hours. These may include, but are not limited to, medical emergencies and medication questions. Find out which of the companies you deal with have twenty-four-hour hotlines or weekend telephone-assistance programs, such as insurance or mail-order medication companies. If they have twenty-four-hour hotlines, then you can reserve those calls for after business hours. You will immediately be reducing the number of calls you have to make during the workday.

3. Ask a family member or a friend to help you out with some of your telephone duties. Be very clear and specific about what you want and need. Consider hiring a home health aide for your dad. Before you hire her, find out if she is willing and comfortable to help you out with some of the telephone calls, such as confirming doctors' appointments.

4. Communicate your dilemma to your boss. Tell her you have made some adjustments to help you through this difficult time. Instead of making the calls when she isn't looking, ask her permission to use the office telephone only for emergency situations. Offer to purchase a telephone card or use your cell phone if she prefers.

You can save time and energy to do your work by organizing your telephone numbers, prioritizing the most important calls, asking for help, and being open and honest with your boss.

Help for the Working Caregiver

Many caregivers juggle several jobs at one time: caregiving, work, and family. You can learn how to reduce some of the stress associated with your responsibilities by making a few changes that will put you in control of your hectic schedule.

- **I will prioritize my tasks.** I will make a list of the things I have to do. I will figure out how many hours a day and how many hours a week I have to handle my responsibilities. I will handle the most important things first, and I will reserve the rest for another time.

- **I will not overschedule.** When I consider my schedule, I will think about the time I need, how I feel, and if I am asking too much of myself. If I feel that I am pushing my limits, I will rethink and reschedule.

- **I will set limits.** The more I do for my family, friends, and boss, the more people will expect. I will be very clear on what I can and cannot do and remain firm and steadfast to my decision.

- **I will take care of myself.** I will schedule time for myself every day. It may mean having a cup of coffee in front of the television or listening to talk radio. Whatever I do, I will be sure it gives me peace of mind and body.

Essential Telephone Numbers

Create your own telephone directory. Keep it organized. Have important numbers close at hand to help decrease your caregiver burden. Periodically update this list for your convenience.

IN AN EMERGENCY, ALWAYS CALL 911 FIRST

1. Family members to contact in an emergency:

Name_____Tel._____

Name_____Tel._____

Name_____Tel._____

2. Physicians:

Name_____Tel._____

Name_____Tel._____

Name_____Tel._____

3. Pharmacy:

Name_____Tel._____

4. Friends:

Name_____Tel._____

Name_____Tel._____

Name_____Tel._____

5. Neighbors:

Name_____Tel._____

Name_____Tel._____

6. Others (social service agencies, hospitals, insurance companies)

Title_____Name_____

Tel._____

Title_____Name_____

Tel._____

Title_____Name_____

Tel._____

Title_____Name_____

Tel._____

Title_____Name_____

Tel._____

7. Others (repair services, telephone company, electric and gas, etc.)

Title_____Name_____

Tel._____

Title_____Name_____

Tel._____

Title_____Name_____

Tel._____

Title_____Name_____

Tel._____

The Working Caregiver's Journal

One working caregiver provided us with her helpful journal that contains important information regarding her parent's care. She writes in her journal every day. It takes her just a few minutes, but it saves a great deal of time and energy when she needs specific medical information or updates. It also provides her with a private venue to express her feelings.

This is a guideline on how to begin your Working Caregiver Journal. For example, fill in the date, time of day, whom you spoke to, and the telephone number. In the section "What happened today?" write a note about a conversation, a hospital report, or any important information you want to remember. Express how you feel in the "My feelings" section.

Date: ____/____/_____   Time of day: _____

Contact: _____   Tel: _____

Contact: _____   Tel: _____

What happened today?

_____

_____

_____

My feelings:

_____

_____

_____

_____

_____

_____

_____

Date: ____/____/_____ Time of day: _____

Contact: _____ Tel: _____

Contact: _____ Tel: _____

What happened today?

_____

_____

_____

My feelings:

_____

_____

_____

_____

_____

_____

_____

_____

Date: ____/____/_____ Time of day: _____

Contact: _____ Tel: _____

Contact: _____ Tel: _____

What happened today?

_____

_____

_____

My feelings:

_____

_____

_____

_____

_____

_____

_____

8

LIVING WITH ALZHEIMER'S DISEASE

Dear Eldercare 911,

I care for whoever is in my mother's body twenty-four hours a day. I've watched her change from someone who never found a minute she couldn't fill with a hobby, taking care of her house, her family, or her friends, into a stranger who wears diapers and answers every question with a blank stare or a smiling "Yes." While I was watching her, my friends and family watched me morph from a happy wife and mother with a career that I loved to a stay-at-home stressed-out wreck. Her friends and mine have both stopped visiting us. I guess they're uncomfortable . . . or maybe they're just afraid they'll be next. And our poor dog . . . he is as lost as I am and shedding clouds of fur out of stress . . . or is that my own hair flying around?

—Ellen, Utah

Dear Eldercare 911,

My parents are amazing. My sisters and I recently found out that about six months ago our father was diagnosed with Alzheimer's disease. They didn't deliberately hide the news from us; they just didn't know how to tell us. Mom joined a support group. Then she dragged Pop to a family support group with other couples who have Alzheimer's. That's what Mom called it—"couples who have Alzheimer's." She says she'll be the caregiver; so as far as she's concerned, "they" have it. Last week, they asked the three of us to come home for the weekend and told us. I can't imagine how hard it was for them to stay calm. Pop had a lot to say, as he said, "while he could still keep his thoughts together." He told us to never forget that although he might not be able to say the words, he would always love us and his grandchildren. He didn't want us to ever doubt his love even when he couldn't show it anymore. It took a few days for our brains to restart, but when they did, we decided that if they could be this brave, so could we. We agree that what matters most now is finding out how we can help our parents cope with their future, but that's where our abilities end. The truth is, we're still overwhelmed and have no idea where to start. How do we know what help to give or when to give it?

—Brian, Alabama

Whether your parent is in the early stages of Alzheimer's, like Brian's father, and can still communicate and participate in many activities, or is in the third stage and has more advanced symptoms, like Ellen's mother, Alzheimer's caregivers have a commonality in needs and issues. In a very practical sense, caregivers who live with Alzheimer's dementia are often also held captive by the disease. Friends may stop visiting, their personal time may be severely limited or disappear entirely, and careers may be put on hold or canceled. Exhaustion or overwhelming anxiety may replace interesting conversations and quiet pillow talk; headaches, stomach aches, depression, and difficulty sleeping are almost routine. Can you avoid these debilitating experiences? It may be impractical to expect to care for an Alzheimer's patient without feeling sad or frustrated, or without wondering how you will cope. However, it is not unrealistic to believe that you can improve your quality of life and help control some of the impact that the disease has on you and your family. Mastering the four topics in this chapter can help improve your chances of regaining or maintaining your quality of life.

- **Educate yourself.** What is Alzheimer's disease (AD)? How many stages of the disease are there? What changes will you and your parent experience as the disease progresses? *Knowing what to expect is critical to your understanding of unfolding events and to planning for both your parent's future and your own.*
- **Learn coping and communication skills.** Dementia often breaks down caregivers' emotional and physical reserves more quickly than other types of illnesses. *Without new coping skills, every Alzheimer's day can devour another piece of your quality of life.* Call your local Alzheimer's organization for skills training and read "Coping with Cognitive Changes" at the end of this chapter.
- **Find relief with help and services.** It is in your best interest to work with professionals who specialize in dementia care: this includes board-certified physicians, daycare and respite workers, and professional homecare workers and sitters. *This is the wrong time and the wrong disease to go it alone.*
- **Caring for yourself.** How do you maintain your balance when your parent's needs keep increasing but the number of hours in the day

remains finite? Finding time and space to care for your own mental and physical health may be your most important caregiving duty.

A. THE THREE STAGES OF ALZHEIMER'S DISEASE

Dear Eldercare 911,

My father has had Alzheimer's disease for three years. He still lives alone and manages with help from me and my brother. When he stopped driving, I started taking him with me on errands and shopping trips so that we could get the things he needed and so that he could get out of the house. Last week, while we were out, I had to go to the bathroom. I left him at the door to the ladies' room and told him to wait for me. I felt it was safe because he has never wandered off—he usually stays right by me. You've already guessed what happened—when I came out of the bathroom, he was gone. Luckily I found him still in the store. Unluckily, he was standing there as calm as you please peeing in a plant in the furniture department! We went to the doctor and he said Dad had progressed to Stage II. How can I see to it that I don't get any more embarrassing surprises?

—Mortified in Texas

Dear Mortified,

Alzheimer's disease (AD) is a progressive neurological disease that develops slowly. People with AD become increasingly more impaired as the disease passes through its three primary stages: Stage I (mildly impaired), Stage II (moderately impaired), or Stage III (severely impaired). The "What to Expect: The Three Stages of Alzheimer's Disease" chart at the end of this topic will help you understand what to expect at each stage. AD is very unpredictable and you are likely to experience more surprises, but to avoid embarrassment in the future, you only have to remember two words: "admit" and "accept." Turn to the person who may have been offended and say, "My father has Alzheimer's disease." Most people will understand and the tension will disappear. If you meet someone who isn't sympathetic to that explanation, we suggest that she cannot be moved, but you can and should—so move on without further statement or explanation and try to leave her and the incident behind!

To help your peace of mind, try to create a secure environment for your dad. To understand his decreasing ability to maintain his own health and safety, try this exercise: as you go through your daily activities, notice how many of your functions are based on *memories and experiences*. It's the simplest of concepts: first we *learn* and then we *remember* what we learned and use those memories to successfully navigate daily activities and to understand experiences. AD destroys or renders inaccessible parts of the brain, in effect, erasing some memories and preventing access to others. This has a dramatic impact on your parent's safety.

For example, your dad may no longer be able to access the stored knowledge and memories he needs to automatically *remember* what a bathroom is for, or how to fill a glass with water, or how to use or turn off the stove, or that he has to eat to remain healthy.

In reality, his brain is no longer telling him that to remain safe he needs to lock the door, that a red traffic light means *Danger—Stop!* and a green one means *Safe—Go!* He may no longer possess access to the fact that he should not drink bug spray or put motor oil in the coffee pot instead of water. Telling him "that will burn you" won't keep him from putting his hand on a red-hot stove if he can no longer reach into his memory bank and find the definition he once learned for the word "burn." Helping your dad requires that *you remember* that the damage to his brain from Alzheimer's disease means *he can no longer remember* how to safely perform many of the simplest activities that he needs to successfully navigate through the day.

In Stage II, it's important to consider these issues:

- **Supervision:** Dad may not remember to eat. Or if he can no longer discern between a visitor and a stranger, he may put himself at risk by opening the door to strangers. He will more than likely be unable to evacuate in case of fire or retain enough control and judgment to remember how to call for help in an emergency.

- **Household safety:** Assume Dad is at risk for injury from all poisons and sharp objects: alcohol, ammonia, cleaning and laundry supplies, ladders, matches, cigarette lighters, knives, tools, and open stairways and balconies. Remove items that aren't needed, and add baby locks on cabinets for the remaining supplies or tools. See the end of the next section for "Basic Safety Measures for an AD Home."

- **Personal grooming:** Your dad will become increasingly less concerned with hygiene. He may need assistance to remove unclean clothing or use the toilet and will eventually become incontinent. If your father no longer recognizes streams of water, he may become fearful of showers, which may make cleanliness a serious issue.

- **Financial risks:** Protect your dad's finances by removing them from his control. Leave him a small amount of spending money to help preserve his dignity and feelings of independence. It's important to remove credit cards as well.
- **Driving:** Even if he voluntarily stopped driving, *remove the car.* Seniors often have duplicate keys. A caution: as hard as this may be to believe, unless you remove savings and checking accounts, and credit cards, your dad may find a way to purchase another car. (If you're wondering if you *really* have to take the car, take the ultimate test: *would you want your father driving your daughter to school tomorrow?*)
- **Social interaction:** Provide an alternative means for visiting friends, running errands, shopping, doctor visits, and other needs, or enroll Dad in an appropriate daycare program. Without outside activities, he is likely to become more confused because of lack of stimulation and personal interaction.
- **Caregiver assistance:** Call the Alzheimer's organization or the local Area Agency on Aging nearest you and talk to a family counselor for information on respite services, caregiver support groups, and in-home assistance.

Dear Eldercare 911,

My mother just received a diagnosis of First-Stage Alzheimer's disease. She lives alone and desperately wants to maintain her independence for as long as she can. We checked the car and couldn't find any dents, but she won't let us see her checkbook or tell us anything about her financial affairs. She forgets things now and then, but for the most part, she really seems okay. My brother Don and I want to help her, but we have different ideas of what to do. He says leave her alone. He says she looks the same and sounds the same so she doesn't need us to remind her she's sick and make her feel worse.

Don says to wait, but I can't help feeling she must need something from us. How could someone with Alzheimer's not need help? Should we jump in and take over or just wait until she begins acting like she needs help?

—Marilyn, Oregon

Dear Marilyn,

You and Don are both right: your mother can still function independently for many of her activities of daily living but she needs help now with others.

184 THE ELDERCARE 911 QUESTION AND ANSWER BOOK

The best way to help now is to learn which tasks are causing her frustration because they are becoming progressively more difficult for her.

Stage I of AD often presents one of the most difficult periods for caregivers and their parents. Your mother may look the same (no outward physical changes) and, for brief periods of time, may act the same. She may carefully avoid embarrassing moments by using social skills she acquired over decades of dealing with people. For example, she may draw attention away from herself and onto you or others, or avoid the question/problem entirely by changing the subject. The more control she loses because of progressively greater disorientation or confusion, the more afraid she will feel. As trying to act "normal" becomes increasingly difficult and stressful for her, she may try to keep the extent of her decline a secret by withdrawing from social activities with family and friends.

To help *now*, begin with these steps:

1. Let your mom continue to do as much for herself as she is able. Offer *assistance* for problem areas. For example, if you see mail piling up, offer to go over it *with* her rather than do it all yourself. If your mom shows agitation or frustration with a task, then offer to take care of it for her.

2. Pick a quiet time and explain that she can have a voice in her future by making her wishes known *now* and appointing someone to make financial, legal, and healthcare decisions when she is no longer able to do so herself.

3. Post reminder notes around her house. Tape a list of frequently dialed numbers near each phone to help Mom call her friends and family more easily; tape Mom's name, address, and telephone number to each phone to help in emergency situations. It is important to "tape" the numbers because if you simply place them near the phone, your mother may pick them up and move them.

4. Schedule time yourself or hire someone to drive your mom on both mandatory (doctor and grocery store) and pleasure outings (social gatherings and casual shopping). Count yourself lucky that you didn't find dents in the car *now*, or worse. But Mom's judgment is impaired, and it is dangerous for her to continue driving. Remove her car and remember to provide an alternate means of transportation.

5. As the disease progresses, your mom will become frustrated trying to remember how to cook and simply stop trying, leaving her at risk

nutritionally. She may also inadvertently start a fire if she forgets how to safely use a stove. Hire someone to help assure that she has balanced meals available every day. Don't forget to check to see if she actually eats the food.

6. Join a support group. Comparing notes with other caregivers and benefiting from their acquired skills will help improve your mother's quality of life and your own.
7. Communicate with your mom's physician for the latest information and medication breakthroughs.

What to Expect: The Three Stages of Alzheimer's Disease

The course of Alzheimer's disease can vary significantly with each individual. However, some changes are more typical and so you can reasonably expect to experience them. For example, the behavioral changes that usually dominate Stage I are joined with overriding physical problems in Stage III. Educating yourself to the flow of Alzheimer's can help you communicate better with your parent, your family and friends, and your parent's physician.

Use the box to the left of each symptom to check those that apply to your parent. Check all that apply, even if you cross over to another stage. Feel free to check off symptoms in more than one stage. This information can help you create plans to keep your own mental, physical, and financial future intact. Taking this list to your parent's physician will provide her with an insider's clear written account of your parent's behavior and abilities. The physician will be more able to prescribe appropriate lifestyle and medication changes that may help improve the entire family's quality of life.

CHANGES COMMONLY EXPERIENCED IN STAGE I

Although Stage I is called the "mild" stage, it is actually one of the most difficult periods of the disease process for you and your parent. Most people in Stage I AD realize that they are losing control and fight back by denying the existence of the problem. Their children also find it easier to deny the disease and attribute problems to "getting older." These combined denials mean delayed diagnosis and treatment, often putting the person with AD at more risk. An early diagnosis by a board-certified neurologist specializing in AD can result in Mom receiving medications that may help slow the progression of the disease. Treatment at an early stage gives Mom the potential to retain a higher functioning level for a longer period of time.

Short-Term Memory Loss, Confusion, Focus

☐ My parent is beginning to forget recent experiences such as appointments made yesterday or last week.

☐ She has trouble with new experiences such as a new telephone number or area code, or meeting someone new.

☐ My parent sometimes has trouble finding familiar places like her home or mine, the grocery store, and the doctor's office.

☐ My parent finds it difficult to follow sequential directions like recipes, projects, or greetings such as "come in, take your coat off, sit down."

☐ My parent has a shorter attention span and sometimes finds it difficult to focus on specific tasks or finish activities.

Speech/Conversation

☐ My parent has had word-finding problems and has filled in the sentence with a nonrelated word or made-up words that sound like gibberish to cover the difficulty.

☐ My parent seems to be talking less. (This may help avoid having to find words or making another embarrassing mistake.)

Initiative/Self-Care

☐ My parent has difficulties with decisions on menus or selecting clothing to wear.

☐ My parent has begun to make inappropriate driving decisions.

☐ My parent has begun to make inappropriate financial decisions.

☐ My parent has lost interest in hobbies, friends, and other activities.

☐ My parent is not as well groomed as she used to be.

☐ My parent doesn't appear to bathe as often as she used to.

Personality/Mood Changes

☐ My parent has mood swings that he didn't have before AD.

☐ My parent makes excuses to avoid friends and family.

☐ My parent has become depressed.

☐ My parent has experienced a reversal in personalities from kind to nasty, outgoing to reclusive, gentle to sharp tongued, or other obvious and significant changes.

CHANGES COMMONLY EXPERIENCED IN STAGE II

Memory and cognitive ability continue to deteriorate in Stage II, which make supervision and assistance a primary need. Preparations for this stage include considerations for twenty-four-hour assistance, transportation, housing, financial and legal matters, and long-term care.

Medical assistance and caregiver respite are mandatory for your parent's safety and yours, and to control your quality of life.

Increased Confusion

☐ My parent has difficulty remembering to lock the door.

☐ My parent cannot remember how to call me if she needs help.

☐ My parent cannot formulate complete thoughts and sentences.

☐ My parent cannot read.

☐ My parent may mix up identities or forget names and identities (daughter, son, grandchild, friends, and deceased relatives).

☐ My parent doesn't recognize or remember the use of objects like a chair or a bed.

☐ My parent shows frustration at not being able to understand or at not being understood.

Speech/Actions

☐ My parent repeats questions or statements many times.

☐ My parent makes repetitive motions.

☐ My parent paces in circles or wanders from room to room.

☐ My parent often becomes unmanageable in the afternoons or evenings with verbal outbursts or physical activities such as masturbating or disrobing in public or running away.

☐ My parent makes up stories to fill in memory gaps.

Hygiene Changes

☐ My parent refuses to bathe or becomes fearful and agitated when we bathe her.

☐ My parent wants to wear the same clothing for extended periods of time without washing them.

☐ My parent is incontinent.

Sleep/Paranoia/Fear

☐ My parent sometimes or always sleeps during the day and stays awake at night.

☐ My parent has accused us of trying to kill her or of stealing her money.

☐ My parent is sometimes aggressive or combative and has tried to kick, hit, scratch, or bite other people.

Safety Risks

☐ My parent lives alone and gets lost when he goes outside his home.

☐ My parent no longer understands what poison is or does.

☐ My parent is unsure of himself on stairs or balconies.

☐ My parent's balance is off, and he is at risk for a trip or fall.

☐ My parent can no longer dial my number on the phone. (Try this test: hand your parent the telephone and say "Dial my number, Mom.")

☐ My parent could no longer evacuate in a fire.

☐ My parent could no longer remember how to call 911 in an emergency.

CHANGES COMMONLY EXPERIENCED IN STAGE III

Stage III is also known as "end-stage" Alzheimer's, because it signifies the final years of the disease. At the end of this stage, your parent will pass away. Assistance from a counselor at your local Alzheimer's organization and hospice, and a physician specializing in Alzheimer's disease and related dementias can help you and your parent enormously during this very difficult time.

Assistance

☐ My parent needs total assistance with feeding, transferring from bed to chair, eating, walking, and every activity of daily living.

☐ My parent has difficulty swallowing.

☐ My parent refuses to eat.

Memory

☐ My parent no longer recognizes himself or family members.

Speech

☐ My parent rarely or never communicates.

Body and Functions

☐ My parent sleeps most of the time.

☐ My parent has had a significant weight loss.

☐ My parent's skin bruises or tears easily.

☐ My parent is completely incontinent of bowel and bladder.

Alzheimer's can be a long-term disease. Look for additional information and assistance to help with your planning and caregiving needs in chapter 13, "Resources."

B. COPING WITH COGNITIVE CHANGES

Dear Eldercare 911,

I've read a bunch of books, but something was definitely left out of my Alzheimer's education. My wife and I have been caring for my dad since he was diagnosed with AD about five years ago. I thought we were managing okay, but lately our lives have been full of dread. It started last Christmas when my dad walked over and fondled my Uncle Ralph's penis. My uncle yelled, "Harry, what the hell's wrong with you?!" slapped Dad's hand, and walked right out the door! Then, during our anniversary party, Dad did it again to his other brother, Uncle Bob, who screamed, "Harry, are you c-cr-r-r-a-zy?! Get your hand off me!" and did exactly what Uncle Ralph had done before—steamed right out the door. Dad just kept saying, "But I love you. Why can't I hold you?" Now we're terrified he'll do it to someone else, so we don't ask people over and we don't take him anywhere, even out to the mall or dinner. I don't know what to think about my dad. Is there a sign we should be looking for to tip us off that he's going to do it again? Is he going to get worse? Am I next?

—Harry Jr., Michigan

Dear Harry,

Alzheimer's disease lowers inhibitions, both sexual and nonsexual. You don't tell us anything else about your father, but we'll guess that his confusion has progressed to the point where he regularly has difficulty making himself understood and often uses language and gestures that neither you nor your wife can decipher. If so, then your father may have been trying to use his limited capabilities to tell his brothers that he loved them the only way he had left—by holding or touching them. In your father's perspective, he was acting appropriately and without sexual thoughts.

If your father touches you or anyone else inappropriately again, don't overreact. Gently remove your father's hand while touching him back in a nonsexual manner on the arm or shoulder. Talk to him in a soothing voice. You can say "I love you, too," or "Come look out the window with me," or "let's walk." Your goal is to distract him from what he was doing by gently redirecting his attention to something else. The incident should be over. But the original two are not. It's time to explain your father's actions to Uncles Harry and Bob and help them understand that people with Alzheimer's still have a great need to give and receive love and affection from their families and friends.

Dear Eldercare 911,

Can anything you read or hear ever really prepare you for the emotional reality of this monstrous disease? No one told me that eventually my mother might bite me when I insisted she take her sweater off. Or that she'd rip the checkbook from my hands while I'm writing a check and throw it across the room in anger. Or be overjoyed to "help" me open the mail, and then collapse in tears after the first letter or two. During these horrible moments there is absolutely no reasoning with her. I just try to keep us both safe. Ten minutes later, she looks at me with clear eyes and the smile of an angel. I know the illness causes all this, but these ups and downs are making me ill, too. Can't anyone do something to alleviate her pain and mine?

—Pauline, Toronto

Dear Pauline,

From the consistency of your mother's actions, she appears to be demonstrating her frustration with her declining ability to function—in these instances, to write her own checks and to open her own mail. She wants to take care of herself and may have enough cognitive function left to know that she can't and never will again. Her reactions to her continuing decline are actually quite logical and mirror the feelings we'd all have in those circumstances: a boiling over of rage and resentment, anger at her inability to function, and anger at the person who can still complete tasks that she can no longer handle. The smile "a few minutes later" may be her only way of letting you know that she's sorry, or more likely may signal that she's forgotten the entire incident.

Aggressive or combative outbursts are a red flag to see your parent's physician for medical attention to help rule out causes other than AD (two common examples are adverse drug reactions and urinary tract infections, however there are many others), or to help temper your mother's behavior through medical intervention. It's also in your best interest to learn the cause of the outburst and distraction techniques to help dissipate it quickly and soften its impact on both of you. Yelling or arguing with your mother is useless: she has no control over her actions. *Alzheimer's is in command.*

For distraction, try turning on soothing music or tunes from her past, perhaps the 1930s or 1940s. If she always attended religious services, try singing or playing hymns that she used to love. Parts of her long-term memory may allow her to recognize and react positively to the music. If she likes to dance or sway to music, then slowly start swaying and moving to the music in the hope that she will join you. You can also try pointing to the window and saying "Look, Mom, . . ." and mentioning something to see outside. If your mom likes to have her hair brushed, bring out her hairbrush. If it's necessary to avoid serious injury, leave the room, but make sure Mom is safe before you leave. You have every chance that if you return in a minute or two, your mother will have forgotten the whole incident.

After a bad incident, try to remember what triggered the outburst. Then try to eliminate future problems by removing the cause from your environment. You may have to repeat this scenario with many different real or potential triggers, but it's certainly worth the effort. Use these examples to begin your detective work.

- Was your parent trying to communicate with body actions? Was she swaying back and forth and holding herself near her pubic area? Perhaps she had to go to the bathroom and didn't know how to tell you.
- Did someone startle or frighten her by approaching her from behind?

Remember to remind people to walk around in front so that your mother can see them before they speak to her or touch her.

- Did she hear a whistle or another loud noise that frightened her? Sirens and violence often frighten people with AD, so avoid watching violent or disruptive TV programs when your parent is in the room.
- Was she frustrated because she tried to tie her shoe or button her clothing and could no longer manage the task? Try buying shoes and clothing with Velcro closures.

There are many communication and distraction techniques that will improve your quality of life. Networking with other caregivers can serve as a continuing education course. The more connected you *stay*, the more tools you'll acquire to help your parent and yourself. Ask your local Alzheimer's organization for help or for a support group to help you master additional techniques.

Coping with Cognitive Changes

Some professionals believe trying to cope with cognitive changes may produce some of the most exhausting, frustrating experiences that family caregivers encounter as AD passes through its three stages.

The list of debilitating effects caregivers suffer is long and painful to read: health problems include depression, isolation, anger, sleeplessness, headaches, stomach aches, anxiety, fear, and more. Meanwhile, family relationships often suffer and husbands, wives, and children may become resentful or incommunicative. We can't stop your parents' cognitive decline, but we can offer coping strategies that may help reduce some of the debilitation and anxiety you feel. These suggestions are a good start, but be sure to check with your local Alzheimer's organization or the resources in chapter 13 for additional suggestions.

1. Provide a calm, soothing, safe space for your parent by reducing loud music and noise; remember to eliminate background noises while you and your parent are talking. These sounds or noises may distract or confuse your mother and make it more difficult or even impossible for her to concentrate on your conversation.
2. Create a memories box, a scrapbook, or a photo album of old photos and mementos that you and your parent can look at together. Reminding him of familiar faces and places may help calm him.

3. If your parent uses profanity or inappropriate sexual behavior, use gentle distractions to divert his attention, and then ease your own stress by "admitting and accepting": simply explain to those present that Alzheimer's is in control, not your parent.

4. Look for a daycare program that is suitable for your parent. The physical and mental stimulation and comfort of a controlled routine supervised by professionals may help him stay calmer and more manageable at home, and may help him sleep through the night. It will also provide a much-needed respite for the caregiver.

5. Finding simple activities that your parent can help you with or manage alone may help improve her self-esteem. Don't add stress by overreaching: folding two or three towels is enough for helping with the laundry; use place mats or napkins only for help with setting tables; and provide only one small flower pot with a small bag of soil for gardening assistance.

6. If your mother talks to dead friends and relatives, don't distress her by reminding her they are dead. Say something like "Aunt Helen was wonderful," then distract her and change her focus.

7. Help your parent remain calm by reducing clutter and avoiding hectic activities such as renovations or workout groups.

8. Be certain your parent is treated by a board-certified physician specializing in dementia. Don't be afraid to ask questions or to ask for assistance regarding behavior modification or medication reactions. An AD specialist will welcome your involvement.

9. Do not try to teach your parent a new activity or expect your parent to retain new experiences. For example, don't drop off a microwave oven if your parent has stopped eating or can't remember how to cook or use a regular oven. Take your parent out to dinner, but don't expect her to remember what she ate or the restaurant decor the next day.

10. Structure your parent's day with tasks and activities that focus on pleasure and enjoyment along with accomplishments. Examples include getting dressed, listening to music, and reminiscing with the memory box; eating lunch and playing cards or other games; getting dinner ready or watching a movie; getting ready for bed in the evening; and *conversation* throughout the day.

11. Visit restaurants and malls at off-peak hours to avoid crowds and noises that might upset your parent. Don't expect your parent to make choices or decisions from the menu; suggest "Mom, would you like me to order the roasted chicken for you?"

12. Do not lose your temper. Your parent is not trying to act difficult, and no amount of your yelling or anger will change the situation. *Alzheimer's is in control.*

13. Try to ask short, simple questions that can be answered by *yes* or *no* so your parent will not have to struggle for the correct words to form a sentence. Try to use the same words in the same order every time you ask the same question. Be concise. Too many added words or associated details may confuse your parent or cause him to focus on the wrong part of the message.

14. Ask one question or make one request at a time and wait patiently for your parent to comply. Then continue, always one request at a time. Avoid sequential directions such as "come in, take your coat off, and sit down." There are three requests or commands in that sentence, and your parent may not be able to remember them all. This will make it difficult or impossible for him to do as you ask, which will frustrate you both.

15. Avoid accidents and other problems by taking appropriate safety measures in your parent's home or your home. ("Basic Safety Measures for an AD Home" follows these coping tips.)

16. If your parent is in Stage III Alzheimer's, help yourself and him by consulting with your local Alzheimer's organizations and talking to his physician about assistance from hospice.

17. *Don't argue. Listen.* If your parent argues or doesn't respond to your requests, try to determine if your parent is upset or afraid or just doesn't understand what you want her to do. *Remember, your parent is not deliberately ignoring your request, Alzheimer's is.*

18. If you find yourself losing your temper often or becoming too frustrated to continue effective caregiving, immediately call your local Alzheimer's organization for respite help and other assistance.

19. Don't take your parent's words or actions personally. Your parent isn't deliberately trying to hurt you. Aggressive physical episodes and emotional outbursts are two of the symptoms associated with AD.

20. *Touch, hug, and kiss your parent and smile at her regularly.* These simple acts will help your parent feel wanted and safe. *People with Alzheimer's still need love.*

BASIC SAFETY MEASURES FOR AN AD HOME

As your parent progresses through the three stages of AD, it's important to change his environment to help keep him safe from harmful accidents. This beginning list will get you started. You can obtain a complete list of safety suggestions from your local Alzheimer's organization or online at many of the resources listed in chapter 13.

FALLS AND TRIPS

- Your parent's decreased awareness and other symptoms of AD put him at risk for trips and falls from scatter rugs and electrical cords in walking areas. Remove them.

- Professionally install grab bars in toilets, bathtubs, and showers to help your parent use them safely.

- Check your lamps for wattage tolerance, and whenever safe and possible provide more light: add night lights, more lamps, or change bulbs to a higher wattage. Avoid halogen lights.

- To help impaired senses and balance, make certain your chairs are heavy enough not to skid or tip backward when your parent sits down.

WANDERING

- Use safety gates for open walkways, stairs, patio doors, and pools.

- Raise the lock on outside doors or cover the inside doorknob with Velcro in the same color cloth as the wall to camouflage the door and prevent your parent from opening the door and wandering out alone while you are busy in another room. Do not put your parent at risk by using this technique to lock your parent in the home alone without supervision or the ability to evacuate in an emergency.

MEDICATIONS, HOUSEHOLD CHEMICALS, AND FIREARMS

- Store all medications out of reach in locked cabinets.

- Secure cleaning supplies, insect sprays, and other chemicals out of reach in locked cabinets.

- Secure firearms, knives, scissors, and tools out of reach in locked cabinets.

Ask your local Alzheimer's organization for information on a support group or find one on the Internet. Discussing your problems will help you acquire many of the different coping skills that Alzheimer caregivers need to help keep their lives on track.

C. FINDING RELIEF WITH HELP AND SERVICES

Dear Eldercare 911,

I love my parents, but I hate going to see them. My father has Alzheimer's disease and he mostly paces from room to room or snoozes off in his chair. My mother refuses to leave his side. She changes his diaper, cleans up his mess, feeds him, talks to him, helps him move around, and from the looks of her, she'll die before he does. I asked her doctor for help and he said he had recommended that she hire someone to help her, or that she talk to someone at the Alzheimer's Association, but that she wouldn't listen to him. He said there was nothing more he could do. They don't have a great deal of money, but I'm willing to chip in. Do I have to lose both my parents to this disease?

—Stan, Colorado

Dear Stan,

It sounds like convincing your mother to accept help will be difficult, but you're right to continue to try. Most professionals agree that full-time caregivers need respite, and those who have it are better caregivers in every way, including maintaining better emotional and physical health. To help your mother, you have to discover the root cause of her resistance. Are you sure your parents can afford to hire help even if you "chip in"? Don't rely on what your mother tells you; she may be too embarrassed to let you know they need assistance. You need firsthand knowledge of their finances. Is your mother so dedicated to your father that she feels it is her job, and hers alone, to care for him? Has she had experiences with hired caregivers that have left her less than satisfied or even frightened? Does she believe that she can provide better care for your father than anyone else? Are you sure your mother knows where to find help? Remember, what seems a logical and simple phone call away to you may seem beyond the strength of an elderly caregiver who is so overburdened that she would rather just plug on day after day than take on the difficult task of creating a care plan and managing the homecare worker.

- Start by visiting and talking quietly with your mother. Say, "Mom, you do such a wonderful job of caring for Dad, but I'm worried about you. I don't want to lose you to sickness, too."
- Ask her what her main resistance is to bringing in help. Listen carefully to her answer and *don't interrupt her*. Your rebuttal can wait. When she finishes telling you her *main* point, say "What else, Mom? What other problems do you see if we bring in help for you?"
- Use the information she gives you to form a response. Part of your response might be "Mom, if you really want to do this, then you've got to stay healthy. Because if you wear out or get sick, there is no one else. If we get even a little help for you, you'll be stronger for a longer period of time. How about trying help for just two afternoons each week?"
- Another approach is "Mom, I know Dad wouldn't want you to work like this. He loved you too much. So do I. So let's work together to get the best help we can. Even for just two afternoons a week. Please Mom, I'll help you. Can we try this together?"
- If she says no, then stop for the day and try again in a week or two. Hopefully, she will finally says yes. When she does, call the local Alzheimer's organization and ask a family counselor for help in finding assistance for two afternoons a week: look for respite care or a home-care worker or whatever services your mother agreed to try.

Eventually, ask the Alzheimer's organization or a private geriatric care manager to help assess all your parents' needs. The care manager's recommendations should help improve your parents' quality of life and also help access benefits and community services that your mother might not be aware of. Often the financial savings are significant. You can find a care manager and a local Alzheimer's organization in the resources in chapter 13.

Dear Eldercare 911,

I am a professional healthcare advocate with a story that your readers need to hear. Today I met a new client. This is the description I got from her children when they called for assistance:

We think Mom may need a little help. Probably just someone to come in and make dinner for her. Otherwise, she seems fine. She takes care of the house pretty well. She still drives. She's pretty much in control and her memory seems good. It's just her diet. When we talk to her about what she eats, she says "eggs." We asked about meat and vegetables and she said, "No, just eggs." We know she's depressed because Dad is in a nursing home in the end stages of Parkinson's disease. She should move to an assisted living community, but she refuses. She wants to stay home. She doesn't have much money and we can't afford to help much, but would you assess her needs and see if you can set up someone to cook for her—someone we can afford?

Here's what I found when I met her. The temperature was in the nineties for the fourth straight day (we live in the South) and the air-conditioning was off. I asked Mrs. P. if she was hot, she said "yes," but the air conditioner had been broken for a while and she'd called several times and no one came to fix it. Her TV didn't work. Same story: she wanted to watch TV and she'd called several times but no one came to fix it. There were piles of clothes on the floor, some clean, some dirty. The refrigerator was filled with decayed, smelly, moldy food. (We eventually took out several full bags.) I asked her if she was hungry, she said "not really." I said, "if you could eat anything you wanted right now, what would it be?" She smiled and answered, "turkey, gravy, and mashed potatoes." I convinced her to let me take her to lunch, and she ate her turkey and potatoes as though she hadn't eaten in days—which was partially true. After she ate, we talked. She cried when she told me about her husband and how sad and lonely she was. "This," she said, "is the nicest afternoon I've had in a long time." She admitted that she didn't drive too much anymore because she kept getting lost. Later, the TV repairman told me he'd been there several times, but Mrs. P. kept pushing the wrong buttons on the control. (I asked the man to make those buttons inoperative.) The A/C company said Mrs. P. had made two appointments but was never home when they got there—Mrs. P. didn't remember any of them.

We see this all the time. Adult children who are financially unable to afford help for their parents often deny the need because they don't know where to find assistance. I feel certain that eventually Mrs. P. would have joined her husband in the nursing home because she appeared to be unable to care for herself, when the reality is that she may be confused due to nutritional problems or isolation and depression. I'm not blaming the family. They are under enormous pressure and assume there is no way out. They may be right, but I thought you'd like to let them know that there are a number of places they can call for help before they give up.

—Healthcare Advocate, Alabama

Dear Healthcare Advocate,

Thank you. Read on.

Dear Caregivers,

Your family and thousands of others share the same fears and frustrations. You know your parents need help, and neither you nor your parents can afford the fees. You may have tried to obtain help from community services without success or simply not known where to call for assistance. As our parents' lives expand, they require more assistance. Because of this and budget constraints, the waiting lists for community services in many areas grow longer each year. But there is hope. Try the steps below. If you don't find help on your original contact, *don't give up.* Before you end the call, ask your contact for a referral, by name, to another source. When you call the referral, remember to say, "Marie Jones at the Alzheimer's Association gave me your name because she thought you might be able to help me." In some cases, that simple sentence will help you begin a dialogue that may set you apart from other callers.

1. Your first call should be to the nearest Alzheimer's organization or the Area Agency on Aging nearest you to make an appointment to speak with a counselor. These organizations specialize in helping caregivers find assistance and respite care. They usually have access to services with a sliding scale fee structure that is *based on your parent's ability to pay.* There is no cost for speaking with the counselor, and if you can't leave your mother at home, the counselor may come to you. There are two huge benefits to making this contact:
   - Caregivers are frequently too overwhelmed to thoroughly consider their options. Ask the counselor to help you determine *what kind of assistance* would be most helpful to you and your parent. Often, one of the major obstacles to obtaining help is a lack of clarity on what type of help would be most effective. Depending on your parent's needs and cognitive abilities, you may discuss either a companion/sitter or a home health aide, transportation to and from physicians' appointments, daycare, meal preparation, or other similar assistance. Alternatively, the counselor may help you realize that your parent needs more services than he can reasonably expect from the community organizations if he remains at home and may help you find an affordable alternative for him.

- Second, most of those organizations have dedicated AD caregiver support groups and ongoing caregiver education; some have on-site daycare for your parent while you're attending the meeting. Again, there is usually a sliding scale fee based on your parent's ability to pay. No matter how much you think you know, you *owe it to yourself and your parent to take advantage of this offering*. Both of your lives will measurably improve because you will learn about resources, coping skills, and caregiving techniques from caregivers, many of whom have tested them with their own parents.

2. Ask the Alzheimer's organization or the Area Agency on Aging for a referral to an elder law attorney *who you can afford*. You can also use the Internet to locate an elder law attorney near you by logging on to the Web site for the National Association of Elder Law Attorneys (www .naela.com). Elder law attorneys are trained to help clients with the legal and financial planning necessary for long-term care that is hampered by deteriorating assets. For example, your parent may be eligible for state or federal government benefits that you might not be familiar with. You may also need to take specific steps to protect your assets. It's always best to use an attorney in the state your parent lives in because many benefits are governed by complicated state laws and you'd want your attorney to be an expert in her state's regulations and requirements.

These two calls should start you on the road to finding relief. Remember that it took a while for your situation to get this difficult, so try to be patient as you begin creating your plan.

D. TAKING CARE OF YOURSELF

Dear Eldercare 911,

When my head begins pounding, I start wondering if I have a brain tumor. The good news is that thought doesn't really add much more stress. I'm already so totaled out from caring for my mom and trying to keep my job that I hardly ever have time to finish a whole thought about "me," so I feel as though "taking care of me" really isn't an option anymore. I have a huge family, but they're no help. One brother sends money, but that's it. My other brothers do nothing, and my sisters live too far away to help.

—Carmen, New York

Dear Carmen,

You sound like you've tried to find time for yourself before and it didn't work out. But if you're reading this chapter, you're signaling your desire to try again. Why put it off? We know you have time for this much: *Stop and take the time right now* to take in a deep breath through your nose, hold it for a few seconds, and then *slowly* exhale through your mouth. Repeat your deep breathing twice more. Now, let's go forward and take the next step toward improving your quality of life.

Think back. Do you recall the date that you promised to forsake all others for your parent? To not spend any more time with your friends? To jeopardize your own health? It's probably difficult to remember the exact moment you made those pledges because you almost certainly *never agreed* to any of those conditions!

Let's work on the premise that *whether you became a caregiver by accident or choice, you didn't agree to care for your parent in lieu of caring for yourself.* With that in mind, let's try to create a strategy for you to use every day to help you care as much about yourself as you do for your mother. This strategy is only "what" to do. After you check off your agreement to the different parts of this strategy, read the answer to the next question for step-by-step instructions on "how" to make your new life a reality.

Until this new strategy replaces your old habits, you may need support. Make a copy of your personal *caring for myself* affirmations to carry with you and use it to help you stand firm as you rebuild your life.

My Caring for Myself Strategy

The most effective way to benefit from these affirmations is to read them out loud each morning or every time you feel the need for support—perhaps before a family meeting or during extremely stressful moments. The sound of your own voice reaffirming your worth and importance as a person is an extremely powerful tool for reclaiming your life.

☐ I will make it a point to find time for myself every day. I will start with only ten or fifteen minutes each day and try to increase that time as I go along. I can do this because I believe that I am as important as everyone else in this house.

☐ I will relearn how to say *No*. I can do this because my "needs" and safety are as important as my parent's. I've thought deeply about this and I see now that after my family's safety is assured, other things (their "wants") can wait until I've taken care of my health and safety.

☐ I will ask for help to ease my frustration and burden. I will do this because I have decided to continue my job as caregiver for as long as I want to, but I resolve not to do it alone. I will call the nearest Alzheimer's organization to help me find physical, practical, and emotional support.

☐ I will reconnect with one or more friends. I will do this because I realize that I didn't agree to cancel my life to care for my parent.

☐ I will make a primary care doctor appointment today and follow through with the physician's instructions. I will do this to stay emotionally and physically strong. I want to enjoy the quality of life that I'm about to restore.

Dear Eldercare 911,

I love my parents, but I've had enough! I was reunited with a high school friend on the Internet and we were catching up on our lives via e-mail. When I started to describe my life, I freaked out. I don't have one! Just to get a grip on myself and reassure myself that I was still the attractive, interesting, vibrant woman that I remembered, I went and looked in my bathroom mirror. For the first time, I saw what my friend would see. Oh, my God! The picture staring back was definitely me; it's just that I don't want to be this "me" anymore. The woman in the mirror is a pitiful mess—she and I know she's only 63, but she looks more like 163! I can reconstruct how I got here, but what I don't know is how to get out of this hole! I never saw "me" this way before because it never mattered. I never get dressed up or go anywhere. I guess I'm asking you how I can bring myself back. How do I get rid of "I have to get them..." or "You promised you would ..."? I'm caring for an eighty-five-year-old mother with First-Stage Alzheimer's and an eighty-seven-year-old father with diabetes and a number of other problems. How am I going to get through this and have a life before I need a caregiver for myself?

—Linda, Indiana

Dear Linda,

We don't doubt that handling all the needs of two ill parents overwhelmed you enough to cause you to finally quit trying to care for yourself! We applaud both your spirit for wanting to reclaim your life and your dedication to your parents, but we agree with you. It's time to repair the damage. Let's start with a little reorientation.

The first step in your recovery is the absolute recognition that *caregiving is a job*. As such, you are entitled to some time off. (The labor laws of this country mandate time off for all workers.) If you called a professional home-care agency and asked for one person to live in your home and care for both your parents twenty-four hours each day, with no time off, the agency would refuse. The agency would tell you that the *job* requires at least two people. Each of them would need eight hours each day for sleep or respite and one or more days off each week to keep them mentally and physically healthy enough to provide optimum care. We can hear you laughing, but we hope you're beginning to get the idea.

To find help that you can afford, read topic C in this chapter, "Finding Relief with Help and Services." To get yourself ready to accept and benefit from help, use the STOP technique to help you set realistic goals: *Step Back, Think, Organize*, and *Proceed*. For example, caregivers often come to believe that their way is the *only* way, or that no one can care for their parents as well as they do, or that everything has to continue to be done *exactly* as they have done it. This is a recipe for failure. Your help should be competent, experienced, communicative, and compassionately attentive to your parents. After that, it's time for a little realism. You must acknowledge that at times something may not get done or someone's dinner may be twenty minutes late. When that happens, *Step Back* and review the issue: *Think* about the damage you perceive, and then decide if your parent's safety has been compromised. In other words, was a significant need ignored or did your parent have to readjust to something a bit aggravating but basically minor? *Think* about the merits of regaining your life as weighed against dinner at 6:00 PM on the dot because "that's the way it's always been." Then *Organize* your thoughts and prioritize your actions to deal with your parent's objections or consult with your helper about the problem. Now you're ready to *Proceed* to resolve the issue. You'll find that once you *Step Back* and look at the problems realistically, many will resolve themselves.

STOP

1. *STEP BACK* 2. *THINK*
3. *ORGANIZE* 4. *PROCEED*

1. STEP BACK

    a. Acknowledge reality: *caregiving is a job.*
    b. Set realistic goals: accept the fact that at times someone or something will not receive immediate care or attention.
    c. Learn to recognize the people who manipulate you and the times you act out of anger, frustration, or guilt.

2. THINK

    a. Begin to regain control by stepping back and assessing your immediate wants and needs.
    b. When your path is unclear, ask questions. You cannot identify priorities unless you have enough information to make informed decisions.
    c. Use your natural body rhythms to your advantage. Make difficult decisions at your peak time of day.
    d. Don't "shoulda, woulda, coulda" yourself after the fact. Once you've done your best, believe your best is good enough. If you've made a mistake, learn from it and move on to your next priority.

---

3. ORGANIZE

    a. Grab a pad and pencil. Use a separate page for each of these headings: Today, Tomorrow, This Week, and Next Week.

    b. Now, create your to do lists. What do you have to do today? Tomorrow? Next Week?

4. PROCEED

    a. Focus only on what you have to accomplish today and tackle your list one item at a time.

    b. At the end of the day, take a moment to review what you've done. If you haven't completed all today's tasks, reschedule them for tomorrow or later in the week. If you are a "planner," review tomorrow's tasks, but don't take action.

    c. Leaving items on the rest of your list until the time you've scheduled them for may help you find time to spend on yourself!

As of this writing, there is still no cure for Alzheimer's disease. When a "breakthrough" occurs, it may still take years for approval and testing before it reaches the general public.

One of the reasons Alzheimer's continues to plague us is because it has always existed in the shadows. Families may not have been as open about or may have been ashamed of grandparents who "acted strangely." Most were reluctant to admit that someone in their family talked to dead people or wandered naked around the house. Others believed AD was a "judgment and punishment" for prior sins. With all this denial and secrecy, it's easy to understand why in past decades there was little or no research and even less funding to find a cure.

But we have found our voices. Alzheimer's is now a very public issue with a megaspotlight shining on it day and night. And, for the first time since Dr. Alois Alzheimer discovered the disease in 1906, *there is hope. You are no longer alone.*

9

BREAKING AWAY FROM BURNOUT

A. CHECK YOUR BURNOUT QUOTIENT

Dear Eldercare 911,

I am an elder abuse prosecutor. I see the horrible things that happen to old and frail people at the hands of family members and professional caregivers. But my anger at my father grew and grew because he could not admit that Mom was suffering from dementia. She was confused and it was difficult for her to communicate. I told Dad over and over that he needed help in the house to take care of her. Over time Mom appeared very thin and poorly groomed. One day when I was visiting Mom, I noticed a huge, bloody abrasion on her arm. To me it could be an innocent bruise or one that is consistent with abuse. Dad said he did not know what happened. I was really angry because he did not want to take her to the doctor. I insisted. As the doctor examined Mom, I knew he thought Dad did it to her, but I knew in my heart that he didn't. The doctor admitted Mom to the hospital and Dad left us alone. He was a very angry man. I felt abandoned, lonely, and scared. I was exhausted and burned-out, but I continued to make myself available for three years. I called every day to check on both of them. I wanted Mom to hear my voice. I didn't want her to forget me. Day after day I tried so hard to convince Dad that he needed help. Finally, I told him that if he didn't get help in the house, I would report him to social services. For so long he didn't listen to me, then he did. I was exhausted not only because he was so resistant, but because of my job I am supposed to know what elderly people need to stay safe. It was so hard for me for such a long time.

—Carol, Minnesota

Dear Caregivers,

Carol is not alone. Her eventual success is a tribute to her fortitude, caring, and persistence. But what is the cost to her physical and emotional health? Many strong, educated people find themselves so stretched and strained by their sense of responsibility that they feel overwhelmed and frustrated at the very least some time during their caregiving experience. Some of you describe yourselves as self-assured and in control, the one person everyone in the family depends on—the rock. But what if you begin to lose control? What if you feel like everything is falling apart? How can you protect yourself from caregiver burnout?

Read the following questions and think about your answers before you respond. There are no right or wrong answers and no one is going to grade your paper. This is tool for you to take a look at yourself from a different perspective. Your individual responses will give you a picture of how you think and feel about your caregiver responsibilities and how they are affecting you. Burnout is not a permanent condition. It is actually quite treatable, and more important it is avoidable. Remember, this is just a personal guideline to help you measure your own "Burnout Quotient."

Burnout Quotient Quiz

1. Do I ask for and/or get help with my caregiver duties?
2. Do I know and understand what is worth fighting for and what I have to let go?
3. Do I ever take time-out for myself?
4. Do I say *yes* to everyone else's needs and *no* to my own needs?
5. Can I set limits with family and friends who may demand a great deal of my time and energy?
6. Am I experiencing stomach aches, headaches, or other physical problems? Do I laugh less and cry more? Is it harder for me to cope with my family and job?
7. Do I feel angry and frustrated with my loved one because of my role as a caregiver?
8. Do I ever give myself credit for all my accomplishments?
9. Do I ever take a step back and reevaluate my situation and see how I can make it better?
10. Am I ready to step forward and make a positive change in my life?

How did you respond?

1. If you don't ask for help, it is likely that you are doing too much and you don't have any time for yourself. You may feel that if you ask for help you are acting weak or incapable of doing your job. The truth is that it takes courage and strength to admit you need help. If you answered "no," you are taking a first step toward helping yourself cope with your role as a caregiver.

2. If you feel that you understand which battles are important, you are probably able to prioritize your responsibilities. This approach can help you save time and energy. If you answered "no," you are probably exhausted. No one can fight every little battle and still have physical, emotional, or psychological energy left.

3. If you take time out for yourself, you are way ahead of millions of caregivers. Congratulations! Burnout can often be avoided when caregivers take time out to play and think. If you said "no," then you are probably feeling isolated and deprived. This is not a healthy state of mind or body. It is time to put yourself at the top of your priority list.

4. If you say "yes" to everyone else's needs and "no" to your own you may become resentful of your parents and family. Reviewing chapter 2, "Saying *No* to Toxic People," will help you understand that saying "yes" all the time is not in your best interest. If you said "no," you are a true champ, because so many caregivers find it easier to say "yes," in the short term but they do not benefit in the long term.

5. You are protecting yourself from burnout if you can cut a visit short with Dad because he becomes abusive, or you've asked your teenager to lower his stereo system so you can rest. If you said "no," you are probably ready to explode with anger and frustration and you are on the road to burning out very quickly.

6. If you have physical problems, anxiety, or depression, get help immediately from an appropriate healthcare professional. Even if your answer was "no" and you are feeling well, everyone needs and deserves a routine physical examination to maintain optimum good health.

7. If you often feel angry and frustrated, be aware of your temper and frustration level. At times a bad temper and loss of control may lead to abuse of a loved one. If you said "no," then think about the rest of your family. Even if you are able to keep your emotions in check with your parent, you may take your anger out on someone else, that

is, a spouse or a child. Before the problem escalates, contact your local social service agency or Area Agency on Aging for a referral.

8. Bravo, if you can give yourself credit for all the wonderful things you're accomplishing. If you answered "no," then it is about time you thought about all of the things you do for your loved ones and friends. Make a list of the outstanding things you've accomplished. Give yourself a hearty congratulations and a pat on the back. You deserve it.

9. You are very fortunate if you have the ability and insight to try to see things clearly and to know when they need to change. If you said "no," then you might want to stop and make a list of the things that you are doing. Ask yourself: What do I want to do? What do I actually need to do? Review the list and consider making some changes. Making any change in your life takes time and patience, but you can do it.

10. If you are ready to leave burnout behind and begin the process of recovery, take a step forward toward making a positive change in your life. Help yourself and the people you love. Talk to a counselor, a friend, or a clergyman about your situation. Work on a plan that gives you a new outlook, a new path to follow, and peace of mind. If you said "no," you still might want to talk to someone you trust. Reach out to someone who you believe has your best interest at heart.

No matter how you answered these questions, the fact that you took the time to read them and think about them is a start in the right direction. Burnout is not a given; it is a harsh reality in the lives of millions of you who care for an aging relative. Burnout does not have to be a permanent part of your life. It is avoidable. It is preventable.

B. GETTING HELP

Dear Eldercare 911,

I am a forty-six-year-old woman and I come from a very large, close family. My dad is ill and my mom is his primary caregiver. My parents are from another culture, and it is Mom's belief that you do not accept help from outsiders; therefore, she refuses any professional help in the house. One of my immediate problems is to get past her pride and get the help she needs. My parents are both in their seventies and Dad has been bed-bound for years. Because Mom was always busy with Dad, at an early age I experienced role reversal. I mothered my younger siblings and helped around the house. About a year ago I began to experience a change in my mom. She was always so loving and full of life, but suddenly she became someone else. I was losing the person I knew. She still doesn't sleep or eat properly and it is affecting her health. Her entire demeanor changed and she is always irritable and angry. I realized that after so many years as a caregiver she was burning out. I didn't know when or if her "light" would ever come back. I want my mom to have a life that is not completely defined by her role as a caregiver. I love my parents. How do I help Mom find her way back?

—Charlotte, Nebraska

Dear Charlotte,

As you describe your mother, we picture a woman filled with love and kindness. Unfortunately, years of self-neglect and self-deprivation can transform even the most loving person into someone who is angry and frustrated. Your close relationship with your parents and siblings is heart-warming, but you alone may not be able to help Mom redefine her thinking about getting help in the house. Your parents' cultural background also plays a strong role in her decision to do this alone. Breaking through this barrier will take understanding of your family's customs and beliefs.

Here are several ways for you to begin the process of helping your mom regain the "light" in her life.

- Arrange a family meeting as soon as possible. The power of a supportive family may help to convince your mom to get the help she needs before her own health completely deteriorates.
- Talk to Mom about making an appointment with her physician. Anyone who is deprived of adequate sleep and nutrition over a period of time is bound to experience some physical, emotional, and psychological problems. If possible, alert the physician to Mom's demanding caregiver responsibilities. This will provide him with an entree to speak to her about her present condition. Try saying: "Mom, you are amazing the way you take care of Dad, but we are worried about you. You work so hard and nothing stops you from helping him. We are afraid if you don't take care of yourself, your health will suffer and that will stop you. Then what? Please do us a favor and get a checkup." If your mom rejects the whole idea, let it go for now. Nagging at her will probably

not make her respond any more favorably. However, you have planted a seed in her mind about her present situation and that may just be enough of a catalyst to get her to see the doctor.

If she says "yes," then offer to help her make the appointment and go with her for the checkup. Your support will mean a great deal to her.

- Hire a geriatric care manager to assess your parents' situation and prepare a care plan with specific steps on how to help your mom. You can contact the National Association of Professional Geriatric Care Managers at www .caremanager.org for a referral in your mom's community. Once you have the names of the care managers, take the time to interview each one by telephone. You will want someone who is not only knowledgeable of community services but sensitive to the cultural barriers that may stand in Mom's way of getting the help she needs. Find out exactly when the geriatric care manager is available, the fees, and when you should expect a written report. Visit with Mom and talk to her about this person you found to help her. Explain to her that a consultation does not mean that she has to do anything other than listen. Assure her that you will be present at the consultation for support. If she rejects the idea, leave the information you gathered with her. Try again to approach the subject when the two of you are alone.

- Talk to your mom about hiring a home health aide. There are agencies that specialize in culturally sensitive home health aides who understand your Mom's native language, dietary likes and dislikes, and other special needs. Having someone in her home who she can relate to and who will provide this type of comfort level may add to her peace of mind.

Dear Eldercare 9 I I,

You will not believe my story, but it really happened. I am ready to throw in the towel, give up, and walk away. My eighty-one-year-old father is a character. From the time I was a young girl I remember Mom complaining about him. She always said he acted just like a little kid. Well you'd think by the time you hit eighty-one, you'd grow up. Well he hasn't, and I doubt that there is much of a chance he will change. Let me tell you about the latest insanity. He attends a senior center program three times a week two blocks from his house. Dad is very bright and alert, but he has difficulty walking without a cane or someone holding his arm. He reluctantly agreed to take the handicap van to the center. The rest of the time he manages pretty well. The van usually arrives thirty minutes before the program. On one particular day the van did not arrive on time, and for Dad that was a green light to walk the few blocks by himself. He would never think of missing the program or calling and asking about the van. As one of the staff members was exiting her car, she happened to look up the street. There he was walking in the middle of traffic! The poor woman raced up the block in order to lead him back onto the sidewalk and then she escorted him to the senior center program. Fortunately, he wasn't hurt, but I can't take it anymore. I am mentally burned out and emotionally exhausted. Please help me.

—Kathy, New Hampshire

Dear Kathy,

Your dad sounds like quite a character, but he requires an evaluation and supervision. You need a break from worrying about him. Although you describe him as "bright and alert," his behavior is not simply foolhardy but reckless and dangerous. Dad likely needs medical and psychiatric attention. You can get him the help he needs to remain safe in his home and take time out for yourself. You may be suffering from mental burnout. Unfortunately, it is sometimes more debilitating than physical burnout. Many caregivers find that they can't turn off their worries, not even when they try to sleep. You might want to begin turning this situation around by having a talk with your dad.

- Try this dialogue to get the conversation jump-started. "Dad, you are something else. I guess you really like the daycare program because you took quite a chance with your safety. I am really worried about you, but I have two things I need you to do for me. First, I want you to promise me that you will never do that again. Second, I want to get someone in the house to help you out. It would really give me peace of mind knowing you are well cared for. How about it?" Dad may sometimes act childlike, but he probably will not like the feeling that you are trying to take charge of his life. No matter how he responds, here are a few more suggestions to help you along the way.
- Arrange an appointment with a geriatric psychiatrist. Get a referral from your dad's physician, the daycare program staff, or the local hospital. It is important to have Dad's cognitive status evaluated so that you have a clearer picture of his abilities now and in the future.
- Talk to the staff at the daycare program. You have a built-in profes-

sional staff of geriatric specialists. Because they know your dad well and his idiosyncrasies, they can guide you regarding a homecare attendant and other preventative measures.

- Hire a home health aide through a licensed, bonded homecare agency. The daycare program staff, the nearest Area Agency on Aging, the local hospital, or Dad's medical doctor can make appropriate recommendations. Interview the home health aides without your dad present. Be prepared with questions regarding their experiences with male patients. Give them the specifics about your dad and how important it is for him to continue to attend the daycare program. Make sure to check the home health aides' references.

- Choose two or three home health aides that you like and then arrange for a time for you, Dad, and the aides to meet. This will give him an opportunity to be an active participant in the decision-making process. Observe the interactions between Dad and each aide. Does he appear comfortable with her? Is she empathetic and caring? When she leaves, talk to him about how he feels. If he appears even somewhat satisfied and you are comfortable with his choice, ask him to give it a try. You might want to start with four to six hours a day, five days each week, and then increase the hours as is needed. Dad may not be overly receptive, but you know this is the best way to keep him safe and in his own home.

Kathy, worrying about your dad is mentally exhausting and will take its toll on your physical health and well-being. As you help your dad to remain safe and sound in his home, you need to think about your needs as well. Try to be as honest with yourself as you can. You don't have to make drastic changes or do everything at once. You are in control. Begin by taking one small step at a time. Soon you will feel better, and your quality of life should improve.

C. REBUILDING YOUR QUALITY OF LIFE

Dear Eldercare 911,

I have devoted the past five years to my ninety-year-old mother. To this day she is sharp and alert, and only recently she has had some serious physical complications. She fell in the house and fractured her hip. The surgery was successful but she did not do well in the rehabilitation center, and she is now in a nursing home. My problem is that I am an only child and I did everything for Mom. I took care of her finances, shopping, and social engagements. She always expected more and often manipulated me into getting it for her. For example, one day after a six-hour visit she began to cry when I was getting ready to leave and go to my home. At the time I knew what she was trying to do, but I also knew that she was safe. So I left the house. As I approached the top step of the front porch, I heard her crying. I opened the door only to find her standing there with a smirk on her face. She said to me, "I want you to stay and never leave me." This story is only one of many that highlight her ability to get to me at any time. But that was then and this is now. She is in a nursing home and my day-to-day involvement is different. I don't have as much to do for her and I am grateful. But I am exhausted, and after five years of taking care of her, I am not just feeling burned out, I feel barbecued. I want to regain the pieces of my life that were lost for so many years. Can you help?

—Melanie, Ohio

Dear Melanie,

Wow! You are amazing. Experiencing your mother's manipulative behavior for so long is not only exhausting but depressing, yet you seem to have the foresight to see that there is a better life ahead. You recognize that you are still involved in Mom's life, but the extent of your involvement is somewhat limited since she is in a skilled nursing facility. Regaining the pieces of your life that you lost during the past five years will take some effort on your part. Often when a conscientious caregiver loses some or all of her caregiver responsibilities, she struggles to fill the void, because the caregiver role often consumes so much time. Try some of these ideas to help you maintain the appropriate contact with Mom and the nursing home staff. Several suggestions will help you to refill your time with activities that bring you peace and pleasure.

- Visiting Mom on a regular basis will help you maintain contact with the staff as well as check on her status. Schedule your visits at times that are convenient for you like a Wednesday morning or a Sunday at lunch hour. Try to alternate the times you visit in order to meet with different staff members and to see Mom at different times of the day. Visiting at mealtime or during an activity will provide you with important information regarding her status and condition.
- Try to attend team meetings at the nursing home. Family members are usually asked to join the meeting a few times each year. Team meetings are comprised of various staff members such as physicians, nurses,

physical and recreational therapists, and social workers. At this time you will get to know the staff and their plans for your mom's care, and they will get to know you.

- Be an advocate for your mom when it is necessary. If you observe or hear something that makes you uncomfortable, or Mom complains about a particular person, listen to what she has to say and meet with the appropriate staff member. For example, if she complains about a particular attendant, you might want to have a private conversation with that person. Try to begin your conversation with something positive and nonaccusatory. Discuss Mom's complaints with her and ask her to try to make the appropriate changes. If Mom continues to complain and you don't see any improvement, request a meeting with the attendant's supervisor and so on until you have the appropriate results.

- Think about what you want and need to do to take care of yourself. Make a list of the things you have not done for a long time. The list can include something uncomplicated like reading a book or something more involved like taking a long-overdue vacation. As one caregiver said after she found a homecare worker for her father: "I finally never have to postpone a vacation or reschedule a doctor's appointment. They call to schedule something and I say that I am available anytime. I used to only dream about my dreams, now I fulfill them. I finally feel free to do what I want. I feel well again." It's your turn to feel well cared for again.

- Renew relationships with old friends and family members whom you lost contact with because you were always so busy. Sometimes people want to contact you or include you in a social activity but they feel uncomfortable "bothering you" when you are occupied all the time with other responsibilities. By reaching out to them you are opening the door to be included once again. You will be surprised at how many people will be happy to hear from you after such a long time. Plan a small dinner party for a few friends to let them know that you are available and ready to socialize.

- Relax, relax, relax. Try to remember a time when your body did not feel so tense and your spirits were high. Join an exercise, meditation, or yoga class to renew your physical and emotional strength and stamina. See the resource section of this book (chapter 13) for appropriate Web sites on women's issues.

Dear Eldercare 911,

Everywhere I look I see clothes, bedpans, walkers, wheelchairs, and diapers. Mom lived with us for over ten years, and I was her only caregiver. She was physically sick and bed-bound for the past three years. Each year the situation was more hopeless and I just kept on going. In retrospect I remember reading an article on caregiver burnout, but I was too involved to pay attention. Mom died eight months ago. The remnants of the last decade of her life are piled in a room that was once my sewing room, then her bedroom. It is so difficult for me to throw these things away because someone can certainly use them. The walker and wheelchair are in wonderful condition, and I have dozens of adult diapers in unopened packages. I want my room back, but I don't know where to begin and how to decide what to do with the room. This may seem like a simple job, just throw the stuff out and start again, but starting again is not so easy after ten long years. I feel stuck. Help me find a way to start fresh and maybe in the process help someone else.

—Susan, Washington

Dear Susan,

For ten years you have invested a great deal of time and energy in your mother's care. Coping with the loss of your mother and your role as caregiver is a difficult process. This may take some time, and you may want to reach out for help from a bereavement counselor or group to help you through the stress and pain. Ask for a referral from your physician, local hospital, church, or synagogue. Your mom's room may have been her world for ten years, but as a caregiver it was also your world. The door to that room is not only a wooden object, but now that she is gone it is the door that you can open to a new room full of new opportunities. Try this four-step action plan to help you rebuild not only your room, but also your quality of life.

1. Contact your local hospital, the nearest Area Agency on Aging, or a charitable organization of your choice to discuss your options for contributing many of the assistive devices, clothes, and other homecare aids. Clothing items that are in good condition, wheelchairs, walkers, and boxed adult diapers are often items that are welcomed and accepted by charitable groups. By giving away these items, you are helping yourself accept the process of letting go. It is an added bonus knowing that a less fortunate person will use Mom's things.

2. Select any pictures or personal belongings you want to keep for yourself. Then share pictures or other mementos with family members. This is not only a way of distributing your mother's belongings, but it gives other people a concrete way to remember her. Sally from Utah said that her parents had lovely family portraits in their hallway, but after they died no one wanted them. She decided to auction off the pictures and give the proceeds to her parents' favorite charity. There are many ways to dispose of a loved ones belongings. It is important for you to feel comfortable and good about what you are doing. Take all the time you need to handle the situation the best that you can.

3. Look with a new eye at the room that served as a sewing room and a hospital room for ten years. What do you see? Do you see a den with a comfortable couch and a big screen television? Or do you see a library with lots of books and special reading lamps? Maybe you see a quiet sitting room or an exercise area. The options are endless and limited only by your imagination. The most important thing is to take back this space and make it your own. A caregiver of thirty years said, "When I finally finished my room, it became my sanctuary. I do everything in there, read, pay bills, and look at beautiful magazines. The world revolves around me and I am safe in my room." Decide what you want and then take the next steps to make it happen.

4. Visualize what you want in the room and then make a list of the things that you will need for the transformation. Decide on a budget and then do a little leg work to find just the right stores to buy what you want. For example, if you want to make your room into a tranquil sitting room, you may want to select colors that are serene and calm, such as light blue or coral. Purchase furniture that has an outdoor feel such as a light color wicker with floral cushions. If you want to create a library, you may select deeper colors like burgundy or hunter green. The choices are endless, and the possibilities are enormous. Enjoy your ability to create a space that is just for you.

Complete your project at your own pace. You can always add little personal touches as you go along. The process of creating a new space has many implications. It is the end of one phase of your life and the beginning of something new. Once the room is ready, place a ribbon across the door, and before you enter ceremoniously cut the ribbon. Enter your room with renewed hope and uplifting expectations for the future.

Thirteen Ways to Reduce Your Burnout Quotient

These supportive statements will help you reduce your burnout quotient. Begin each statement with I will:

Request the help I need from my family and friends.

Enhance my life by taking time out for myself every day.

Decide which battles are important to me and which ones I can let go.

Use my common sense to help make appropriate decisions for my family and me.

Conquer day-to-day problems by tackling things one at a time.

Enhance my quality of life by being as kind to myself as I am to my loved ones.

Believe in myself every day the way others believe in me.

Uplift my spirits by listening to music, reading a magazine, or taking a walk in the park.

Remember to get a routine medical examination to insure my good health.

Nourish my body, mind, and spirit to help me maintain the balance in my life.

Often take the time to pat myself on the back for all my accomplishments.

Utilize my numerous strengths to help me face my caregiver responsibilities.

Trust myself because I am doing the best job that I can for the people I love.

Read these statements out loud, silently, or share them with a friend. Choose one idea at a time, or as many as you feel comfortable with, to enhance your quality of life.

10

LESSONS IN FEELING GOOD ABOUT YOURSELF

Dear Eldercare 911,

So many times I think enough is enough, when will it be my turn? I look around and see my demented seventy-eight-year-old mother and my chronically ill seventy-nine-year-old father and I know it may not end for years. I feel trapped, with no escape in sight. Will I ever feel cared for again? Please help me.

—Miranda, Vermont

Dear Miranda,

The idea that you can be a caregiver and still feel "cared for" must seem incongruous. You may feel that you are not entitled to feel good when your family members feel so bad. You may not see an end in sight, which can take a toll on your body and your mind. Unfortunately, the reality of the burden of caregiving combined with many deep emotional feelings often results in healthy caregivers becoming chronically ill patients themselves developing headaches, stomach aches, backaches, and emotional problems.

The road to taking control of your life and feeling good again starts with a willingness to accept the fact that not every day will be everything you hoped for and some days will be better than you ever expected. Being prepared for the ups and downs and the highs and lows of caregiving will help you navigate this "journey." As Janet from Iowa said: "It took me a long time to accept the unexpected. When I first began on this journey, I answered each and every phone call with trepidation, always feeling that something was wrong. After two decades of caring for parents, an aunt, and an uncle, I realized that I can't anticipate the bad news. I have to assume that everyone is OK until I hear differently. That's how I go about my life, that's how I feel good."

Although caregivers share many of the same experiences, you must search for the things that in particular make you feel good. Read on for the many thoughts and ideas of your fellow caregivers that may help you on your personal journey.

A. TIME OUT

Dear Eldercare 911,

I am a very guilt-ridden man. I never intentionally hurt anyone, I pay my taxes, and I always wait for the light to turn green. My guilt stems from my relationship with my father. Dad was never very nice to me; you might even say he was very cruel. He only hit me once when I talked back to my mom, but he always said very hurtful things. I really never liked him. Mom died a few years ago and Dad lives in an assisted living facility in our hometown. He was weak after a car accident, and at eighty-two years old he is very forgetful. He seems to be well cared for at the facility, and I try to visit him when I can. That's part of my dilemma. I have two homes, one a few miles from the facility and one in the south. I like my home down south because I enjoy the warm weather all year round. But I think what I like the best is the fact that I am away from Dad. I am at peace with myself when I know he is not nearby. On the other hand, I feel so guilty because when I am not there, no one else is visiting him. After all, he is my dad. Can you help me?

—Traveling Son, Michigan

Dear Traveling Son,

Everyone is entitled to time off from caregiver responsibilities. It sounds like your second home is a place you enjoy and gives you some peace of mind. Or does it? In order truly to enjoy your time away from your caregiver duties, you have to come to terms with your situation. Your ill feelings toward your dad are compounded by the fact that you seem to feel guilty since there is no one else to visit him. There are several options to fill the visiting gap when you are not there. Because you said that your relationship with your dad has always been poor, you may find some relief from your emotional struggles by speaking to a therapist who specializes in family problems. Here are a few additional steps to help you on the way.

- Make an appointment with the social worker at the facility to discuss your feelings and what you can do to ease your mind. She can also assist you with many of the concrete problems you are facing. Ask her if she can recommend a not-for-profit agency that provides services for free or a sliding scale fee based on an individual's income. Some agencies can provide a "friendly visitor" to visit your dad at the facility. A friendly visitor is someone who visits the elderly who are homebound, in assisted living facilities, or in nursing homes.

- Contact your dad's church or synagogue. Many clergy are happy to visit their parishioners on a regular basis. A caregiver from California shared her story: "When Mom was in a nursing home, her priest visited once a week. Because they grew up in the same neighborhood, they had so much to talk about. My mom always said how much she looked forward to his visits."

- Hire a geriatric care manager to visit Dad as well as to handle any problems that arise when you are away. Prior to hiring a care manager, be clear on the fees, what you expect, and what she can provide. If Dad calls you to complain about the food or an aide at the facility, the geriatric care manager can meet with the appropriate staff members and report back to you. Decide in advance whether you expect written reports, telephone calls, or e-mail updates. See the resource section in this book (chapter 13) for more information about geriatric care managers.

Time away from your caregiver duties is very important to your well-being. Making the time is one thing, but enjoying the freedom is something else. Until you come to terms with your feelings and provide alternative visitors for Dad, it will be difficult for you to just sit back and enjoy yourself.

Dear Eldercare 911,

My husband doesn't like my family. I know that's not something new or earth-shattering, but it is a problem for us. He always tolerated everyone, but he says his tolerating days are over. We are both in our fifties and my father is in his mid-eighties. Dad had a few heart attacks, but he is still very independent. We live in beautiful Connecticut and Dad lives in a tropical location. When the summer comes, he wants to get out of the heat and stay with us. The problem is that for two consecutive summers he came to "visit," but he didn't leave for six months. I thought my husband was going to kill Dad and me. On top of that, my brother lives a few towns away from us, farther north, but he never offers to help out. Sure, he invited Dad for a day or two, but he quickly returned him to our home. I have to do something and fast. I don't know if our marriage can withstand another six-month "visit." How do I keep my hubby happy and not completely insult my dad?

—Visitor's Blues, Connecticut

Dear Visitor's Blues,

As caregiver responsibilities increase, there is a greater need to be clear on what it is you can and cannot do for your parent. Otherwise, a six-month visit may continue for another six months and another. Why does Dad feel a need to stay for three additional months if the hottest time of the year is June, July, and August? The answer to that question may help you with your next steps. If Dad is staying with you because he is too anxious to be alone, then it may be time to discuss housing alternatives. If he is staying because he is lonely and wants company, you don't have to be it, but you can help provide him with some options. The first thing to do is to have a talk with your dad. Because your husband is upset, we wouldn't include him in this first discussion. Try saying, "Dad, I'd like to talk to you about your visits. When you first asked if you could come up for the summer, we thought it would be fine, but your visits seem to be getting longer and longer. Is there something we can talk about? Is it hard for you to live alone anymore?" Wait until Dad responds. He may feel very uncomfortable and not say very much. If he says he really enjoys his home and independence, suggest that he visit for three months. Set the boundaries and stay firm. If Dad admits that he is lonely or afraid, then you can present him with the following options.

1. Talk to Dad about a roommate. Through his church or synagogue or the local senior center he may be able to find a compatible roommate to socialize with and to share the expenses.

2. Suggest to your dad that he may also find an appropriate companion through a licensed homecare agency. For an hourly fee the companion may visit him at home and accompany him to the movies or out to dinner.

3. Talk to Dad about moving to an assisted living facility. Discuss the option of remaining in his hometown or moving north closer to you. Explain to him that assisted living provides him freedom, independence, and socialization options within a safe and secure environment. If he appears interested, ask him to think about which location he prefers and then arrange a few tours of specific facilities.

4. Talk to Dad about moving into a studio apartment in a senior housing community. If he has the funds, he can maintain his home for vacations and live near you, but not with you. If this appeals to him, contact your local Area Agency on Aging for senior specific housing alternatives or check chapter 13 in this book for more information.

5. Talk to your brother about his role in helping out during the time Dad is with you. Ask him to invite your dad to visit for one week a month over the three months. If he is unwilling to commit to one week each month, ask him if he is willing to have Dad visit for two or three long weekends. This will provide you and your husband with some of the time-outs you need.

Dad may want to keep his options open for now and remain with you for three months at a time, but you can always present the alternative options in the future. Keep in touch with your brother and gently remind him about his role in your dad's life. Setting boundaries and expressing your needs will help you and your husband achieve a schedule that provides you with time-out from your caregiver responsibilities.

B. MENDING YOUR MIND

Dear Eldercare 911,

I tried very hard to keep my mom in her home. Although she was declining and she spent a big part of her day in bed, I wanted her to stay there for as long as possible. I felt that was her roots. I believed it was in her best interest to stay at home with an aide to provide the care that she needed. I struggled and I didn't give in to moving her to a nursing home until the aide actually said to me that she just couldn't handle Mom's care anymore. That's when I knew that Mom's Alzheimer's condition had deteriorated and she needed a different level of care. I moved her to a facility that had a very good reputation, and I know in my heart that they did everything they could to keep her clean, comfortable, and safe. But for me, the day I moved her was the day I lost her forever. She didn't seem to respond to me in the same way and she grew less and less communicative. The staff said it wasn't because she didn't love me or that she was angry at me for moving her. She was old, sick, and dying, and I just couldn't accept it. She lived for a few months, and that was two years ago. I am still holding on to the feeling that the day I moved her out of her house was the end of her life. Can you please help me find a way to come to terms with my feelings?

—Marie, Oregon

Dear Marie,

Your words, of having "lost her forever," are so powerful. Many caregivers express those feelings when they describe a parent in the end stages of

Alzheimer's disease or another type of dementia. When you transferred her to a nursing home, your suffering increased because you felt as if you let her down. The reality is that you did what you could for as long as it was physically possible. A caregiver from New York summed up how she felt when she placed her mom in a nursing home, "I tried to keep her home, but I couldn't. I made sure she was well cared for and when I close my eyes every night I sleep well, because I know in my heart that I did the best I could do for her." You did the best you could do for your mother. The staff at the nursing home was right; you moved Mom because she was deteriorating and at the end of her life. Most likely she would have reacted the same way to you in her own home. It may have been easier for you to accept if she remained at home, or it may have been just as difficult. Many caregivers tell us that the most painful emotion to experience is when a parent doesn't recognize who they are anymore.

You don't use the word guilt, but your expressions reveal the fact that you feel so burdened by your decision. We cannot take the guilty feelings away from you, but we can make some suggestions that we hope decrease their intensity. Your mom died because of an illness, not because you moved her to a nursing home. Consider the following suggestions.

- Think about speaking to a therapist who specializes in caregiver issues. She may help you work through your feelings and discover an inner dialogue from which you can draw to help you heal.
- Contact your local Area Agency on Aging, community hospital, or social service agency for a referral to an appropriate support group.
- Read chapter 11, "Life after Caregiving," and chapter 12, "Words of Hope and Comfort," for some very helpful suggestions and encouraging thoughts from other caregivers.

Dear Eldercare 911,

My eighty-year-old dad is in an assisted living facility because I couldn't stand it anymore. It boiled down to one fact: he had no one else to take care of him and keep him company except me. I love him, but I can't say I like him very much. I asked myself over and over, how can I fill up his life? So instead of trying, I moved him out of the house he loved and into an assisted living facility. I thought I'd be off the hook, but I'm not. I can't sleep, I forgot what it is to laugh, and basically I'm miserable. My mind never seems to rest because I know that he is so angry at me for moving him. He said that I abandoned him and that he hates me. I try to visit once a week, but he doesn't really say anything to me. I guess the problem is that I don't know if I moved him because he was driving me crazy or it was really the best thing for both of us. Can you please help me sort this out?

—Franklin, Idaho

Dear Franklin,

So many caregivers ask themselves the very question you posed: how can I fill up his life? The answer is no one can fill up anyone else's life and no one should be expected to. As a parent ages, his friends die, move, or suffer from a variety of medical problems creating losses that cannot be filled by an adult child. Sometimes the adult child tries to fill the void, and because this is not something he wants to do, he begins to resent the time and energy it takes to "papa-sit." Hiring a companion or a home health aide sometimes helps the situation, and sometimes it is just not enough.

You are no different than many other caregivers who feel that in order to maintain some semblance of a life you need to move a parent into a facility where other people can take over the care. In many cases the move to a facility is probably the best course of action because the parent receives the care he needs and the adult child is not the primary source. This move may even help to preserve some of the most tenuous relationships.

You said that you don't know if you moved your dad because he was "driving you crazy" or because "it was good for you." The answer is probably that it was a combination of both, because eldercare decisions are often based on want and need. Dad needed companionship and full-time care, and you were not able to provide either for him. You did not abandon him; you wanted him to have everything he needed.

Dad is angry now and he may be for some time. Try these few steps to help you cope with the present situation.

- Continue to visit and try to communicate with him. Bring him a little gift or some magazines he enjoys. When you are with him, try to keep the conversation light. If he becomes verbally abusive, leave and try again another day. It will take time for Dad to come to terms with his new environment and how he feels about you.
- Keep in contact with the staff for your peace of mind and ask them to help you during the transition period. Let the staff members know that you are available and that you welcome their advice and input. Most facilities have team meetings where the staff gets together to discuss

how to help each client. Often family members are invited to the meetings to listen as well as to participate. Try to attend these meetings and be open and honest with the staff.

- Talk to the social worker about meeting with your Dad to help him sort out his feelings.

You've done the best you can for yourself and Dad. You did nothing wrong. It's time to sleep well and with a clear conscience.

C. SHARING YOUR FEELINGS

Dear Caregivers,

Many caregivers find that talking to an understanding friend, a family member, or a counselor helps to alleviate some of their caregiver stress. Others find that writing is a very helpful way to express their feelings, thoughts, and concerns. Writing also provides a diary of events and a simple way to keep track of the things you have to do. Sherrie has been a caregiver for over eight years. Although her caregiving experience has been difficult over time, she found wonderful help for herself and her parents: a geriatric care manager, home health aides, excellent medical care, and a caregiver support group. She has agreed to share some of her reasons for using a journal, and through some of her writing she provides us with a glimpse into her personal caregiver journey.

Sherrie's journal helps her to do the following:

1. Remember things. When there is a medical crisis, she can easily follow the medical history in her journal. She logs hospital and doctors' names, telephone numbers, and addresses.
2. Have access to information. She keeps track of medical issues, home-care information, the names and telephone numbers of repair services, and even the contact at the local grocery store.
3. Keep track of doctor appointments. Sherrie used to write things on little pieces of paper and leave them taped to her desk or attached to the dashboard of her car. With easy access to her journal, every appointment is in one place.
4. Provide documentation. As you read some of the journal excerpts, you will see that she keeps track of her parents' medical conditions, who treated them, where, and when. This is extremely helpful to her when her parents see a new doctor or they require hospitalization.

5. Vent her feelings. Writing her thoughts helps Sherrie to relieve a little of the day-to-day pressures and frustrations she feels and experiences as the primary caregiver for her parents.

Dear Eldercare 911,

I am sharing excerpts from my caregiver's journal hoping that other women and men will benefit from this process. It is where I express my thoughts, concerns, and feelings. I use my computer to input everything I have to say, but some people may want to use an actual journal or diary.

As you read my journal, you will understand that this is my way of coping with many of my caregiver duties. I hope you will try this technique and see if it works for you.

—Sherrie, Ohio

Dear Sherrie,

We have selected random sections of your *journal* to share with our readers. Each section highlights different problems that you experienced as a caregiver.

9/17/97

Dad told me he hasn't taken his medication for 1–2 months because "there is too much pressure." His blood pressure is up. I read him the riot act. Spoke to Dr. L. He says Mom has a skin condition, psoriasis. They are treating her for an upset stomach. He says she doesn't need antidepressants. She is taking: Iron sulfate, Lasix, Flagel, and Tylenol.

2/19/98

When I got home last night, there were two messages from Dad. One message said to call back right away, my mother wants to speak to me. I called back and the aide answered.

She said my mother was too tired to talk to me. I said, OK, and then Mom started to relay messages through the aide. Message was Mom wants to come live with me. I said for how long. She said as long as she lives. I said sorry. I said no one will be home because I work. I said why can't they hire someone for her now. She said because Dad is with her when the aide leaves. She said Dad resents taking care of her. I said maybe he's not up to it. She said well, he's up to doing other things. I said like what? She said he goes to the grocery store and the library. I said maybe he's doing that just to survive. She said they are killing each other.

In the meantime, Jack's [Sherrie's husband] father had a stroke last night.

10/30/98

It's bad enough that Dad and Mom abuse me, but I won't tolerate their abusing my husband. He has been nothing but good to you. You ask him for advice all the time, but you don't trust what he tells you though you ask for advice from everyone from the bank manager to the carpet man. I'm tired of knocking my head against a wall. I'm going to take the sign off of my back that says "KICK ME." I won't let you abuse us anymore. We have made every effort to salvage your lives, we can't do anything more for you.

8/29/03

Mom died several months ago and Dad is living on his own. He called this morning. Here was the conversation:

> Dad: Did you go swimming this morning?
> Me: No Dad, I'm at work.
> Dad: I brought the laundry in this morning. Now what do I do?
> Me: Go to the senior center.

I wonder if this was a good time to bring up activities at an assisted living facility? But if he won't go to the senior center, why should he be interested in that?

3/18/04

Dad has been in the hospital. I had a meeting with the hospital social worker. She gave me a list of the things I should do: 1. Go to a support group. 2. Get a geriatric care manager. 3. Get an elder law attorney. After each item I said, "Been there, done that!" I am so ahead of the game. I really am quite good at this! She asked Dad if he would be interested in going to a group (she had in mind an adult daycare center) and he said yes.

But the aide said she tried to get him to go to the senior center and he wouldn't go. I'm trying to arrange for a van to pick him up for the senior center and once it's arranged I will try to convince him to go.

Sherrie, we thank you for your candor and your willingness to share your private thoughts with all of us. When you wrote about the difficult choices you had to make and the emotional turmoil you experienced, we all felt the depth of your commitment to your family. Many caregivers experience so many of the raw emotions and day-to-day experiences that you endured and will be able to relate to you and gain strength from your personal journey. Your writing is a tribute to the fortitude of all caregivers and beautifully expresses the feelings, concerns, and frustrations of so many.

Dear Eldercare 911,

My father lives in an assisted living facility. He is slowly becoming more frail every day. He is over ninety and his short-term memory is poor. I always tried to talk to him about school, my work, or my family, but he always made it difficult because he felt the need to control me. He expressed his control by not showing any interest in my life and he made every attempt to outdo me. As an adult I am still intimidated by him, but my husband keeps telling me that it's time to make peace with Dad and my feelings. My husband has never been very close to my dad and he understands how I feel. I guess I have mixed feelings. I would like to tell him off, but I also would like to tell him how much I love him. Believe it or not, I really do. I would like to do something to let him know how I feel, but I honestly can't talk to him. Do you have any suggestions?

—Millie, Georgia

Dear Millie,

Our first instinct is to suggest that you try to talk to your dad. However, given your strong feelings about your past and present relationship and your mixed emotions, it may not be helpful at this time for you or him. If you are interested in exploring your feelings, contact a therapist who specializes in family matters. She may be able to help you come to terms with your situation and prepare you to have a talk with your dad. If you feel that therapy is not an option or answer for you, try one of these alternatives to express your feelings. Any one of these projects may be a catalyst to help you communicate with your dad.

- Create a family history through a scrapbook. There are stores that specialize in the materials you may need to create a beautiful memory book. Add anything you like to tell your story, such as mementos from high school, a special award, a poem, or a letter of recommendation you received from a boss. Make copies and keep the originals for yourself. You can add some old and recent pictures to help you enhance your story. Decorate the cover with colors and things your dad likes, such as sports figures or cars. If he likes things simple, just place a family picture on the front cover.
- Design a photo album or collage. Gather as many pictures as you can that reflect your life. If you include pictures from your youth, try to display ones that have your dad in the photos. Add pictures of places he may have visited or enjoyed. This may help trigger a pleasant memory or event.
- Produce a family video. Bring your family together and have each person say something special to your dad. If he has sisters or brothers who can participate, ask them to join in. Bring the camera to the home and include him in the production. If he doesn't have a VCR or a DVD player in his room, ask the recreational specialist at the facility to have one available for you.

Once you create a special communications technique, try to enjoy it with your dad. Don't get discouraged if you try one of these ideas and you are not successful the first time. Try again at another time when your dad may be more receptive. If he does not respond to your overtures, keep in mind that this is *his* problem. *You* are not a failure. You tried your best and that is all you can ask of yourself.

D. CAREGIVER RIGHTS

Dear Caregivers,

Many caregiver groups and organizations have written Caregiver Bills of Rights. The purpose of these documents is to empower caregivers with the strength to do what they have to do for themselves and their families. For example, as a caregiver you have the right to have respite or you have the right to say no to a family member if you are too tired or overwhelmed to comply with a request.

We asked several caregivers this question: As a caregiver, what are your rights? But before showing the results, it is important to establish this one basic point—a right is a privilege, a basic freedom to do what you want to do in a particular situation. The first step is to acknowledge and own your rights, and then you can decide what you want to do or not do with them. Owning your rights allows you to ask for help, to take time for respite, and to vent your feelings and concerns. Denying that you have rights may not give you the same freedom to do what you want and need to do for yourself. Some of you believe that caregivers do not have rights; you have a job, a duty, or a responsibility. Other caregivers feel strongly that their rights are essential to their well-being and their ability to take care of an elderly parent. One caregiver said, "I have a right to maintain a balance in my life, because if there is no balance I am no good to anyone." Here is what some of you think in your own words.

Caregiver Rights

I have the right to:

1. Maintain an interest in my own life while I care for my parent. Matt, Illinois
2. A break. Judy, New Hampshire
3. I need respite. Sally, New Jersey
4. I can't think of my rights, I have a duty to my parent. Joe, South Carolina
5. Determine how much I want to do. Ed, California
6. Respect from healthcare professionals. They have rules and regulations, but sometimes the hair on my neck goes up. Healthcare professionals need more sensitivity. Lauren, New York
7. Take time off. Sylvia, Texas
8. Not be second-guessed. My responsibilities, my decisions. Ira, New Mexico
9. Keep structure and sanity. Bob, Washington, DC
10. I have no rights. Wendy, Ohio
11. Not get too consumed with my caregiver duties. Steven, Pennsylvania
12. Peace and joy in my life. Mary, Idaho
13. Responsible help. To hire a qualified caregiver who does a responsible job. Sue, Nevada

14. Not to feel guilty when I do what I think is right for my parent. Charles, New York

15. Ask for help, although it is hard for me because I have always been independent. Jackie, Maine

Each of you sees your rights or lack of rights from an individual perspective. There is no correct answer. What you all share in common is the bond of being a caregiver. You may live different lives and have different stories, but you all feel the emotional pain and the physical exhaustion of taking care of a family member or a friend.

If you feel that you have rights but you are uncertain how to express what you want and need, take the time to create a list.

- Label column A *Wants* and label column B *Needs*. Add to the list every day for a few days. Review both columns and select something that you want or need to do. For example: I want to take my friend out to lunch on Tuesday. I need to get a haircut on Thursday.
- Think about how much time you will require to do these things and who can help you if you need someone to assist you with your caregiver duties.
- Take the time to enjoy one or more activities away from your caregiver responsibilities.

If you don't believe you have rights as a caregiver, ask yourself why you feel this way. Consider talking to a licensed therapist who specializes in caregiver and family issues. It may be a very difficult question to answer and you may need a little help to give you new insight and perspective.

But no matter how you feel about this issue, you can decide the role that you will assume in your parent's life. You have the power, the right, and the insight. We ask only that you consider the fact that a "cared-for" caregiver is usually healthier, stronger, less stressed, and more effective.

Dear Eldercare 911,

When you asked the question: What are your rights as a caregiver? I thought to myself, I don't have rights, I have a sense of responsibility. But then I started to think more about your question and I realized that I do certain things during the course of a week, but I never thought about them as a right, just some things I do for myself. I take time off twice a week to go swimming and once a week at least to visit my daughter and grandson. I guess the word "rights" threw me off and maybe even put me off. I take care of my dad and mom, because I want to and because they are my parents. There is no great love or relationship, just years of being their daughter. Rights or no rights I do what I have to do and I take a little time off to keep my sanity.

—Diana, Michigan

Dear Diana,

Thank you for your honesty. Several caregivers questioned our sanity when we asked the question. In the context of a Caregiver's Bill of Rights, women and men learn that their health and well-being is as important as the health and well-being of a parent, grandparent, aunt, or uncle. Caregivers who are entrenched in their caregiver duties often have to be reminded to take care of themselves as well as they care for their loved ones. If the word "rights" makes you uncomfortable, think about what you do for yourself that you consider as "necessary." It is necessary because anyone who has cared for a family member for any length of time knows that taking time out to play and relax is essential to the job. The prerequisite for *all* caregivers should be a lesson in feeling good. We hope you will read and practice "Ten Steps to Feeling Good about Yourself" in this chapter to help you continue to find ways to give yourself respite and relief from all you accomplish.

Feeling Good

All caregivers need an opportunity to talk about how they feel, to think about what they want and need, and to take time-outs from caregiver responsibilities.

- **I will rest, relax, and rejuvenate myself.** I will use the three Rs when I feel stressed, anxious, or fatigued. I will feel better and stronger and more able to cope with many of my responsibilities.

- **I will be kind to myself.** I will take time off from my caregiver duties. It is not only a smart thing to do; it is necessary for my well-being.

- **I will share my feelings.** I will reach out to friends, family, and support groups for an opportunity to talk about how I feel. I will gain peace of mind by venting my concerns.

Ten Steps to Feeling Good about Yourself

This exercise is designed to help you focus on yourself in a positive way. Use these ten statements to help you begin to think about yourself, what you do, and how you do it. Are you ready to feel good about yourself?

1. Every day I will take the time to plan my day's activities. I will do everything possible not to overplan or overextend myself.

2. I will try to do one thing each day that gives me inner peace and satisfaction. I may spend thirty minutes exercising, ten minutes on the telephone with a friend, or I may enjoy both activities. It is my choice.

3. I will not wait for a crisis to strike before I get my own medical attention. I am going to maintain my good health by having preventive medical checkups and by exercising.

4. I am a strong person, but I sometimes neglect my needs. To keep my strength I will sleep as much as I can and eat properly. I can then best handle many of my caregiver and family responsibilities.

5. When I look in the mirror, I will see myself clearly. If I need a haircut, I will find the time to go to the hairdresser. If I need to lose or gain weight, I will consult with my doctor on an appropriate nutritional and exercise plan.

6. My family is very important to me, but I will not consume myself with my responsibilities. I will make an effort to take time off and time out when I need it.

7. I know I cannot do everything by myself, even though I try. I will try to remember to step back, assess my situation, and find the help I need.

8. I will not deny my need to talk about my feelings. I know my emotional health is important, and when I talk about how I feel, a burden is lifted from my heart and my mind.

9. I am the best daughter, son, grandchild, husband, wife, niece, or nephew that I can be. When I make an important decision to help my family member, I will try not to be second-guessed.

10. I choose to help my family. I choose to love myself. These two choices are not mutually exclusive.

11

LIFE AFTER CAREGIVING

Dear Eldercare 911,

First my wife and I were caregivers for my mother until she lost her three-year battle with cancer, and then for her father through eight years of Alzheimer's disease. We've been "free" of those responsibilities for the past year. As much as we loved our parents, we looked forward to the time when we could restart our lives together and have time to enjoy each other again. But here we are, one year later, still finding it difficult to travel or make plans with friends. We've talked about this and we agree that we still love each other. That makes it even more perplexing because we have very little desire to make love. I feel as though we've both run out of gas, only we don't know where to fill up again!

—Gus, Nevada

Dear Eldercare 911,

A few weeks after my mother died, I called my brother and sister and suggested that we all meet and go through Mom's personal items to decide what we wanted to keep, and we could give the rest to her favorite charity. She volunteered for that group for years, and I knew she'd want them to benefit from her things. My brothers and sisters were furious! They said, "It's too soon," "How can you be so unfeeling?" and "Have you already forgotten her?" They refused to even think about it; they said I "should be ashamed." I think they're being unreasonable and unnecessarily cruel. Mom lived with me. I was her primary caregiver for three years. I gave up my personal life, my time, and my space, and now I want them all back. I want to move illness and death out of my house and replace it with bright colors and happiness. What's wrong with my brother and sister? Are they really shallow enough to believe that redecorating that room means I love Mom any less? Don't they know she's not in that room anymore?

—Doris, Pennsylvania

Dear Gus and Doris,

Your stories teach us a valuable lesson: people experience and recover from grief differently and on their own timetables. This is in line with everything else we do in life because each of us creates our own reality. In other words, we dream differently; we approach problems in our own unique way. And most of us are also dealing with different levels of emotional and physical stress from problems *other than* caregiving or the loss of a parent. All these factors combine to form one basic truth: we love and mourn individually within the boundaries of our own personality, and when we do, we are being true to ourselves. It would be cruel to force us to do otherwise.

Caregivers often develop a unique relationship with their parents because of the responsibilities inherent in keeping them safe, the amount of time spent with them, and the intimacies involved in caring for them. Then, when our beloved parent dies, we are surprised that we sometimes feel as though we have lost a part of ourselves.Shock, anger, anxiety, fear, and sadness are only a few of the emotions that can overwhelm us after a death. Our bodies may run through a range of physical problems, including headaches, backaches, loss of motivation, fatigue, inability to focus, or other ailments.

Because of the stress and strains of caregiving, many caregivers are physically and emotionally drained *before* their parent dies. As a result, they may have additional healing to do and may take considerably longer to mend. There is no timetable for recovering from the loss of a parent.

Some caregivers simultaneously feel great loss and great relief because the enormous load and responsibility has been lifted from their shoulders. All too often, when they act on these normal, justifiable feelings, they are met with rancor and accusations from siblings and family members. Because these family members did not carry the same burden, they may not understand the caregivers' need to turn away from the darker feelings of sadness that they've carried for so many years and the need to let the sunlight shine on them. It's important to take the time that you need.

Siblings or other family members who enjoyed a different relationship with your parent may experience and show their grief any way they choose, but they should not influence your actions. Grief and mourning are based on history and emotional attachments. It is unreasonable to expect everyone to experience a loss in exactly the same way. Each of us manages our feelings differently. There is no right or wrong method. We are *wrong* only when we judge others who do not respond *our way*—when we deem their way unacceptable.

However we show and act on our feelings, there is one universality that transcends our differences and binds us together: the goal of recovery. *Grief and mourning are the emotional tools we use to recover from the shock and pain of a tragic loss.* We hope that this chapter eases your way through your next journey.

A. WHO ARE YOU NOW?

Dear Eldercare 911,

I changed so much in the years I spent caring for my father. It's not just that I'm older. That doesn't thrill me, but I can handle it. My problem is I don't know who I am—or even who I was. I was devastated and had no enthusiasm for anything for almost a year after Pop died. I've never experienced pain like that. I finally got grief counseling and it helped me work through my feelings. I had no idea death could be so complicated. Last week I timidly called an old friend and had lunch with her. It had been years since we spent time together, and we were both looking forward to our reunion. It was awful. I know nothing of her "normal" world of shopping, restaurants, and lunches with friends. I haven't been to the theater in years (I don't know one show from the other) and my vacation isn't "all set." All I know is diapers, doctors, medicines, wheelchairs, and hospitals. When I returned home, I realized that my house still "smells" like sickness. My father was ill for years and lay near death for five months. I wasn't prepared for him to die, and it looks like I haven't finished preparing myself to live. I don't regret one minute of the years I invested in caring for my father, but now I'd like to invest the same amount of love and energy in "me." Where do I start?

—Lynne, California

Dear Lynne,

You can start in the middle or at the beginning—it's your choice. Our suggestion is to start slowly, one step at a time. What's most important is your knowing that the rest of your life depends on you starting somewhere!

If you could "wish upon a star," what would you ask for? Think carefully: if you could wake up tomorrow and experience one change in yourself or your surroundings, what would it be? Perhaps a good place for a new beginning is to replace the "smell" of sickness in your home with a new, welcoming feeling. We're sure that once you begin, you'll create your own list. In the meantime, here are some basic suggestions to get you started.

- If you can afford it, call a professional cleaning service and ask them to estimate the cost of a thorough top-to-bottom cleaning. That includes the shelves, baseboards, louvered doors, cupboards, windows, stove, refrigerator—everything!
- Buy a few beautiful scented candles in your favorite aromas and colors and put at least one in each room, including the bathroom. Keep one or more lit in the room you're working in when you're cooking, dressing, putting on makeup, reading, or watching TV. (For safety, remember to extinguish candles when you leave the room.)
- Unless money is no object, create a monthly budget. In addition to retail stores, shop flea markets, consignment stores, and outlets to stay within your budget.
- Begin with the room you spend the most time in. Paint it a different color; buy a new piece of furniture. Think about a chair, a table, an area rug, an armoire, or anything else you'd like. If you feel up to it, redecorate the entire room.
- Buy yourself at least two new outfits: one for quiet times at home and one for going out with friends.
- Buy yourself a new set of sheets and towels in your favorite colors.
- Make an appointment to have your hair professionally cut and styled. After your haircut, visit a cosmetics store for color and makeup tips to go with your new "do."
- Join a group: volunteer to raise money for a worthy cause; join a dinner society, a political group, a horticultural society, a book group, a music society, or a "learn to ski" group—anything that interests you. Learn to socialize with those who like the same things you do.

Start slowly, and if one idea doesn't work out, keep going. Try another one and use each success to gain confidence for your next move. Use the "Everyday Tools for Living Forward" segment at the end of this chapter. Remember your goal: devote the same amount of love and energy that you gave to your father to yourself. Your reward will be a wonderful new life.

Dear Eldercare 911,

I'm fifty-five years old. My wife and I cared for my mother for two years before she died, and I thought I was okay with her passing, but now I'm not so sure. I'm almost embarrassed to admit this—I've never said it out loud— but I've finally figured out my problem. My mother was the last person alive who ever called me by my childhood nickname. Isn't that silly? I mean, at my age? I go to work and take part in my community, but I just can't shake the feeling that something of myself died, too.

—Antonio, New Jersey

Dear Antonio,

When a parent passes away, we lose much more than a physical presence: we often lose the support and stability of the person who helped mold our personalities, taught us right from wrong, instilled our sense of ethics and/or religious beliefs, developed our tastes for food, and helped put together numerous other pieces of the puzzle that makes us whole. The nickname is a symbol of all your memories from childhood and all that you experienced with your mother. Instead of losing your childhood nickname, why not bring it back to life?! You don't have to use it every day, but you can continue to enjoy it by sharing with those who are special to you.

Can you think of projects to help you stay more connected to your mother and to your childhood? These three examples may help you begin.

- If your mother valued education, you might get involved in a literacy program. Teaching others to read could add to the legacy she left for you.
- Consider creating a small (or large) scholarship in her name. Helping others in her name is a wonderful way to show your love and respect.
- Perhaps you can collect old family photos and have them made into a video tape or a CD so that you can share your memories with your family. The key is to revive those memories so that you don't lose the warmth and pleasure you can draw from them.

If you find that these recommendations do not help, we hope you will consider contacting your local hospital or hospice organization for a referral to a professional grief counselor. The coping skills you can learn in counseling may help you honor your mother and your past by replacing your sad or debilitating feelings with loving memories.

B. TIME FOR HEALING

Dear Eldercare 911,

My mother was sick for years, and since I was an only child, I was "it." I was at her side so often that I finally packed a suitcase and moved in to her house. Every day that I went "home" to her from trying to run my company was more and more depressing. I grew to hate going there. My personal life disintegrated and my health suffered. I don't know how, but I managed to stay in business. Carving out the time that my mother needed was hard, but I always did it. At the end, it was a runaway train and there was nothing I could do but watch it happen. Finally, there were so many emergencies, so many procedures that I lost any clue as to what was happening medically. Now, all this time later, I received a sympathy card and it all came back because of a stupid poem and "so sorry for not having contacted you since...." This card had been sitting on my friend's table for eight months, and she finally got around to mailing it. I've had some big hurts in my life; it's almost like you measure your life in how much you can handle. Is it always going to be this level of pain? ...after eight months, on some level it's even worse.

—Ramona, North Dakota

Dear Ramona,

We are in awe of your ability to carry on and run your business under the circumstances you describe. You also show your amazing emotional strength by finding the courage to express your feelings to us. The answer to your unasked question is, "Yes, there is hope for your future." "Will it always be this level of pain?" No, we would expect your pain to subside over time and through the help you can receive by reaching out to a bereavement specialist. No one can tell you that your pain will totally disappear, but it will lessen and soften with time and will no longer be debilitating.

A traumatic death can continue to disrupt our lives for many months after our loved one leaves us. The love and comfort of family and friends is less available and sustaining as they return to their own lives. This often leaves caregivers alone in searching for answers. After eight months, some of the numbness that you used to protect yourself from the unbearable shock and pain of death may have lessened. Without that insulation and protection, your pain feels "even worse." Recovery from a traumatic death is a long-term process, sometimes taking years. The best way to help yourself through this painful period and the quickest return to a good quality of life is to reach out for help. It's important to end your emotional isolation. Look for a counselor (social worker, therapist, or psychologist) who works with bereaved *caregivers*. Your body and mind have been relentlessly assaulted for several years with new and traumatic life-threatening situations, so they need time and assistance to heal. We also sensed some guilt about losing control when your mother's medical situation became a "runaway train." People who are used to being "in control" feel especially vulnerable and powerless when they cannot intervene and prevent harm to a loved one. Without counseling, these feelings may often develop into long-term debilitating guilt. A professional can try to help you manage all your feelings.

In conjunction with counseling, these recommendations may help you feel more focused and able to face each day.

- Eat regular, nutritious meals. The appropriate foods can help provide the fuel that your body and mind need to continue their work toward recovery.
- Make the time for long walks or an exercise program to help relieve emotional and physical stress, and remember also to relax your body and your mind.
- Try writing a journal or meditating to relieve your emotional pain. Writing your feelings down or using a guided meditation tape or CD often provides peace of mind and may allow you to sleep or rest more peacefully.
- Be frank with your physician about your feelings. This will help the physician monitor your health.

Ramona, try to feel the love and peace that you brought to your mother through the continuity and dedication of your help and determination. You were there when she needed you. Now, it's time to dedicate the same amazing determination and inner strength to your own needs. Call for help and begin rebuilding your peace of mind.

Dear Eldercare 911,

It's simple: I was my mother's caregiver for two years. Although she lived in my home, my two sisters and one brother contributed time and money. This was a family project. She loved us all and we all loved her back. When she died a month ago, she left a hole in my heart that was almost unbearable. My brother and one sister stayed with me until the funeral, and for one night after the funeral and then they went back to work leaving me and my other sister to mourn alone. I was so hurt about how they handled Mom's death that I have hardly spoken a word to them since. I think they should have stayed at least another day or two out of respect for our mother. She loved them with all her heart, and I don't think a few days are long enough for them to grieve. My brother said, "I didn't go to a party, Ginger, I went back to *work!* I don't see any disrespect in that." He's a good guy and I know he loved her, but how could he leave like that?

—Ginger, Missouri

Dear Ginger,

We're sorry for your pain, but we're glad you asked for help before the rift between you and your siblings widens further. It's far from "simple." You are correct in your desire to show respect for your mother and continue mourning in the privacy of your home for a longer period of time than your two siblings seemingly are. *But your brother and sister are equally correct* in wanting to grieve in their own manner and in their own familiar surroundings.

The reality is we all mourn and grieve differently, and there is no disrespect in that. Grief is among the most personal and private feelings any of us will ever have. Some feel better when they recall memories with friends and families; others find it difficult to talk about their departed loved ones and find peace remembering alone. Many memories bring smiles and laughter to mourners, but that laughter is usually warm and loving, not disrespectful. While remaining in your home was more comfortable for you, the reverse may have been true for your brother and sister. They may have needed the balance of their own homes and families or their jobs to help them through their pain.

You write that your mother loved your siblings: why not fill the hole in your heart with her love? Consider honoring her memory by replacing your anger with understanding and becoming the glue that holds this family together. The best way to start is to pick up the phone and call your brother and sister to reopen the lines of communication.

C. FILLING THE VOID

Dear Eldercare 9 I I,

This will be my first holiday season without my mother. I don't know how we'll get through it. I started thinking about decorations and who's coming to dinner, and the memories almost overcame my senses. I could actually see myself with her in the kitchen or when I was little. I never realized how traditional we were during special times or how much those traditions meant to me. I just burst into tears. I volunteered to have Dad, my brother, sisters, and aunts and uncles for dinner this year, but now all I can see is a long miserable evening full of tears and sadness. How do we fill the emptiness she left in our lives?

—Penny, Virginia

Dear Penny,

You have experienced a terrible loss, but you are lucky that your family traditions remain such a strong and warming influence in your life. There is no reason they cannot continue to sustain you and provide the support and meaning that you need so badly now.

It's likely that your entire family is feeling the same fear and anxiety that you describe. They must all be wondering how to manage the first gathering without your mother. Why not get together with your father (if he's able), brothers, and sisters, and talk about the situation openly *before* everyone gathers for the holiday. Talk about ways to make the evening more pleasant and how to fill the time with love and wonderful memories of your mother and the times you all spent together. Tears are an honest expression of your sorrow at losing your mother. When you're with so many family members, you may find that you all support each other and that conversation and warmth may replace many of your tears. Try to involve your children in the actual events to help them feel more connected and less afraid. These suggestions may help you and your siblings think of others.

- Ask every family member to bring food to fill a box and donate it, in your mother's name, for less fortunate members of your community.
- Ask the children to create a poem or song about Grandma.
- Ask each adult to tell a story or write a poem about something fun or meaningful you did with your mother.
- Before the day of the dinner, ask everyone to select a memento. Choose

items that each of you love from Mom's possessions. After dinner, create a memory box that you can look through next year or whenever you want to reminisce.

- Bring out old holiday photos and choose photos to go in a special holiday album.
- Toast your mother with a glass of wine or soft drink: give everyone a chance to speak.
- Send memorial flowers to her church, synagogue, or senior group.

Inviting your family to join you in remembering your mother, as she would want to be remembered, may help ease your burden and theirs—and help you continue enjoying the warmth and love you've always felt during holiday gatherings.

Dear Eldercare 911,

My parents were married for sixty-four years. My dad died almost a year ago and my mother still cries every day. After Dad left us, I brought her to live with me. I was, repeat "was," happily married with two reasonably bright and well-adjusted teenagers. Now my husband spends more and more time at his office, and my kids just want to leave the house and delay returning as long as they possibly can. I feel the same way they do. It's like torture. We can be sitting through a peaceful dinner and something—usually nothing that we can see—will trigger Mom's weeping. We never know when it's coming or why. It's the same scenario everywhere—the mall, the movies, it doesn't matter. The other day I took her to the grocery store. She went to another aisle to pick up something we forgot. When she didn't come back, I went looking for her. When I saw two people with their arms around her looking like they were helping hold her up, I almost died of fright. I ran toward her thinking she'd fallen or fainted. The two customers with her said they found her standing there with tears running down her face. I love my mom, but my family and I are being hammered to the ground. Gary and I have worked so hard all these years to create the life we wanted for our children and ourselves. I want to continue caring for her, but I'm afraid she's going to drown all of us with her tears.

—Robin, Washington

Dear Robin,

How fortunate your mother is to have a daughter who recognizes her need for assistance to manage her grief. There are a number of details missing, but we'll try to fill in the blanks as best we can. When your father died, your mother suffered multiple losses that changed her life in many ways. First, of course, she lost her partner of sixty-four years—the person she may have woken up with, ate with, watched TV with, who was always there to talk with, and with whom she shared an entire lifetime of experiences and adventures, like conceiving and giving birth to you, and then raising you into the loving, responsible woman you are. She may have lost the person who knew the most about her likes and dislikes or the last person who ever knew her as a beautiful young woman.

You don't say if moving into your home was a crosstown move or across the country. You were wonderful to bring her home with you, but she may also feel the loss of her home and independence. She can no longer take comfort from the memories of your father that she might have found in *their* home or from being surrounded by their own furniture and belongings. Perhaps she left friends behind and the familiarity of merchants and physicians she had known for years. Your mother is lucky to have family that invites her into their home, but friends are priceless and essential as well.

It can easily take several years to recover from the loss of a partner of sixty-four years. Add her move away from her home and friends, and the impact is even more devastating. There is no set time for this process. One memory of your father or an evening with friends in their home can retrigger her pain. When you consider your mother is dealing with memories that span over six decades, you'll find it easier to understand how she can continue to weep for her past. However, you and your family need a more positive environment in which to nurture each other. We hope these suggestions help ease your way through this very difficult time.

- You didn't mention your own feelings of loss. Your mother's continuing sorrow may take you back to a more painful time or may make it even more difficult to help her. If you find yourself sinking emotionally, make an appointment for *yourself* with a bereavement counselor who works with adult children.
- If your mother has friends in her old neighborhood, try to arrange regular meetings with them. She may find it easier to talk to peers, many of whom have experienced a similar loss.
- Look for a bereavement support group for *spouses*. She will find many women and men who are suffering from the loss of their partners, and the open conversation and memories may help her begin to manage her loss.

- Consider a mental health therapist who is experienced in helping elderly spouses through periods of bereavement.
- Be sure that she continues attending to her physical needs. The stress of grief can impair the immune system, and your mother may become ill without a physician monitoring her health. It's also important for her to eat well-balanced, nutritious meals and exercise in moderation.
- The combined disorientation from your father's death and your mother's move to new surroundings may cause her to become a little confused or forgetful. Use notes and gentle reminders until your mother regains her focus. If this does not happen, call her physician for an evaluation.
- Allow your mother to express her grief. It's important to acknowledge her feelings. If you can't talk to her, the support group and conversations with friends will help. If it's not too painful, share memories of your father with your mother through photographs and quiet talks.
- When she's ready, give your mother a tape recorder and ask her to record her life so that your children can share it with their children. Start by asking her questions about her life as a child, then how she met your father, and continue.

You are all in the midst of one of the most painful experiences life presents to us. Be patient and be sure to remember to help yourself and your family while you are helping your mother.

D. EVERYDAY TOOLS FOR LIVING FORWARD

Many caregivers are obligated to continue caring for their families or to return to their jobs before they have had time to deal with their own feelings of grief and loss. We hope our *Everyday Tools for Living Forward*—"Helping Your Parent," "Who Are You Now," "Returning to Work," and "When to Ask for Help: Warning Signs"—will help you develop new coping skills during this difficult period.

Helping Your Parent

Losing a spouse or partner presents special issues and encompasses a different pain and healing process than losing a parent. Use these guidelines to help your parent.

1. Do not rush your parent through her grief. This is a long-term process, which can take many years.
2. Be alert for significant ongoing changes in your parent's routine such as lack of self-care, increased alcohol or drug use, and others listed in the "Warning Signs" worksheet that follows. If your parent exhibits these symptoms, call her physician.
3. Expect guilt, anxiety, fear, and anger as part of your parent's response (and yours as well). They are considered part of a normal reaction to the loss of a spouse or parent.
4. Call the nearest Area Agency on Aging, your local church or synagogue, or hospice for a referral to a bereavement support group for spouses.
5. If your parent attended religious services regularly and stopped abruptly after a spouse's death, call her clergy, ask a friend of hers to take her, or take her yourself until she can resume attending on her own.
6. If your parent withdraws from family and friends for a significant period of time, speak to her physician. Be certain your parent eats regular, nutritious meals and gets enough rest. The combination of age and grief can exhaust an older person's resources very quickly.
7. If your parent has dementia, you may see a significant decline in cognitive ability. This may be a good time to get involved and set up a safe routine.
8. Help protect your parent's assets. Your mother may have never been included in managing your parents' financial or legal matters, and this is not a good time to expect her to learn new skills or make decisions on matters she isn't familiar with.

While you're providing for your parent's basic material necessities (medical, transportation, meal preparation, in-home assistance, etc.), try to remember that her most important need now may be someone to listen without judging, and to respond with kindness when she expresses her feelings.

Who Are You Now?

Caregivers often find many changes in their lives after a parent dies. Writing down your thoughts can help you identify and acknowledge how (or if) you have changed, or how (or if) you want to change. Recognizing your feelings may help you manage your grief and plan your future.

1. Who am I now? How am I different from when my parent was alive?

_____

_____

_____

2. What changes, if any, would I like to make in my life?

_____

_____

_____

3. What is my first step toward making these changes, and when will I be ready to begin?

_____

_____

_____

4. What changes, if any, would I like to make in my home or job?

_____

_____

_____

5. What is my first step toward making these changes, and when will I be ready to begin?

_____

_____

_____

6. Other things I would like to experience now are:

_____

_____

_____

Use your written thoughts as a guide to stay focused while you heal. If you change your mind, simply write down your new goal. *When you're ready*, taking one step at a time may help you reclaim your sense of self and begin *living forward.*

Returning to Work

Returning to work can be a helpful step in healing, but the thought of talking to coworkers about your feelings may also create anxiety. Responding to their well-meant (but sometimes poorly articulated) condolences may be difficult, but a little emotional preparation may help soften the experience.

1. If your office has a counselor or therapist available or a referral program to an outside counselor, set up an appointment before you return to work for help with some of your emotional issues.
2. If you have special friends at work, ask them to intercede for you by talking to coworkers before you arrive. For example, you may tell them you don't wish to discuss the accident or funeral, but a simple "I'm sorry" or "I'm glad you're back" would be appreciated.
3. If you do want to share your feelings, be careful not to overburden your coworkers or take advantage of their support. If they become tired of listening, they may begin avoiding you, and that will add to your pain.
4. If you're still experiencing bouts of tears or your temper is short and you're worried about it, speak to your supervisor on the first day. Explain that you're mending well and ready to work, but you might "tear up" periodically for a little while longer and you don't want her to become alarmed.
5. If you are concerned that you may not be able to function at full capacity, ask for help (remember to say "thank you") or try working part time until you're ready to take over all your previous responsibilities.

For many people, returning to the routine and normalcy of office life enhances healing by offering a different emotional and physical focus. When you're ready, it can be an important step in the process of *living forward*.

When to Ask for Help: Warning Signs

Grief is a natural response to the loss of loved ones. There is no time limit on mourning and no deadline to "finish" grieving and "get on with your life." However, there are danger signs to alert us that we may need help from others to process our grief and manage it without endangering our own health and future. If you check any of these boxes, talk to your doctor or clergy for a referral to a bereavement counselor or bereavement support group. Remember, these boxes represent changes in habits after a death.

☐ Increased intake of alcohol or drugs; abusing nonprescription medications; borrowing other people's prescriptions.

☐ Increased physical problems, such as headaches, stomach disorders, fatigue, inability to sleep, or fear of sleeping.

☐ Refusing to eat, eating significantly increased amounts of food; changes from eating nutritionally balanced meals to mostly "junk" food.

☐ Continuing sense of hopelessness; continued withdrawal from friends and family; continuous crying.

☐ Increased and excessive anger at family members or the deceased.

☐ Increased lack of awareness or interest in personal safety, hygiene, or appearance.

If you experience any of these warning signs, it's time to meet with your doctor or a bereavement counselor and talk about your feelings. If you get help when you need it, you are helping yourself to restart your progress back to a good quality of life and begin *living forward*.

The authors and the caregivers who shared the stories for this chapter offer you their best wishes and hope their experiences will help bring you out once again into the sunlight.

12.

WORDS OF HOPE AND COMFORT

Dear Eldercare 911,

Somehow when this book is done, you must get the words out that "when the time comes, we are here for you." A book of encouragement by my bed at night, filled with words of comfort about this maelstrom which has no road maps, no absolutes, will help me feel less alone and lost.

—Annie, Arkansas

Dear Annie and all Caregivers,

It is our pleasure. *You are not alone.* Your gifts to others are bountiful: love, kindness, sympathy, and encouragement are only a few of the wonderful contributions you make on a daily basis. We are honored to return some of those wonderful feelings and experiences to you.

Draw strength during the night or soothe your disquieting thoughts at any hour with the love and warmth that you'll find in this chapter. Find peace in every caring thought. Listen to the music of hope. *We are all in this together.*

Comfort

Dear Caregivers,

You have created hope where there was precious little of it, brought joy back when it was absent. You have been good to those who needed you. Now, be kind to yourself. Take comfort from the expert in giving it—yourself.

Dear Eldercare 911,

My mother has Alzheimer's and doesn't always know me anymore. She often looks at me with a blank stare, and I assume she's wondering who I am. So

253

often she bears no resemblance to the woman I knew that I frequently wonder who this person is in my mother's body. The pain of feeding and dressing and changing the diapers of a stranger every day was destroying me. I was sure I'd never know another moment of peace. One day, she was refusing to let me change her clothes and I was nearing my breaking point when I suddenly felt a memory I hadn't thought of in decades. It was almost as though she was willing me to remember. When I was small, Mom would make up songs for me about how much she loved me as she washed my hair, helped me go to sleep, cleaned up my crayons, prepared my food, and other things. She made all the things I fought her on seem like fun with her playful and loving songs about them. The words were just a couple of sentences sung to the tune of one or two songs she knew, but they all repeated my name over and over and they all ended with kiss. I began softly singing to her exactly as I recalled her singing to me, except I substituted her name for mine. I started smiling at my silly song, and my frustration eased off a little. Her eyes lit up and she smiled her beautiful smile that I hadn't seen in so long, and then she hummed and started moving to the music. We actually danced a little, laughed, and sang a few times together before she agreed to change her clothes. The words I used for her songs didn't make much sense, but her smile and the hug she gave me told it all. She still has Alzheimer's, and she may still look at me without knowing who I am—I can't change that. But now, when I look at my mother, I don't have to wonder who she is anymore. I recall the loving woman who taught me to brush my teeth and color inside the lines. My heart has found a little comfort enjoying the thought that my mother is helping me master yet another of life's challenges.

—Sandra, Illinois

Courage

Dear Caregivers,

It takes a special kind of courage to walk the caregiver's road. There is no shame in feeling fear. Whether you acknowledge the fear or deny it, the fact that you move forward with the day's responsibilities *in spite of your fear* quietly demonstrates your enormous courage.

Dear Eldercare 911,

Please share this with other caregivers. I actually had a few free moments the other night and my husband and I watched an old World War II movie on TV, complete with spies who were captured and tortured. I said, "It's amazing. They were ordinary men who left their homes and families and went to war. I don't think I'd have the courage they showed." My husband looked at me and said, "You?" He said, "You're amazing. You're the most courageous person I know." I was surprised and he told me how much he admired what I do for my parents—all the problems I take on and the effort I put into trying to win better care for them from all the support people I deal with. The more I thought about what he said, the more I tended to agree with him. Caregivers, too, are "ordinary people" faced with extraordinary challenges. Yet somehow we keep going and try to prevail. We try to keep our balance in what often seems like a world that's out of balance, at least when it comes to care for the elderly. Other caregivers' husbands and families may feel the same way but may not have the opportunity to say so. Please share my husband's words with all caregivers. He's right, we are amazing!

—Bella, Wisconsin

Dear Eldercare 911,

Now that I am no longer a caregiver, I often wonder how long it will take my emotional bruises to mend. My expectations were so high, and the reality of what I could do so different, that in the end, my own limitations just confused me. However, in the same moment I would say that I may have been one of the lucky ones—that's a thought that will take some time to digest—because I developed the strength and courage I needed to be an advocate for my father during his ordeal. I never expected to become that strong; in fact, you might say I exceeded my wildest expectations. And now I expect to be a better person for having done so.

—Charlotte, Oregon

Dear Eldercare 911,

I have been married for thirty-three years. My wife, Brenda, and I have a won-derful relationship—after all this time, we still make each other laugh. I don't recall either one of us ever actually saying, "That's *your* job," but I recently real-ized that I always relied on my wife for caregiving duties. It was Brenda who got up most nights when our kids were sick. I'm embarrassed to say this, but deep in my heart I felt she was better suited to it, so I let it become "her" job. When my mother was sick, it was Brenda who took her to the doctor and hired a homecare worker. When my dad recently became ill, one of the guys at work said, "You're lucky to have Brenda. What would you do if *you* had to take over the caregiving responsibilities?!" It hit me like a ton of bricks. I always loved my parents. Why didn't I think it was my responsibility to care for them? I realized that I should be the one caring for them. So I took over one responsibility and then another, until I was in charge of Dad's care. My friends are flabbergasted. They want to know why I would voluntarily take on this burden when someone else was available to do it for me. That's the point, I tell them. It's "my" burden or, at least, "our" burden. I've thanked Brenda over and over again. I never realized the amount of time that caregivers devote or the emotional impact they withstand every day. I won't say it's easy or that I'm comfortable with my new role yet. In fact, I find the role of caregiver unnerving and frightening, but I'm determined to live up to the example my wife and other caregivers like her have set for me: I'll accept the fear and just do what needs to be done. In the end, I know I'll make a difference in my father's life, and that will make a positive difference in my life.

—John, Florida

Dear Eldercare 911,

My mother has much more courage than I'll ever have. I'd have thrown in the towel years ago. I don't know where it comes from. Do you have to be that sick before you get that way? Or is her bravery more for her family than for herself? It will take me years of quiet contemplation to recognize all the pieces of my mother's legacy, but one lesson is with me all the time . . . I will never lack courage again.

—Sadie, New York

Hope

Caregivers impart their own special message of hope that springs from deep within them. That doesn't exclude moments of concern or even despair—no one goes through this experience without experiencing sadness. But then we dig into our souls and bring forth the promise of tomorrow, even during the most painful times. Here is Ed's story.

Dear Eldercare 911,

My father taught me to be an optimist. My family used to tease us saying "Look out, here come the 'good news guys.'" A few months ago, on a miserably cold and rainy night, my father lay dying, and my daughter, who had been ill for most of her pregnancy, struggled with the difficult birth of her first child. My wife stayed with my daughter and I stayed with Dad. I had no idea how I would handle my beloved father's dying and my grandson being born in the same night. How could I be desolate and joyful at the same time? I had lost any sense of the future. I didn't have an ounce of optimism in my body. Dad tried to console me by telling me "It's my time, Ed. Who knows what great adventure I'll find." But I just couldn't be comforted. As he lay dying, the nurse came to tell me my wife was on the phone and had said it was "urgent," that she had to talk to me immediately. I could barely breathe thinking something had gone wrong and I might lose two people I loved that night. When I returned, my father opened his eyes and said "red." It wasn't a question, it was a statement. I was surprised but I instinctively knew what he meant. "Yes," I answered and he smiled, "I knew it. Good News Guy." Then he passed. My father had eight siblings and I have five. He and I were the only ones in the family with red hair. Until my grandson was born. That night I learned that optimism is who you are, not what you are experiencing. Hope lives within you, and if it's in your heart, you can keep it there forever. As for Dad's hopes to keep the Good News Guys alive and his potential for a great adventure—I'm one hundred percent optimistic!

—Ed, Alabama

Dear Eldercare 911,

My mother and father were always very affectionate with each other, but they didn't show that physical warmth very often with me or my siblings. So we grew into a "non-hugging" family. I discovered how much I'd missed when I became an adult and began receiving "hello" and "good-bye" hugs from my friends and coworkers. I've made it a point to be very physically close to my children and husband. Although I hoped my physical relationship to my parents would change, I never had the courage to be the one to change it. My mother recently had a stroke. She recovered to a great degree, but she still has problems with the left side of her body. We spend a lot of time together, and we try to continue doing the things she so loved to do before the stroke. One of her favorite hobbies is needlepoint. She's right-handed, so she can still stitch, but she needs help threading the needle, cutting, and knotting. Last week while we were working together on her latest needlepoint, I found myself intently looking at her. She asked me if anything was wrong. I said, "No," and went back to stitching. A short while later, I was staring at her again, and she put her thread down and said, "Kim, what is it?" Without thinking, I said, "I love you and want to hug you." She smiled at me and said what I'd always hoped to hear. She said, "I love you too" and opened her arms. Since then, we've been on a hugging binge! It's as if a gray cloud that was over my head just blew away! I never realized how much this meant to me and how wonderful I would feel from following my heart.

—Kim, New Mexico

Peace

If you sometimes feel as though as you haven't given enough, Marjorie's story will help you see how much your supportive thoughts and everyday kindnesses mean to your parent. It's the simplest of equations: *you cannot give what you do not possess.* Giving what you have to give is all anyone can ask of you.

Dear Eldercare 911,

My mother has advanced Parkinson's disease and lives in my home. Sometimes I feel useless because I can't help her. Recently, the only way I could describe my feelings was that for the first time in my life I was without joy or hope. My mother's sister asked me why I felt that way. When I told her it was because I couldn't help Mom, she said you mean "cure" her. Then she opened my eyes to the help I give Mom every day. She said that I provided warmth, love, support, kindness, comfort, shelter—in her words, "everything that was within my power to give." I had always thought that my contributions were insignificant, that I just did what needed to be done. I know now that I haven't failed, that no one expected me to "cure" Mom, just to be there for her when she needed me. My aunt helped me see how much I've brought to Mom's life. I finally realized that what I considered minor kindnesses meant the world to her. Understanding the reality of what I can and cannot do is very comforting. It helps me realize that what I do makes a very large difference in my mother's life.

—Marjorie, Nevada

Dear Eldercare 911,

The small miracles continue even today. I often feel my parents' presence at critical moments that some would consider ridiculous if I told about them about such things. Sometimes I find joy in remembering the poignant moments and amazing things that brought us closer. I would not have missed our relationship for the world, as odd as that sounds.

—Abigail, Vermont

Strength

Dear Readers,

Some caregivers are blessed with parents who realize the enormous emotional and physical sacrifices their children make when they accept the role of "caregiver." To those caregivers, we offer this poem on behalf of their parents as another "thank you" for their sacrifices.

Too many caregivers live with the hurt of giving their all without ever hearing a simple "thank you." That injustice ends here. For those of you who were never were properly thanked for all you gave, we offer these thoughts that were surely in your parents' hearts as a thank you for your hard work.

To all caregivers, we offer these sentiments and pay tribute to the positive difference you've made in so many lives.

TO MY CAREGIVER

Judith Rappaport-Musson

Have I thanked you for digging deep and being strong for another day? Maybe not, but I should. Because I know that without your strength, I might not have enough of my own.

Have I thanked you for hiding your fears and being brave for one more day? Probably not, but I should. Because I know that without your courage, I might give up and give in.

I'm sure I meant to thank you for looking past my illness to help me remember who I really am. You deserve my thanks. Because I know that without your memories, the "me" that I was might disappear and leave just an old person in my place.

I know I meant to thank you for struggling each day to add my needs to your life's plan.

You deserve my thanks. Because I know that without your sacrifices, the world might forget me without a trace.

If I could give you one gift back as my thanks for everything, it would be this message:

You've shown your colors to me and the world. You have the colors of a true champion, a hero. Were you born with these colors? No. I think you earned them.

Whatever else happens as your life unfurls, you will have the strength and courage you need. Choose your own path. Believe in yourself. You have the power, insight, and wisdom to succeed.

For yours are the colors of a hero, a true champion, a caregiver.

For all you've given, for all you've endured, for all the thankless tasks you've performed, for all your frustration and tears, and for all you've accomplished—on behalf of your parents and the parents of future caregivers who will benefit from your deeds, we offer our sincerest and heartfelt gratitude.

13

RESOURCES

This resource section is divided alphabetically into ten specific categories: Caregiver and Senior Organizations; Elder Abuse; End of Life; Government Agencies; Healthcare; Housing; Medical and Disease-Related Organizations; Professional Organizations; Relaxation for Your Body and Mind; and Travel. Most of the resources are relevant for professionals as well as caregivers. Look for your particular category of interest. If you don't find what you need under the first category, please check under another heading.

CAREGIVER AND SENIOR ORGANIZATIONS

The following Web sites provide caregivers and seniors with comprehensive up-to-date information, education, advocacy, and support.

American Association of Retired Persons (AARP)

www.aarp.org
888-687-2277
601 E Street, NW
Washington, DC 20049

Alzheimer's Association

www.alz.org
800-272-3900
225 N. Michigan Avenue, 17th Fl.
Chicago, IL 60601

Alzheimer's Society of Canada

Web site in English and French
www.alzheimer.ca
800-616-8816 (valid only in Canada)
416-488-8816
20 Eglinton Avenue W, Ste. 1200
Toronto, ON M4R1K8

American Federation for Aging Research (AFAR)

www.infoaging.org
212-703-9977
70 W. 40th Street, 11th Fl.
New York, NY 10018

American Health Assistance Foundation

www.ahaf.com
800-437-2423
22512 Gateway Center Drive
Clarksburg, MD 20871

Benefits Checkup

www.benefitscheckup.org
This National Council on the Aging Web site has a database of federal and state assistance programs for the elderly. This site can help identify benefits your parent is entitled to but may not have applied for.

Canadian Association of Retired Persons

www.fifty-plus.net

Children of Aging Parents (CAPS)

www.caps4caregivers.org
800-227-7294
P.O. Box 167
Richboro, PA 18954

Eldercare 911

www.eldercare911handbook.com

Elderweb

www.elderweb.com
309-451-3319
1305 Chadwick Drive
Normal, IL 61761

Family Caregiver Alliance

www.caregiver.org
800-445-8106
180 Montgomery Street, Ste. 1100
San Francisco, CA 94104

National Family Caregivers Association (NFCA)

www.thefamilycaregiver.org
800-896-3650
10400 Connecticut Avenue, Ste. 500
Kensington, MD 20895-3944

National Hispanic Council on Aging

Web site in English and Spanish

www.nhcoa.org
202-429-0787
1341 Connecticut Avenue, NW
Washington, DC 20036

National Hospice Organization

www.hospicenet.org
401 Bowling Avenue, Ste. 51
Nashville, TN 37205

Partnership for Caring

www.partnershipforcaring.org
800-989-9455
1620 Eye Street, NW, Ste. 202
Washington, DC 20006

Rosalynn Carter Institute for Caregiving

www.rci.gsw.edu
229-928-1234
Georgia Southwestern State University
800 Wheatley Street
Americus, GA 31709

Senior Resource

www.seniorresource.com
877-793-7901
P.O. Box 781
Del Mar, CA 92014

Well Spouse Foundation

www.wellspouse.org
800-838-0879
63 W. Main Street, Ste. H
Freehold, NJ 07728

ELDER ABUSE

The National Center on Elder Abuse

www.elderabusecenter.org
202-898-2586
1201 15th Street, NW, Ste. 350
Washington, DC 20005

The National Center on Elder Abuse is an excellent resource for information about elder abuse, reporting options, the latest research, and resources.

END OF LIFE

Funeral Help Program

www.funeral-help.com
757-427-0220
1236 Ginger Crescent
Virginia Beach, VA 23453

The Funeral Help Program advises consumers of their options and rights. The Web site provides a wide range of resources for education, including books for download, articles, and information on professional funeral consultants.

Growth House, Inc.

www.growthhouse.org

415-863-3045

Growth House, Inc., offers resources for life-threatening illness and end-of-life care. The organization is dedicated to improving the quality of compassionate care for people who are dying. The site offers links to many helpful healthcare Web sites.

GOVERNMENT AGENCIES

Administration on Aging (AOA)

www.aoa.dhhs.gov

800-677-1116

202-619-0724

The AOA is part of the US Department of Health and Human Services that provides a wide range of services and resources for the elderly and their family caregivers. In addition to their services, the AOA can direct you to the nearest Area Agency on Aging as well as many other sources of state and local assistance. This Web site is available in several languages.

Center for Medicare Advocacy

www.medicareadvocacy.org

202-216-0028

1101 Vermont Avenue, NW, Ste. 1001

Washington, DC 20005

Centers for Medicare and Medicaid Services

www.cms.hhs.gov

877-267-2323

7500 Security Boulevard

Baltimore, MD 21244

The Centers for Medicare & Medicaid Services is a comprehensive, user friendly Web site for consumers as well as professionals, providing up-to-date information on Medicare, Medicaid, and related programs.

Department of Veteran Affairs (VA)

www.va.gov

800-827-1000

The Department of Veteran Affairs Web site provides information and programs for veterans who qualify. Benefits and services include healthcare, pension, and burial. The national office can answer questions about qualifying for VA benefits and refer you to the VA nearest you.

Eldercare Locator (Administration on Aging/ US Department of Health and Human Services)

www.eldercare.gov

800-677-1116

The Eldercare Locator helps older adults and their caregivers find local services for seniors. The Web site provides an extensive glossary, caregiver resources, and referrals.

Healthfinder

Web site in English and Spanish

www.healthfinder.gov
P.O. Box 1133
Washington, DC 20013

The Healthfinder is a federal Web site that includes a health library, containing healthcare information organized specifically by age for men, women, and children. The site provides information for caregivers and healthcare professionals on long-term care issues, insurance, and related topics.

National Association of Area Agencies on Aging

www.n4a.org
202-872-0888
1730 Rhode Island Avenue, NW, Ste. 1200
Washington, DC 20036

The National Association of Area Agencies on Aging is the umbrella organization for all the local area agencies on aging. The site provides important information on services for the elderly and advocacy, and supports the dignity of maintaining the elderly at home.

National Institute on Aging (NIA)

www.nih.gov/nia
301-496-1752
Bldg. 31, Rm. 5C27
31 Center Drive MSC 2292
Bethesda, MD 20892

The NIA is a federal government agency that funds and promotes research on life expectancy, age-related diseases, special problems, and needs of the aged, as well as other topics relating to the well-being of older Americans.

National Institutes of Health (NIH)

www.nih.gov
301-496-4000
9000 Rockville Pike
Bethesda, MD 20892

The NIH Web site offers consumers health information, a health database, free fact sheets, brochures, articles, and handbooks with timely information on health maintenance and illness prevention.

Social Security OnLine

www.ssa.gov
800-772-1213
Social Security Administration
Office of Public Inquiry
Windsor Park Bldg.
6401 Security Boulevard
Baltimore, MD 21235

The Social Security Administration's Web site answers questions and provides full information on all aspects of benefits, including statement requests and applications for retirement, disability, and survivors benefits.

HEALTHCARE

Barton Medical Equipment

www.bartonmedical.com
877-8 BARTON
5727 Highway 290 West, Ste. 103
Austin, TX 78735

Barton Medical Equipment specializes in innovative medical equipment to allow one person to securely and safely transfer patients. The site provides pictures of the equipment and specific product details.

Center Watch Clinical Trials Listing Service

www.centerwatch.com

617-856-5900

22 Thompson Place, 47th Fl.

Boston, MA 02210

Center Watch Clinical Trials Listing Service offers a wide range of information related to clinical trials and new drug therapies recently approved by the Federal Drug Administration. This information is offered for patients interested in participating in clinical trials.

Dr. Koop

www.drkoop.com

Dr. C. Everett Koop's Web site provides a wide range of information on physical health, mental health, and fitness. The site also gives information on complementary and alternative medicines and their potential interactions with traditional medications.

Familydoctor.org
(From the American Academy of Family Physicians)

Web site in English and Spanish

www.familydoctor.org

Familydoctor.org provides comprehensive healthcare information for all ages on many illnesses and conditions, including cancer, heart disease, asthma, allergies, stomach problems, and mental problems.

Link to Life

www.link-to-life.com
888-337-5433
297 North Street
Pittsfield, MA 01201

Link to Life's Web site provides Personal Emergency Response Services (PERS) to the sick and elderly. A PERS system provides emergency advice and help at home when needed. These services are available nationwide.

The Mayo Clinic

www.mayohealth.org

The clinic's Web site includes a Healthy Aging Center that provides information on medical conditions, diet, exercise, stress reduction, risk avoidance, and physical, mental, and emotional health. The site also provides Mayo Clinic specialists to answer some of your specific health inquiries at no charge. A free e-newsletter is available.

Pharmaceutical Research and Manufacturers of America (PHRMA)

Web site in English and Spanish

www.helpingpatients.org

HelpingPatients.org is a free, confidential Web site of PHRMA. The site assists patients in finding appropriate programs to acquire their specific medications.

WebMD

www.webmd.com
201-703-3400
669 River Drive, Center 2
Elmwood Park, NJ 07407

The WebMD Web site is a comprehensive health resource for consumers, physicians, nurses, and educators. The site offers free newsletters, up-to-date news and information, chat forums, and special health quizzes.

HOUSING

American Association of Homes and Services for the Aging

www.aahsa.org
202-783-2242
2519 Connecticut Avenue, NW
Washington, DC 20008

The American Association of Homes & Services for the Aging promotes excellence in services to the aging. The association represents 5,600 alternative housing communities and serves approximately one million older persons throughout the United States.

Care Pathways

www.carepathways.com
877-521-9987

Care Pathways provides information and resources about assisted living facilities, nursing homes, and long-term care. Facilities are listed by state. The site includes important links for elder abuse information and a medical and prescription drug dictionary.

Medicare

www.medicare.gov

The Medicare.gov Web site provides extensive information about Medicare and Medicaid nursing homes throughout the United States. Find specific facilities by name, geographical location, or the proximity to your home.

MEDICAL AND DISEASE-RELATED ORGANIZATIONS

The following Web sites provide up-to-date disease-specific information, resources, services, support, research, prevention, and advocacy for professionals and consumers.

About GERD

www.aboutgerd.org

GERD is an acronym for Gastroesophageal Reflux Disease or "reflux." The GERD Web site provides information and education about this disease.

All about Vision

www.allaboutvision.com
610-492-1042

Alzheimer's Association

www.alz.org
800-272-3900 (connects to your local chapter)
312-335-8700 (national office)
Alzheimer's Association National Office
225 N. Michigan Avenue, 17th Fl.
Chicago, IL 60601

Alzheimer's Disease Education and Referral Center

www.alzheimers.org
800-438-4380
ADEAR Center
P.O. Box 8250
Silver Springs, MD 20907

Alzheimer's Society of Canada

Web site in English and French

www.alzheimer.ca
800-616-8816 (valid only in Canada)
416-488-8772
20 Eglinton Avenue W, Ste. 1200
Toronto, ON M4R1K8

The Alzheimer's Store

www.alzstore.com
800-752-3238
Ageless Design, Inc.
12633 159th Court North
Jupiter, FL 33478

American Academy of Dermatology

www.aad.org
888-462-DERM
202-842-3555
1350 I Street, NW
Washington, DC 20005

American Cancer Society

www.cancer.org
800-227-2345

American Diabetes Association

www.diabetes.org
800-342-2383
Attn: National Cell Center
1701 North Beauregard Street
Alexandria, VA 22311

The American Gastroenterological Association

www.gastro.org
301-654-2055
4930 Del Ray Avenue
Bethesda, MD 20814

American Heart Association

www.americanheart.org
800-242-8721
7272 Greenville Avenue
Dallas, TX 75231

American Lung Association

Web site in English and Spanish

www.lungusa.org
800-548-8252
61 Broadway, 6th Fl.
New York, NY 10006

American Parkinson's Disease Association

www.apdaparkinson.org
800-223-2732
1250 Hylan Boulevard, Ste. 4B
Staten Island, NY 10305

American Stroke Association

www.strokeassociation.org
888-478-7653
7272 Greenville Avenue
Dallas, TX 75231

Arthritis Foundation

Web site in English and Spanish

www.arthritis.org
800-283-7800
P.O. Box 7669
Atlanta, GA 30357

Asthma and Allergy Foundation of America

www.aafa.org
800-7-ASTHMA
1233 20th Street, Ste. 402
Washington, DC 20036

Brain Injury Association of America

Web site in English and Spanish

www.biausa.org
800-444-6443
8201 Greensboro Drive, Ste. 611
McLean, VA 22102

Cancer Care

www.cancercare.org
800-813-HOPE
Cancer Care National Office
275 Seventh Avenue
New York, NY 10001

Harvard Brain Tissue Resource Center

www.brainbank.mclean.org
800-272-4622
McLean Hospital
115 Mill Street
Belmont, MA 02478

Hospice Association of America

www.hospice-america.org
202-546-4759
228 Seventh Street, SE
Washington, DC 20003

Macular Degeneration Information Center

www.infoaging.org/d-macu-home.html
212-703-9977
American Federation for Aging Research
70 W. 40th Street, 11th Fl.
New York, NY 10018

The Merck Manual of Geriatrics

www.merck.com/pubs/mmgeriatrics/toe.htm

The Merck Manual of Geriatrics Web site provides the reader with free comprehensive information about geriatric illnesses, specific conditions, and problems.

National Alliance for the Mentally Ill (NAMI)

www.nami.org
800-950-6264
Colonial Place Three
2107 Wilson Boulevard, Ste. 300
Arlington, VA 22201

National Cancer Institute–Cancer Information Service

http://cis.nci.nih.gov
800-422-6237

National Eye Institute

www.nei.nih.gov
301-496-5248
Information Office
31 Center Drive MSC 2510
Bethesda, MD 20892

National Heartburn Alliance

www.heartburnalliance.net
877-471-2081

National Institute of Diabetes and Digestive and Kidney Diseases (National Institutes of Health)

www.niddk.nih.gov
NIDDK
NIH
Bldg. 31, Rm. 9AO4
31 Center Drive MSC 2560
Bethesda, MD 20892

National Multiple Sclerosis Society

Web site in English and Spanish

www.nmss.org
800-344-4867
733 Third Avenue
New York, NY 10017

National Osteoporosis Foundation

www.nof.org
202-223-2226
1232 22nd Street, NW
Washington, DC 20037

The Susan G. Komen Breast Cancer Foundation

www.komen.org
800-462-9273
5005 LBJ Freeway, Ste. 250
Dallas, TX 75244

PROFESSIONAL ORGANIZATIONS

American Board of Medical Specialties (ABMS)

www.abms.org
847-491-9091
1007 Church Street, Ste. 404
Evanston, IL 60201

The ABMS coordinates and publishes information for twenty-four approved medical specialty boards in the United States. It has a list of all board-certified diplomates and provides information to the public on certification status and standards.

American Medical Association (AMA)

www.ama-assn.org

800-621-8335

515 N. State Street

Chicago, IL 60610

The AMA Web site provides comprehensive information for the medical community through medical education, advocacy, and policy issues. The consumer finds helpful information on health issues and a clear and simple way to locate specific physicians through Doctor Finder.

American Society on Aging (ASA)

www.asaging.org

800-537-9728

415-974-9600

833 Market Street, Ste. 511

San Francisco, CA 94103

The ASA provides information, educational programs, training, and other resources to practitioners, educators, administrators, policymakers, business people, and other professionals concerned with the physical, emotional, social, economic, and spiritual aspects of aging.

National Academy of Certified Care Managers

www.naccm.net

800-962-2260

P.O. Box 669

244 Upton Road

Colchester, CT 06415

The National Academy of Certified Care Managers is an organization designed to assure the professional skills of care managers through a standardized examination and to provide quality care management to all. The Web site provides several important professional links.

National Academy of Elder Law Attorneys (NAELA)

www.naela.com
520-881-4005
1604 N. Country Club Road
Tucson, AZ 85716

The NAELA Web site provides addresses for elder law attorneys throughout the United States who work with older clients and their families on issues such as public benefits, probate and estate planning, guardianship, and healthcare and long-term care planning.

National Association of Professional Geriatric Care Managers (GMC)

www.caremanager.org
520-881-8008
1604 N. Country Club Road
Tucson, AZ 85716

The GCM provides addresses for geriatric care managers throughout the United States to help older clients and their families access counseling, treatment, and the delivery of concrete services and dignified care by qualified, certified providers.

National Council On the Aging (NCOA)

www.ncoa.org
800-373-4906
202-479-1200
300 D Street SW, Ste. 801
Washington, DC 20024

The NCOA provides resources, information, and advocacy to consumers and organizations on issues such as Alzheimer's disease, arthritis, heart attacks, personal relationships, and safety. The site also offers a Benefits CheckUp, which helps locate programs for seniors that may pay for some of the costs of their prescription drugs, healthcare, utilities, and other essential items or services.

Nursing Education of America

www.nursingeducation.org
800-234-8706

Nursing Education of America offers nurses continuing education through a large selection of courses, including geriatrics, mental health, and palliative nursing care. There are four course levels to meet specific individual and professional needs and requirements.

The Society of Certified Senior Advisors (CSA)

www.society-csa.com
800-653-1785
1777 S. Bellaire Street, #230
Denver, CO 80222

The CSA educates insurance, accounting, law, clergy, health, real estate, and other professionals to better understand the needs of seniors in twenty-three key areas, including housing, Social Security, Medicare, Medicaid, and financial and estate planning. The Web site helps locate a CSA near you.

RELAXATION FOR YOUR BODY AND MIND

American Yoga Association

www.americanyogaassociation.org

The American Yoga Association Web site provides information, education, and instruction to individuals interested in yoga. Check the online store for videos, CDs, and books.

Ellis Island Records

www.ellisislandrecords.com

212-561-4588

The Statue of Liberty–Ellis Island Foundation, Inc.

Attn: History Center

292 Madison Avenue

New York, NY 10017

The Ellis Island Records Web site provides the ability to search for individual family members, purchase Statue of Liberty and Ellis Island mementos, and as a foundation member create a family scrapbook.

iVillage

www.ivillage.com

The iVillage Web site brings women extensive, timely, information on diet, fitness, health, parenting, home and garden, and much more. Women.com is a free newsletter from iVillage. It features articles on entertainment, beauty, dating, and other diverting topics.

Men's Health

www.menshealth.com

The Men's Health Web site includes timely information and articles on men's fitness, nutrition, and health.

The National Woman's Health Information Center

www.4woman.gov

800-994-9662

The National Woman's Health Information Center Web site—US Department of Health & Human Services provides a wide range of free health information for women.

Women's Health America

www.womenshealth.com

The Women's Health America Web site provides education, advice, and options for women on a variety of healthcare issues such as menopause, bone health, antiaging, diet, and exercise. The Web site includes a health library, mini courses, and an e-newsletter.

TRAVEL

The Society for Accessible Travel & Hospitality (SATH)

www.sath.org

212-447-7284

347 Fifth Avenue, Ste. 601

New York, NY 10016

The SATH Web site helps alert the public to the needs of all travelers with disabilities. The Web site names hotels and helps to provide opportunities for travelers with disabilities all over the world.

GLOSSARY OF ELDERCARE TERMS

AAA (Area Agency on Aging): An organization with offices throughout the United States that provides direct services, information, and referrals for individuals who are sixty-five years of age and older.

Activities of daily living (ADLs): Refers to the ability to perform such tasks as personal grooming, shopping, cooking, eating, using the toilet, dressing and undressing, banking, and doing laundry.

Admitting doctor: The physician who provides access to a hospital for a patient who requires medical treatment.

Adult day center: A structured environment that offers socialization, custodial and respite care, nutrition, exercise, therapeutic services, and support for frail and/or physically or cognitively impaired individuals.

Advance directives: Legal documents that express the wishes of an individual if he becomes incapacitated and unable to make medical, legal, or personal decisions for himself.

Adverse drug reaction: A result occurring when two or more drugs react with each other to create an unexpected side effect that can sometimes be dangerous or even deadly.

Ageism: A misconception that old age in and of itself limits an individual's abilities.

Aging in place: The ability of an individual to remain in his own home because of the availability of supplemental supportive services such as homecare.

Agitation: A behavior that may result from a physical or cognitive impairment or from too much or too little mental stimulation. It may take the form of yelling, hitting, or restlessness.

Alcohol abuse: The overconsumption of alcohol by an individual that interferes with his daily life and ability to function.

Alzheimer's disease: An irreversible, degenerative brain disorder that causes loss of memory and cognitive function.

Assessment: A comprehensive evaluation of an individual's physical, psychological, emotional, social, and environmental needs. A registered nurse or a social worker usually conducts this type of assessment.

Assisted living facility (ALF): An alternative living option that provides a room, meals, personal care, medication management, socialization, and recreational activities in a supervised, safe, and secure environment.

Assistive devices: Any type of equipment that aids an individual and provides increased independence and support, such as a wheelchair, a walker, tub rails, or a cane.

Bereavement counselor: A trained professional or volunteer who provides counseling and support services to individuals who are grieving the death of a family member or friend. This type of counselor is also helpful for people who witness a traumatic event such as an airplane crash or an automobile accident.

Board-certified physician: A medical doctor who completed all medical school requirements and passed a medical qualifying examination.

Burnout: Emotional and physical exhaustion resulting from long-term burdens of overwhelming stress and responsibilities.

Caregiver: Any individual who provides personal, emotional, financial, or supportive care for another person.

Care management: A fee-for-service business that deals with and evaluates every aspect of an individual's daily life and provides an ongoing approach to medical, psychosocial, emotional, and quality-of-life issues.

Care manager: An independent, privately hired and paid for registered nurse or licensed social worker who assesses, plans, coordinates, implements, monitors, and supervises all aspects of a client's daily life.

Case management: A service that is often paid for by government entitlements or some form of insurance. Contact, interventions, and degree of involvement with clients is often time-limited owing to benefit limitations.

Case manager: A registered nurse or a social worker who works for a social service agency or in connection with a hospital or an insurance company and conducts a clinical assessment of an individual's needs and provides services and ongoing monitoring.

Certified nurses' aide (CNA): An individual who earns a state license by completing specific homecare and patient training. A hospital, a nursing home, an assisted living facility, or a private patient may employ an individual with these credentials.

Cognitive impairment: A decline in an individual's ability to perform tasks, make decisions, or think clearly.

Combativeness: Acting out verbal or physical behaviors such as yelling, hitting, or physical aggressiveness.

Companion: An individual or a volunteer who provides company and support for another individual.

Compliant: Able to respond appropriately to another person's directions, such as accepting medication from someone in a timely manner.

Continuity of services: Services provided to an individual without any lapse in time by the service provider.

Custodial care: Personal assistance services including room and board and excluding regular medical care.

Dementia: A neurological condition that results in memory loss, changes in personality, difficulty in learning or retaining new information, language problems, and mood swings.

Depression: A mental illness marked by symptoms that are severe and last for an extended period of time, such as loss of appetite or weight, loss of interest in pleasurable activities, crying, feeling helpless and hopeless, and suicidal ideation, thoughts, and plans.

Diagnosis: An identification of a medical or mental illness or condition.

Disorientation: A state of confusion resulting in an inability to identify or relate to a person, place, or time.

Do Not Resuscitate (DNR): A document that allows a legal representative to make the decision not to allow resuscitation if an individual stops breathing.

Drug abuse: The accidental or intentional misuse of prescription medications, over-the-counter medications, homeopathic products, or any other drugs.

Durable power of attorney: A legal document that allows a competent individual to appoint another individual to make decisions for him or her when he or she can no longer make his or her own decisions. This document remains effective in the event the individual becomes incapacitated.

Durable power of attorney for healthcare: A legal document that allows a competent individual to appoint another individual to make healthcare decisions for him or her when he or she can no longer make his or her own decisions. This document remains effective in the event the individual becomes incapacitated.

Eldercare professionals: Individuals who specialize in the care and needs of the population that is age sixty-five and older.

Elder law: A specialty in the field of law that deals with financial, legal, and personal needs of individuals age sixty-five and older.

Environmental assessment: A comprehensive study of an individual's home to identify and correct safety hazards.

Flextime: An individualized work schedule that allows an employee to work convenient and flexible hours.

Geriatric care manager: An independent, privately hired and paid for registered nurse or licensed social worker who assesses, plans, coordinates, implements, monitors, and supervises all aspects of a client's life.

Geriatric nurse practitioner: A licensed registered nurse who specializes in the care and treatment of the sixty-five and older population after receiving extensive advanced training, education, and clinical experience.

Geriatric physician: A medical doctor who receives extensive training, education, and specialized clinical experience in the care and treatment of individuals age sixty-five and older.

Guardian: A court-appointed individual who makes financial and/or personal care decisions for another individual who can no longer make decisions for himself.

Healthcare proxy: A legal document that allows a competent individual to appoint another individual to make healthcare decisions for him or her when he or she cannot make his or her own decisions.

Homecare: A service business that provides personal care and assistance with activities of daily living in the home environment.

Home health aide: A nonprofessional employee trained to provide personal care and other associated services in the home, such as cooking, light housekeeping, and laundry.

Hospice care: Specialized, compassionate care at home or in a facility for an individual suffering from a terminal illness.

Human resource counselor: A trained professional who works for a small business or large corporation and provides counseling and support services for employees.

Incapacity: A legal term that describes the inability of an individual to make decisions for himself or herself.

Incontinence: The inability to control bladder and/or bowel functions.

Independent living: An alternative living option for an individual who is physically and cognitively capable of residing in an independent environment.

Intervention: Involvement in an individual's life in order to help maintain, rescue, or assist that person.

Living will: A legal document that allows a person to identify in advance the type of medical care he or she wants under specific circumstances, usually relating to serious illness or impending death.

Long-distance caregiver: Any individual who is geographically distant but involved in the care of another person.

Long-term care facility: An institution that provides medical and/or custodial care for more than a few weeks or months.

Long-term care insurance: A private insurance policy that covers some of the costs of extended healthcare needs at home or in a nursing home.

Long-term memory: The ability to remember past experiences, people, places, and things.

Medicaid: A federal program administered by individual states to cover the cost of certain medical care at home or in a nursing home. The purpose and design of the program is to meet the needs of individuals with a limited income.

Medicare: A federal insurance program for individuals age sixty-five and older. It is divided into Part A, hospital benefits; Part B, medical benefits; and Part C, Medicare + Choice.

Medigap: A private insurance plan designed to cover some of the costs not covered by Medicare such as prescription drugs or preventive care and services.

Memorial service: A special tribute to remember the life of a deceased individual. This type of service may take place in a funeral home, a church, a synagogue, a cemetery, a private home, a park, or any place that brings family and friends together.

Memorial society: A nonprofit group that negotiates contracts with funeral homes, crematoriums, and cemeteries. The benefit of this type of group is that members receive discounts on specific products and services.

Memory impairment: The inability of an individual to remember recent and/or long-term events.

Mobility: The ability of an individual to walk independently without the help of another person or an assistive device such as a cane or a walker.

Multi-infarct dementia: A non-Alzheimer's type dementia, sometimes known as vascular dementia. (See **dementia.**)

Neurologist: A medical doctor who specializes in diseases and illnesses of the nervous system.

Nondurable power of attorney: A legal document that allows a competent individual to appoint another individual to make decisions for him or her. This document is generally used for a limited purpose such as providing an attorney the legal power to represent you at a house closing or other business transaction. This document is no longer effective if the individual becomes incapacitated.

Nonverbal communication: An individual's ability to communicate without the use of language skills, such as with the use of eye contact, signing, or body language.

Nursing home: A facility that cares for the specific needs of physically ill and/or cognitively impaired individuals.

Opthalmologist: A medical doctor who specializes in the care and treatment of the eyes.

Paranoia: A mental disorder in which the individual suffers from delusions or disturbances in thinking.

Patient advocate: A social worker or a trained volunteer who acts as an intermediary between the patient and the staff in hospitals or other institutions.

Personal emergency response system (PERS): A device or voice-activated system that connects an individual to emergency assistance.

Preventive intervention: A method of identifying risks and creating a plan to help an individual before a problem actually arises.

Primary caregiver: An individual who takes on the foremost responsibility of the daily care and needs of another person.

Primary care physician: The first doctor that an individual sees for all medical needs and who helps coordinate the individual's medical care.

Private-duty nurse: A registered nurse who is paid for privately and assigned to care for one patient in such places as a hospital, a nursing home, an assisted living facility, or the patient's home.

Professional funeral consultant: An individual who provides families with options and information that allows them to make informed decisions and takes care of all aspects of a funeral.

Prognosis: The possible outcome of a particular medical condition.

Registered nurse: An individual who successfully completed nursing school and passed all of the appropriate licensing examinations.

Respite service: Care provided on a temporary basis in a facility or in an individual's home to relieve a caregiver of caregiving duties and associated stresses.

Self-neglect: An individual's inability to care for his or her personal needs.

Senior center: A building or place for people over the age of sixty-five to join in socialization, education, and nutritional programs.

Sexually inappropriate behavior: Unsuitable or aggressive sexual behavior toward another individual.

Short-term memory: Recall of recent events.

Skilled nursing facility (SNF): A long-term care facility that specializes in the specific needs of a physically frail or cognitively impaired individual.

Sliding scale fee: A fee that is determined by an individual's income level and ability to pay.

Social worker: An individual who completed an accredited school of social work and passed all appropriate licensing examinations.

Specialist: An individual who has expertise in a particular field, such as a gerontologist who specializes in the care of the elderly.

Support group: A group of people who have similar interests and meet together at specific intervals to share experiences, learn coping techniques, and support one another.

Telephone tree: A support system whereby several individuals contact one another on a daily basis. If someone does not answer the telephone within a certain time limit and does not notify the group that he or she will be out of town, an emergency protocol takes effect.

Toileting: Helping an individual to use the appropriate bathroom facilities.

Transferring: Moving from one position to another with or without assistance, such as moving from a wheelchair to a bed.

Urinary tract infection (UTI): An infection of the bladder or urinary tract that is usually treatable with antibiotic therapy.

NOTES

PREFACE

1. National Family Caregiving Alliance Web site, www.nfcacares.org, 2003.

2. Ibid.

CHAPTER 1

1. Harold Kushner, *How Good Do We Have to Be? A New Understanding of Guilt and Forgiveness* (Boston: Little, Brown & Company, 1996).

INDEX